世遗之城：泉州

QUANZHOU: A WORLD HERITAGE CITY

向海而歌——
宋元泉州的交通网络

Navigating the Sea: Transportation
Network in Song-Yuan Quanzhou

中共泉州市委宣传部　编

海峡出版发行集团 | 福建人民出版社
THE STRAITS PUBLISHING & DISTRIBUTING GROUP | FUJIAN PEOPLE'S PUBLISHING HOUSE

目录

引言 …… 001

宝塔导航 …… 003

万寿塔：凝望千年的眼神 …… 004

六胜塔：精美的石头会唱歌 …… 034

扬帆启航 …… 069

石湖码头：送你一片辽远的蓝 …… 070

江口码头：穿越法石港的千里烟波 …… 092

桥梁飞渡 …… 127

洛阳桥：海内第一桥 …… 130

安平桥：天下无桥长此桥 …… 180

顺济桥：诸峰返照潮声远 …… 216

参考文献 …… 238

Contents

Introduction ······ 002

Pagodas: Navigational Landmarks ······ 003

Wanshou Pagoda: A Gaze Spanning Centuries ······ 005

Liusheng Pagoda: A Marvelous Architectural Legacy ······ 035

Docks: Docking Sites for Foreign Merchant Ships ······ 069

Shihu Dock: Facing a Vast Blue Sea ······ 071

Estuary Docks: Amidst the Vast Waves Along Fashi Port ······ 093

Bridges: Connecting Land with Water ······ 127

Luoyang Bridge: China's Earliest Stone Beam Bridge ······ 131

Anping Bridge: China's Longest Extant Cross-sea Stone Beam Bridge ······ 181

Shunji Bridge: A Bustling Transportation Hub ······ 217

引　言

泉州自古就是一座向海而兴、多元共享的城市，是宋元中国杰出的对外经济与文化交流的窗口。沿江、环湾、临海的地理环境，外向型经济贸易业态的实际需求，促使泉州致力于构建完善的水陆联运系统，逐渐形成呼应生产、运输、销售一体化的世界海洋商贸中心交通体系。

宋元时期，泉州港掀起一波令人惊叹的港口码头、桥梁工程建造热潮。能工巧匠们破解诸多技术难题，成就一系列古代海港建筑史上的伟大创举。它们是泉州官方、商贾、平民及宗教人士共同参与的结果，既体现了泉州多元社会结构对海洋贸易的贡献，又反映了海洋贸易给泉州社会带来的经济繁荣与技术革新。

以万寿塔、六胜塔、石湖码头、江口码头、洛阳桥、安平桥、顺济桥为代表，这些宝塔、码头、桥梁组合而成的海洋商贸交通运输网络，勾勒出“温陵城郭枕江开”的气势，浓缩着“涨海声中万国商”的荣耀，形象地展现着泉州人纵横天下的奋斗姿态，闪烁着中国海洋文明的智慧之光和自信之光。

让我们跟随《蓝蓝泉州湾》的优美旋律，一起聆听泉州港通达四海的浪漫故事……

向海而兴的泉州。（陈英杰 摄）
Quanzhou, sailing towards the sea. (Photo by Chen Yingjie)

Introduction

Quanzhou, historically known for its maritime strengths, was once a beacon of diversity and a key center for international economic and cultural exchanges in Song-Yuan China. The city's strategic location along rivers, bays and coastlines, coupled with its strong focus on foreign trade, gave rise to a sophisticated network of water-land transshipment. This network gradually evolved into a comprehensive transport system, seamlessly integrating the production, transportation and trade of a world emporium.

Throughout the Song and Yuan dynasties (960—1368), Quanzhou Port witnessed a remarkable growth in port infrastructure and bridge construction. Skilled artisans overcame various technical challenges, making significant advancements in ancient harbor construction. These achievements were the results of collaborative endeavors among Quanzhou's officials, merchants, residents and religious leaders, underscoring the diverse social fabric's contributions to maritime trade and the resulting economic prosperity and technological innovation that flourished within the city.

Iconic landmarks like Wanshou Pagoda, Liusheng Pagoda, Shihu Dock, Estuary Docks, Luoyang Bridge, Anping Bridge and Shunji Bridge formed a network facilitating maritime trade, symbolizing Quanzhou's grandeur as a city fortified by rivers and open to the sea, with "merchants from all nations amidst the sound of rising tides". This network epitomizes the city's maritime legacy and the spirit of its people engaging in global trade, showcasing their wisdom, confidence and historical significance in global connections.

Let's embark on a captivating journey into the narrative of *Blue Quanzhou Bay* and delve into the enthralling saga of Quanzhou Port's pivotal role in global connectivity.

宝塔导航

Pagodas: Navigational Landmarks

万寿塔：凝望千年的眼神

Wanshou Pagoda: A Gaze Spanning Centuries

六胜塔：精美的石头会唱歌

Liusheng Pagoda: A Marvelous Architectural Legacy

万寿塔：凝望千年的眼神

万寿塔，又名关锁塔，民间也称姑嫂塔，位于泉州湾海岸的制高点。登临塔顶，沿海港口及远近岛屿一览无遗。它是古代商船抵达泉州港的航标，寄托着当地人镇守海口、护佑商旅的朴素愿望。姑嫂望夫的传说，则承载了泉州民众对海洋贸易的历史记忆。

介殊建塔

万寿塔耸立于石狮市宝盖山山顶，左侧遥望泉州湾，右侧直视深沪湾，登之可远眺沧海，为古代“泉州十景”之一，有“关锁烟霞”之美誉。万寿塔高 21.65 米，

关锁烟霞。（陈文丕 摄）
Wanshou Pagoda locking to the mist and clouds. (Photo by Chen Wenpi)

为五层八角仿木空心楼阁式石塔建筑。底层加围廊，塔门前建有一石构方形单檐歇山顶门亭。整座塔看上去十分雄伟，但外观却不华丽，既无精美的雕刻，也无繁杂的纹饰，甚至没有建造者的题字或留名。走近塔身，只见第二层门额上方刻有“万寿宝塔”四字，字并不大，稍不留意，就会错过。但是，当你置身塔上，风吹双鬓，视觉开阔，远眺海天一色，便会有心旷神怡之感。

Wanshou Pagoda: A Gaze Spanning Centuries

Wanshou Pagoda, also known as Gusao (Sisters-in-Law) Pagoda or Guansuo (Lock) Pagoda, sits atop the highest point of Quanzhou Bay. From its summit, you can have a panoramic view of the coastal ports and islands far and near. In ancient times, this pagoda served as a vital navigational landmark for merchant ships arriving at Quanzhou Port. Its presence brought solace to the local community, acting as a guardian of the bay and offering divine protection to traveling merchants. The legend of two sisters-in-law awaiting the husband further preserves the historical memory of Quanzhou's maritime trade.

Monk Jieshu Building Wanshou Pagoda

Wanshou Pagoda stands on top of Baogai Mountain in Shishi, Quanzhou. It overlooks Quanzhou Bay on the left and Shenhu Bay on the right, earning its place among the "Ten Scenic Spots of Quanzhou" during ancient times. Renowned for its picturesque scenery, the pagoda is often described as a "lock to the mist and clouds". Though built entirely of stone blocks, the pagoda's design mimics that of wooden structures. With its octagonal shape and a height of 21.65 meters, the five-story pagoda exudes a majestic aura. However, its appearance is not extravagant, lacking intricate carvings or elaborate decorations. Even the builder's inscription or name is absent. As approaching the pagoda, you may overlook the four Chinese characters "Wanshou Baota" (Wanshou Pagoda) carved above the second-story door. Despite these subtleties, standing atop the pagoda, you will feel a sense of relaxation and joy as the wind gently caresses your face, and you can behold the boundless sea and sky, which creates a truly serene experience.

若是下一番功夫考究的话，可知一位叫介殊的南宋僧人和万寿塔有关。古人认为，“风水”关乎一方之灵气，决定人文之兴衰。史书记载，南宋绍兴年间，介殊发现宝盖山位于晋江东南滨海风口、水口交接处，于是募缘兴建此塔，作为“关锁（风）水口”之用，故称“关锁塔”。

风水之说，姑妄言之，姑妄听之。然而，一介僧人介殊能够募集资金在宝盖山绝顶兴建这一奇观，它所透露出来的社会、经济、文化方面的信息却值得重视。当时，泉州港作为海上丝绸之路的起点之一，海外交通发达，社会开放包容，带来经济与文化的繁荣，才造就了关锁塔这一奇特壮观的建筑艺术瑰宝。

If you delve into research, you will discover a connection between a Southern Song monk named Jieshu and Wanshou Pagoda. The ancients believed that "*fengshui*" (geomancy) was connected to the spiritual energy of a place and influenced the rise and fall of its civilization. According to historical records, sometime between 1131 and 1162, Jieshu discovered that Baogai Mountain was located at the intersection of wind and water outlets in the southeast of Jinjiang River. So, he raised funds to build this pagoda as a "lock of wind and water", hence the name Guansuo Pagoda, or Pagoda of Lock.

The *fengshui* theory may be speculative, but the fact that an ordinary monk like Jieshu was able to raise funds to build this amazing structure on top of Baogai Mountain reveals significant social, economic and cultural information. At that time, Quanzhou Port, one of the starting points of Maritime Silk Road, boasted developed overseas transportation and an open and inclusive society. This brought about economic and cultural prosperity, leading to the creation of the unique and magnificent architectural masterpiece of Guansuo Pagoda.

宝盖山顶关锁塔。（陈英杰 摄）

Guansuo Pagoda on the top of Baogai Mountain. (Photo by Chen Yingjie)

万寿塔地理位置。（黄国炎 摄）
The geographical location of Wanshou Pagoda. (Photo by Huang Guoyan)

而关锁塔屹立于宝盖山绝顶之后，风水一说却并没有引起人们的格外在意。史书上对她的功能另有一番阐释，那就是“高出云表，登之可望商舶来往”。原来，关锁塔实际上是一座航标塔。明代黄仲昭编修的《八闽通志》干脆直截了当地记载：“（关锁塔）甚壮丽，商舶自海还者，指为抵岸之期。”可谓一语道破天机。千百年来，关锁塔默默地为无数进出泉州湾的中外船舶指引航路，阅尽人世间的沧桑变幻。以石塔作为航标，也成为世界航海史上的一大奇观，泉州千年海外交通的文化积淀在关锁塔身上得到充分的体现。明代安溪进士詹仰庇登上宝盖山时，诗兴大发，赞美道：“宝盖峰高控海东，西来金马远争雄。手摩霄汉千山尽，眼入沧溟百岛通。”好一句“眼入沧溟百岛通”，关锁塔守望的正是她眼前这一片蔚蓝色的大海和泉州人延续了千年的海洋梦。

The existence of Guansuo Pagoda on top of Baogai Mountain, however, did not attract much attention due to its significance in *fengshui*. Historical records offer another interpretation of its function, stating that it was "high above the clouds, and from its top, you can see the coming and going of merchant ships", which indicates that Guansuo Pagoda was actually a navigational beacon. This can be proven by the records in *A General Gazetteer of Fujian*, the first extant chorography of Fujian, compiled by Huang Zhongzhao in the Ming Dynasty (1368—1644): "(Guansuo Pagoda) is magnificent, and it serves as a reference point for merchant ships returning from the sea to determine their arrival." For centuries, Guansuo Pagoda had silently guided countless Chinese and foreign ships entering and leaving Quanzhou Bay, witnessing the changes and challenges of life. As a landmark, the pagoda is also a remarkable feat in the history of world navigation, fully embodying the cultural heritage of Quanzhou's thousand-year-old overseas trade. When the Ming Dynasty scholar Zhan Yangbi ascended Baogai Mountain, he was inspired to praise the pagoda in a poem:

"Baogai Mountain stands high, overlooking the eastern sea,

Where Western merchant ships vie for dominance.

With a touch of the Milky Way,

A thousand mountains are within reach,

And the eyes penetrate the vast ocean,

Connecting a hundred islands."

The line that "the eyes penetrate the vast ocean, connecting a hundred islands" perfectly captures the essence of Guansuo Pagoda, who has kept watch over this blue sea, and the millennia-old maritime dream of the overseas Chinese communities.

姑嫂塔传奇

对于关锁塔，闽南民间更习惯称其为姑嫂塔，听着亲切自然，却源自一个凄凉的故事：传说很久以前，闽南天旱，庄稼颗粒无收，一位名叫海生的穷人被迫离别新婚妻子和心爱的妹妹，远走南洋，约定打拼三年后回来团聚。穷哥哥走后，姑嫂俩天天爬上宝盖山，垒石登高，远眺归舟，盼望其平安回来。终于三年期至，穷哥哥乘船回来，姑嫂俩在山上看到亲人的船已近海岸，谁知忽然刮起狂风暴雨，一阵惊涛骇浪把船打翻了。穷哥哥葬身大海，姑嫂俩喜尽悲来，纵身跳下山崖。为了纪念她们，人们就在姑嫂二人垒石登高的地方建起这座姑嫂塔。

因为这个民间传说，宝盖山在明代得了一个很接地气的别称——望郎回山。编撰于 16 世纪的航海指南《顺风相送》记载，望郎回山上有姑嫂塔，是进出泉州港的地标。明代“江南四大才子”之一的祝允明所撰《前闻记》记载，宣德八年（1433），下西洋船队由王景弘率领返航，六月十日，以望郎回山（姑嫂塔）为航标，穿行台湾海峡，这是下西洋船队曾以姑嫂塔作为导航标志的珍贵历史纪录。可见，姑嫂塔故事早在明代初年就广为流传，后来才被明代泉州史学家何乔远载入福建地方志。何乔远《闽书》记载：“昔有姑嫂嫁为商人妇，商贩海，久不至，姑嫂塔而望之，若望夫石然。”虽寥寥数语，但传奇故事的人物、主要情节已经包括在内。

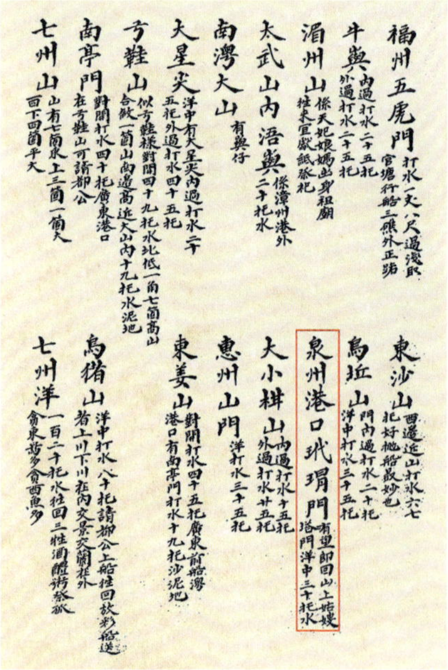
福州五虎門 打水一丈八尺過淺馭 官塘行船三熊外正路
牛嶼 內過打水二十五托 外過打水二十五托
湄州山 係天妃娘媽出身祖廟 往來宜獻紙祭祀
太武山內浯嶼 係漳州港外 二十托水
南澚大山 有嶼仔
大星尖 洋中有大星尖內過打水二十五托 外過打水四十五托
方鞋山 似方鞋樣對開四十九托水北低一角七箇高山 合歛一箇山南邊高近大山內十九托水泥地
南亭門 對開打水四十托廣東港口 在方鞋山可請都公
七州山 山有七箇東上三箇一箇大 西下四箇平大
東沙山 西邊近山打水六七 托好拋船最妙也
烏坵山 門內過打水二十托 洋中打水三十五托
泉州港口玳瑁門 有望郎回山上姑嫂 塔門洋中三十托水
大小柑山 內過打水十五托 外過打水廿五托
惠州山門 洋打水三十五托
東姜山 對開打水四十五托廣東前船澚 港口有南亭門打水十九托沙泥地
烏豬山 洋中打水八十托請都公上船往回放彩船送 若上川下川在內交景交蘭在外
七州洋 一百二十托水往回三牲酒醴粥祭孤 爺東若多貪西魚多

《顺风相送》中关于望郎回山的记载。（李国宏 供图）

The record about Wanglanghui Mountain in *Sailing with the Wind*. (Courtesy of Li Guohong)

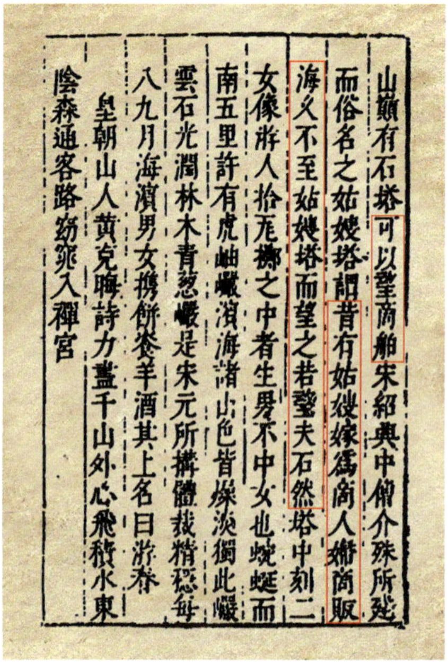
山巔有石塔可以望商船宋紹興中僧介殊所建
而俗名之姑嫂塔䛕昔有姑嫂嫁爲商人婦商販
海久不至姑嫂塔而望之若望夫石然塔中刻二
女像㳄人拾瓦擲之中者生男不中女也蜿蜒而
南五里許有虎岫巖濱海諸山色皆燥淡獨此巖
雲石光潤林木青葱巖是宋元所搆體裁精恖每
八九月海濱男女携餅餈羊酒其上名曰遊春
皇朝山人黄克晦詩力盡千山外心飛積水東
陰森通客路窈窕入禪宮

《闽书》中关于万寿塔作为航标指南及姑嫂传说的记载。（李国宏 供图）

The record about Wangshou Pogoda as a navigational landmark and the legend of the sisters-in-law in *The Book of Min*. (Courtesy of Li Guohong)

Legend of Gusao Pagoda

Regarding Guansuo Pagoda, people of Southern Fujian prefer to call it "Gusao Pagoda" (Sisters-in-Law Pagoda), which sounds more familiar and natural. However, the origin of this name is rooted in a tragic tale. Legend has it that a long time ago, there was a severe drought in Southern Fujian, and the crops failed to yield any harvest. A poor man named Haisheng was compelled to leave his newlywed wife and beloved sister behind to seek work in Nanyang (Southeast Asia), promising to return and reunite with them after three years of hard work. After the poor man left, the sisters-in-law climbed Baogai Mountain every day, piling up stones and ascending to a high point, fervently gazing into the distance and hoping for his safe return. Finally, after three years, the poor man returned by ship. The two sisters spotted his ship approaching the coast from the mountain, but tragically, a violent storm and torrential rain suddenly struck, causing the ship to capsize. The poor man perished at sea, and the two sisters, filled with sorrow, jumped off the cliff. To honor them, Gusao Pagoda was constructed at the location where the two sisters had piled stones and climbed to a high point.

Due to this legend, Baogai Mountain acquired a down-to-earth nickname during the Ming Dynasty, Wanglanghui Mountain (Mountain of Awaiting the Return of the Husband). *Sailing with the Wind*, a maritime guidebook compiled in the 16th century, documents the presence of Gusao Pagoda on Wanglanghui Mountain, serving as a landmark for entering and leaving Quanzhou Port. Zhu Yunming, a renowned scholar in the Ming Dynasty, recorded in his work *Anecdotes in the Early Ming Dynasty* that in 1433, the sailing west fleet led by Wang Jinghong returned. On the tenth day of lunar June, they navigated through Taiwan Strait using Wanglanghui Mountain (Gusuo Pagoda) as a navigation landmark. This historical account is a valuable record of Zheng He's ship fleet using Gusao Pagoda as a navigational aid during their maritime expeditions. It can be concluded that the widespread circulation of the Gusao Pagoda legend traced back to the early Ming Dynasty and was later included in the local chronicles of Fujian by He Qiaoyuan, a historian from Quanzhou. His work *The Book of Min*, mentions that in the past, a lady married to a merchant who traded overseas, and while her husband was away for an extended period, she and her husband's sister would gaze at the pagoda, longing for the husband's return, likening their steadfastness to the unwavering stones. Although the description is concise, it encapsulates the key characters and plot of the legendary story.

郑和下西洋航海图中绘有万寿塔航标。（李国宏 供图）

The map of Zheng He's voyages to the Western oceans shows the navigational landmark of Wanshou Pagoda. (Courtesy of Li Guohong)

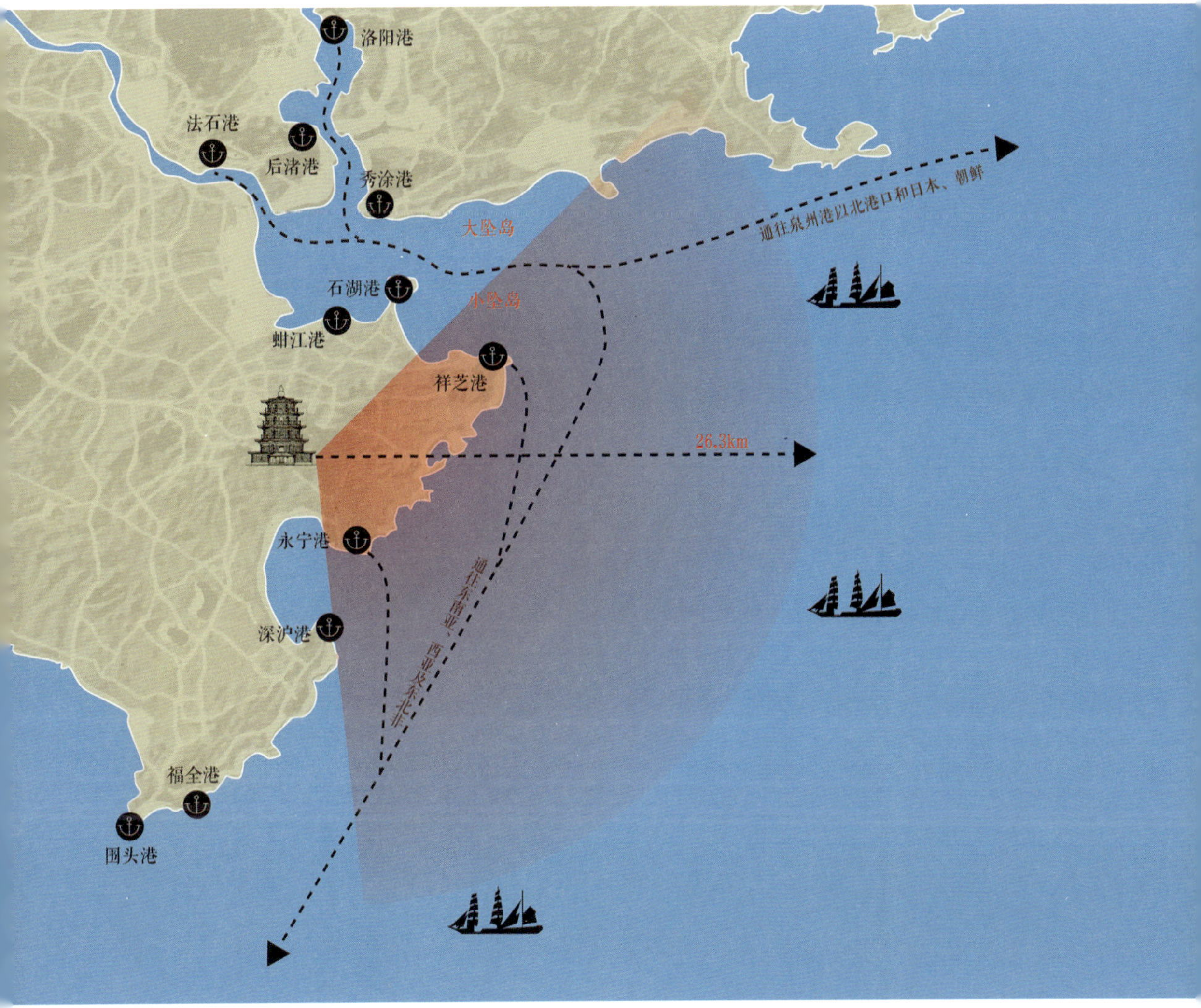

万寿塔作为航标的区位示意图。（李国宏 供图）
The location map of Wanshou Pagoda as a navigational landmark. (Courtesy of Li Guohong)

何乔远还在《镜山全集》中提到，泉州华侨“皆背离其室家，或十余年未返者，返则儿子长育至不相识。盖有新婚之别，娶以数日离者……”。流传于闽南及东南亚地区的姑嫂传奇不同于一般的民间故事，它更像是早期侨乡人民苦难生活的缩影和顽强拼搏的写照。当年，先民们横渡大海，开发台湾，移民东南亚，莫不以姑嫂塔为航标。当姑嫂塔逐渐从视线中消失之际，即游子远离故土之时，不觉令人黯然神伤、潸然泪下。若是远航归来，当姑嫂塔俊俏的身影依稀可见之时，又令多少海外游子悲喜交集、热泪盈眶。因此，姑嫂塔被海外游子视为故乡“摇篮血迹”的象征，令他们魂牵梦萦，挥之不去。

姑嫂传奇是一个纯粹的悲剧，有别于一般以大团圆作为结局的传统民间故事套路。善良而富有想象力的国人在讲故事时，常常追求结局的圆满，甚至不惜采用近乎神话的创作手法，以弥补现实生活中的缺憾。然而，姑嫂传奇的最终结局不是穷哥哥发了大财，衣锦还乡，与姑嫂团圆，美满地过日子，而是一场无名的风浪打翻穷哥哥即将靠港的船只，粉碎了姑嫂三年的等候和满腔的期盼，也让每一个对故事结局有着良好愿望的人感到意外。当穷哥哥的船遭遇狂风恶浪时，没有神仙出手相救。当姑嫂二人怀着对亲人的挚爱纵身跳下山崖的一刹那，奇迹依然没有到来。善良的人们看到了一幕纯粹的悲剧，只留下那座默默无语的石塔孤独地面对千年的岁月轮回。但是，正因为没有奇迹出现，才让姑嫂传奇更接近于事实本身，其悲剧色彩不但没有削弱它的影响力，反而由于原汁原味，更真切地折射出早期闽南先民艰难的生活状态。即便沉淀数百年，姑嫂传奇仍然能够震撼我们的心灵。

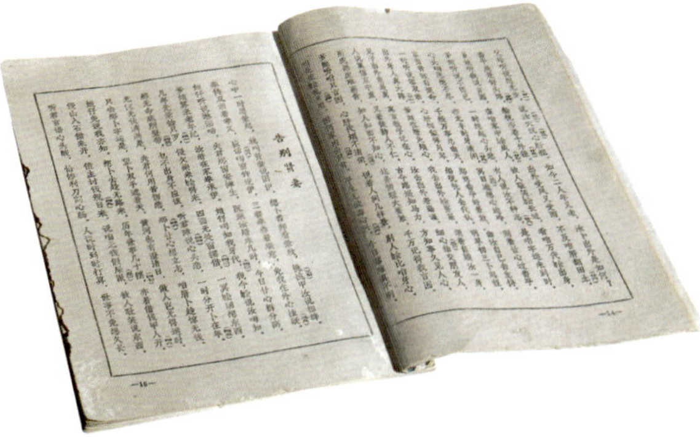
告别贤妻

一首反映丈夫出海打拼前对妻子殷殷嘱托的过番歌——《告别贤妻》。（成冬冬 摄）

Farewell to My Beloved Wife, a song about the heartfelt words of a husband leaving to seek his fortune abroad. (Photo by Cheng Dongdong)

He Qiaoyuan also mentioned in his another work, *Complete Works in Jingshan Mountain*, that Quanzhou overseas Chinese "left their families behind, and some did not return for more than ten years. When they finally return, their sons had grown up so that they could not recognize each other. There were even cases of newlyweds being separated..." The story of the two sisters-in-law, which has been passed down in Southern Fujian and Southeast Asia, is different from ordinary folk tales. It is a condensed depiction of the hardships and tenacious struggle of early overseas Chinese communities. During that time, our ancestors, guided by Gusao Pagoda, crossed the sea, developed Taiwan and migrated to Southeast Asia. When the image of Gusao Pagoda gradually disappeared from their sight, it symbolized their distance from their homeland, bringing a sense of melancholy and sadness, and tears to their eyes. When they returned from their long journey and saw the graceful figure of Gusao Pagoda, these overseas wanderers would be filled with both sorrow and joy, tears welling up in their eyes. Therefore, Gusao Pagoda symbolizes their homeland, a "cradle with bloodstains", which links them with their beloved motherland.

The legend of the two sisters-in-law is a tragic story, different from the traditional folk tales that usually end with a happy reunion. Chinese people are often kind and imaginative, and they seek satisfying endings when telling stories, sometimes even resorting to almost mythical creative techniques to compensate for the regrets of real life. However, the ultimate ending of this legendary story is not the poor man becoming rich, returning home in glory and living happily ever after with his family. Instead, a nameless storm overturns the ship he was about to dock, shattering the three years of waiting and heartfelt expectations of the sisters-in-law, and surprising everyone who has good wishes for the story's ending. When the poor man's ship encountered a fierce storm, no immortal comes to the rescue. Even when the two sisters-in-law jumped off the cliff with deep love for their beloved one, no miracle happens. Kind-hearted people witness a pure tragedy, leaving only the silent stone pagoda standing as a testament over time. However, it is precisely because there is no miracle that the legend of the sisters-in-law is closer to the reality itself. Its tragic color does not weaken its impact, but because of its authenticity, more vividly reflects the challenging living conditions of the early ancestors of Southern Fujian. Even after hundreds of years, the legend can still deeply move us.

历史研究者的视野更多关注的是出外打拼的群体，传奇故事聚焦的则大多是衣锦还乡的喜悦和功成名就的辉煌。只有这座矗立千年的姑嫂塔第一次将侨乡妇女的情怀堆砌在无言的石头上，铭刻在沧桑的岁月里。正是因为侨乡妇女用柔韧的双肩撑起了半边天，闽南的汉子才能这样义无反顾、前仆后继地闯荡江海。姑嫂们却总是悄悄把晚霞都哭红了，留下刻骨铭心的剪影。凝望千年的眼神，就这样深情地盼望着游子的每一次归来。

浩瀚无垠的大海始终带给侨乡人无穷的诱惑，先民们耕海犁浪，出没于风波之中，收获着他们的希望。而大海的变幻莫测，也始终给侨乡人带来严峻的挑战，先民们迎风斗浪，九死一生，付出了他们的血汗。姑嫂传奇的悲剧结局深深地刺痛侨乡人的心，却也坚定了侨乡人的斗志。在狂风恶浪面前，顽强的侨乡人没有停下开拓进取的步伐，每当季风吹响之时，擦干眼泪的侨乡人依旧扬帆起航，乘风破浪。宝盖山顶的姑嫂塔也总是一往情深地目送每一个孤帆远影，默默守护着每一次天际归帆。

Historians often focus more on the group of people who ventured abroad in search of opportunities. Legendary tales often emphasize the joy of returning home triumphant and the brilliance of achieving success and fame. However, it is the ancient Guosao Pagoda that captures the emotions of women in the hometown of overseas Chinese, etching them into the ever-changing passage of time. It is because the women in the homeland have shouldered their fair share of responsibilities that the men in Southern Fujian can fearlessly set sail across the sea and continue to forge ahead. These "sisters-in-law" silently weep until the sun sets, leaving behind unforgettable memories. Their gaze, spanning centuries, is filled with deep affection, eagerly anticipating the return of every wanderer.

The vast and limitless sea always tempts the people in the hometown of overseas Chinese. Our ancestors, driven by hope, fought against winds and waves, risking their lives and paying with their blood and sweat. The tragic ending of the sisters-in-law's legendary story deeply pierced the hearts of the people in the hometown of overseas Chinese, but it also strengthened their determination. In the face of fierce winds and waves, the resilient people in the hometown of overseas Chinese did not halt their exploration and progress. And Gusao Pagoda on Baogai Mountain always silently watches as every sail disappears into the distance, faithfully guarding every return.

宝盖山下舟自横。（杨自强 摄）
Several boats cross under Baogai Mountain. (Photo by Yang Ziqiang)

姑嫂信仰文化传入台湾

姑嫂塔不仅是闽南侨乡的文化符号，也是闽台两岸一家亲的缩影。清代，随着蚶江、鹿港对渡的兴起，石狮与台湾之间的航运交通日益繁盛。搏击风浪的航海人需要来自家乡的精神慰藉和情感支持，因此，姑嫂塔传奇中的“姑嫂”形象，就从一个勤劳勇敢的群体浓缩成顾家兴业的文化意念，逐渐演变为闽台民众虔诚礼拜的祈福旺家的乡土保护神。

台南市后壁乡后廍村正心堂奉祀金府千岁、杨府千岁、福德正神、张府妈祖（张兰）、吴府妈祖（吴秀梅）。其中，张府妈祖和吴府妈祖被尊为“姑嫂神”。据传，后壁黄姓先祖于清代从泉州迁徙至台南开垦，奉请从宝盖山姑嫂塔分灵的姑嫂金身随船护驾来到台南。相传，凡遇凶灾之年，姑嫂即现身拯救民众，乡人尊称大嫂张兰为张府妈祖、小姑吴秀梅为吴府妈祖。起先，神尊由黄家以公厝的形式奉祀，1936 年，后壁村村长黄邦发创议建庙，命名“正心堂”，1983 年重建庙宇。

台南市后壁乡正心堂。（李国宏 供图）
Zhengxin Hall in Tainan City of Taiwan. (Courtesy of Li Guohong)

The Cultural Belief in Sisters-in-Law Spreading to Taiwan

As a cultural symbol, Gusao Pagoda holds great significance not only for the overseas Chinese from Southern Fujian, but also for the close ties between Fujian and Taiwan. During the Qing Dynasty (1644—1911), as trade and transportation between Hanjiang River and Lugang Port flourished, the shipping traffic between Shishi and Taiwan grew rapidly. Sailors who braved the treacherous seas longed for comfort and emotional support from their hometown. Thus, the image of sisters-in-law, derived from the legend of Gusao Pagoda, gradually evolved into a cultural belief symbolizing family prosperity. This belief has become deeply ingrained in the hearts of people in Fujian and Taiwan, who worship the sisters-in-law as guardian deities for blessings and prosperity.

In Tainan City, Taiwan, Zhengxin Hall of Houbu Village, Houbi Township houses various deities, including Mazu of Zhang clan (known as Zhang Lan) and Mazu of Wu clan (known as Wu Xiumei), which are revered as the "sisters-in-law deities". According to legend, ancestors of the Huang family in Houbi migrated from Quanzhou to Tainan during the Qing Dynasty. They brought along golden statues of the sisters-in-law, which were enshrined in Gusao Pagoda, Baogai Mountain, for protection during their journey. It is said that whenever a disaster struck, the sisters-in-law deities would appear to save the people. Villagers respectfully refer to Zhang Lan as Mazu of Zhang clan and Wu Xiumei as Mazu of Wu clan. Initially, the deities were enshrined in a public ancestral hall by the Huang family. In 1936, Huang Bangfa, the village chief of Houbi, proposed the construction of a temple and named it "Zhengxin Hall". The temple was rebuilt in 1983.

类似的故事也在云林县流传。清嘉庆十八年（1813），福建晋江移民迁徙至台湾云林开垦，携带姑嫂金身作为保护神，庇佑航海平安。大嫂张兰、小姑吴秀梅相传为泉州人，夫君航海在外，姑嫂两人登山望海，盼望亲人回航，日久坐化成神，时常显灵，救民疾苦，保佑航海顺利。民众遂在云林县土库乡建造圣安宫，奉祀来自祖家的姑嫂神。

台南信众当中流行“姑嫂神来自福建宜梧”的说法。“宜梧”可能指的是晋江下浯，即霞浯村，这里是晋江吴姓的主要集聚地。值得注意的是，晋江霞浯吴氏祖墓位于宝盖镇坑东村靠近宝盖山的山坡上，而坑东村也是吴氏的重要集聚地。姑嫂信仰中的小姑名叫吴秀梅，与吴姓在石狮、晋江的传衍是有一定的文化关联性的。

台湾地区流传的姑嫂神信仰有几个关键要素都比较明确地指向其信仰的源头来自石狮宝盖山姑嫂塔。比如说，姑嫂登山望海，盼望亲人平安回航，这种文化象征源于石狮姑嫂塔的实物见证与民间传说。再比如说，姑嫂坐化成神后庇佑乡里，保护航海平安，这种信仰文化的塑造符合石狮海上丝绸之路的发展历程和历史解说。

台湾姑嫂信仰文化起源于清嘉庆年间，伴随移民开垦台湾的进程传入，与石狮移民开发、建设台湾的历史背景相吻合。石狮宝盖山姑嫂塔奉祀姑嫂神像始于南宋绍兴年间，延续至清代。姑嫂塔内保留着一件清代石香炉，可作为石狮曾经流行姑嫂信仰崇拜的佐证。

姑嫂信仰在台湾传播之时，被赋予保护航海平安的特殊功能，同时衍生出庇佑乡民、消灾避祸的乡土保护神。姑嫂信仰流传中出现的不同演变，恰恰印证了民间信仰在不同区域必然与当地的政治、经济、文化生态发生联系，并由此出现不一样的传播渠道和信仰的再塑造。但无论如何演变，闽台姑嫂信仰的文化本质都是“唐山过台湾”的历史见证。

Similar stories are also preserved in Yunlin County, Taiwan. In 1813, immigrants from Jinjiang, Fujian settled in Yunlin for cultivation, bringing along golden statues of the sisters-in-law as deities to bless safe voyages. Legend has it that Zhang Lan, the elder sister-in-law, and Wu Xiumei, the younger sister-in-law, hailed from Quanzhou. When their husbands were away at sea, the two sisters-in-law would climb the mountain and gaze out at the sea, praying for the safe return of their loved ones. Over time, they transformed into deities and often appeared to alleviate sufferings of the people and ensure smooth sailing. As a result, the local residents built Sheng'an Temple in Tuku, Yunlin to worship the sisters-in-law deities from their ancestral home.

In Tainan, worshippers believe that the "sisters-in-law deities come from Yiwu, Fujian". "Yiwu" may refer to Xiawu Village in Jinjiang, Quanzhou, which is the main gathering place for the Wu clan in Jinjiang. It is worth noting that the ancestral tomb of the Wu clan in Xiawu, Jinjiang is located on the slope near Baogai Mountain in Kengdong Village, Baogai Town. Kengdong Village is also an important gathering place for the Wu clan. The younger sister-in-law in the sisters-in-law belief is named Wu Xiumei, which shows a certain cultural connection with the Wu clan in Shishi and Jinjiang.

The belief in sisters-in-law deities in Taiwan is deeply rooted in the history and culture of the region. It can be traced back to Gusao Pagoda in Baogai Mountain, Shishi, which holds significant importance in the origin of this belief. One of the key elements of this belief is the act of the sisters-in-law's climbing the mountain and looking out to sea, praying for the safe return of their loved ones. This cultural symbol is derived from the physical evidence and folk legends associated with Gusao Pagoda in Shishi. Furthermore, the belief in sisters-in-law deities protecting the local community and ensuring safe voyages aligns with the development of the Maritime Silk Road in Shishi and its historical narrative.

This belief originated between 1796 and 1820, during a period of immigration and cultivation in Taiwan. It was introduced alongside the historical background of Shishi immigrants contributing to the development and construction of Taiwan. The dedication to sisters-in-law deities in Gusao Pagoda dated back to a period between 1131 and 1162 and continued until the Qing Dynasty. The popularity of the sisters-in-law belief and worship in Shishi can be seen through the extant stone incense burner from the Qing Dynasty within Gusao Pagoda.

As it spread to Taiwan, the belief took on the special function of protecting safe voyages and local deities who safeguards the community and wards off disasters were evolved. The evolution of the belief in sisters-in-law deities demonstrates the connection between folk beliefs and the local political, economic and cultural ecology, resulting in different ways of dissemination and the reshaping of beliefs. However, despite these transformations, the cultural essence of the sisters-in-law belief in Fujian and Taiwan serves as a historical witness to the phenomenon of migration from the mainland to Taiwan in China.

落日余晖下的姑嫂塔。（贾福山 摄）
Gusao Pagoda amid the glow of the setting sun. (Photo by Jia Fushan)

闽台郊商捐资修塔

清乾隆三十六年(1771)，姑嫂塔遭遇雷击，塔顶葫芦状塔刹被击落。鉴于姑嫂塔“位主离宫，焕文明之象；高出海甸，表堤岸之观”，乾隆四十三年（1778），乡绅陈元老、商世楠、高志绍、卢其珊、林振嵩等十二人，捐银一百一十元重修，并由武举人许陈彪捐资镌刻《重修塔峰记》。

陈元老（1724—1781），港塘（今石狮市灵秀镇港塘村）人，从事对台贸易，并在港塘开设典当行。长子陈梦骅，号玉山，以闽县学籍考中乾隆四十五年（1780）庚子科副榜举人。早年，港塘陈家大厝前曾竖立一对旗杆以示荣耀。陈元老父以子贵，又因乐善好施，被朝廷诰封为奉直大夫。陈家珍藏的陈元老画像中，他身着官服，端坐太师椅，显得精神抖擞。陈家大厝外墙尚保存“出砖入石”的砌筑风格，厝边一处残破的小屋为当铺仓库。一棵老榕树倚靠于残墙边，在余辉的映照下，显得格外苍劲，枝叶随风飘动，似乎仍在述说着那段远去的历史。

清乾隆四十三年《重修塔峰记》。（姜玉荣 摄）
The inscription *A Record of Pagoda Restoration* engraved in 1778 during the Qing Dynasty. (Photo by Jiang Yurong)

Merchants from Fujian and Taiwan United to Restore Gusao Pagoda

In 1771, Gusao Pagoda was struck by lightning, causing its distinctive gourd-shaped finial to fall off. Recognizing the cultural and architectural significance of Gusao Pagoda as well as its prominent location overlooking the sea dike, in 1778, a group of local elites, including Chen Yuanlao, Shang Shinan, Gao Zhishao, Lu Qishan, Lin Zhensong and seven others, came together to raise 110 silver taels for its reconstruction. Additionally, Xu Chenbiao contributed funds to engrave the inscription *A Record of Pagoda Restoration*.

Chen Yuanlao (1724—1781), born in Gangtang (now Gangtang Village, Lingxiu Town, Shishi City), was involved in trade with Taiwan and operated a pawn shop in Gangtang. His eldest son, Chen Mengxing, passed the imperial examination and became a *juren* (a successful candidate in the provincial examination) in 1780. A pair of flagpoles were once erected in front of Chen's ancestral home in Gangtang to showcase his achievements. Chen Yuanlao was also bestowed with an honorary position by the imperial court in recognition of his son's success and his own philanthropy. A portrait of Chen Yuanlao, preserved by the Chen family, depicts him wearing official attire, sitting upright on a high-backed chair, exuding a spirited aura. The exterior wall of Chen's ancestral home still retains its traditional architectural style, and a dilapidated small house next to it once served as a pawnshop warehouse. An old banyan tree leans against the remaining wall, appearing particularly vibrant in the glow of the setting sun, as if it is relaying the tales of that distant history.

港塘陈元老画像。（李国宏 供图）
The portrait of Chen Yuanlao. (Courtesy of Li Guohong)

林振嵩（1731—1799），永宁（今石狮市永宁镇）人，又名仕华，号泰侯。往台湾鹿港经商，以从事食盐零售业起家，在鹿港设立日茂行，是清代闽台贸易史上的一位代表性人物。福建社会科学院杨彦杰研究员曾专程赴台湾调查日茂行遗迹，发表《永宁与台湾“林日茂”及其家族文化》。台湾学者张炳南和叶大沛也分别在《鹿港开发史》《鹿港发展史》中介绍过林振嵩家族的历史。

已故历史学家章巽收藏的清代古航海图清晰地标有“姑嫂塔”，注明它是船舶进入泉州港的引航标志，与成书于明末清初的航海著述《指南正法》的描述相互印证，说明修缮后的姑嫂塔作为泉州港外海航标的功能一直得到延续。绘制于清道光元年（1821）的《霞泽乡地图》也标注了“姑嫂塔”，当时朝廷已经正式开放泉州府蚶江港与台湾府彰化县鹿港对渡通商，故该地图特地注明台湾商船进入泉州港时，以姑嫂塔作为导航标志。

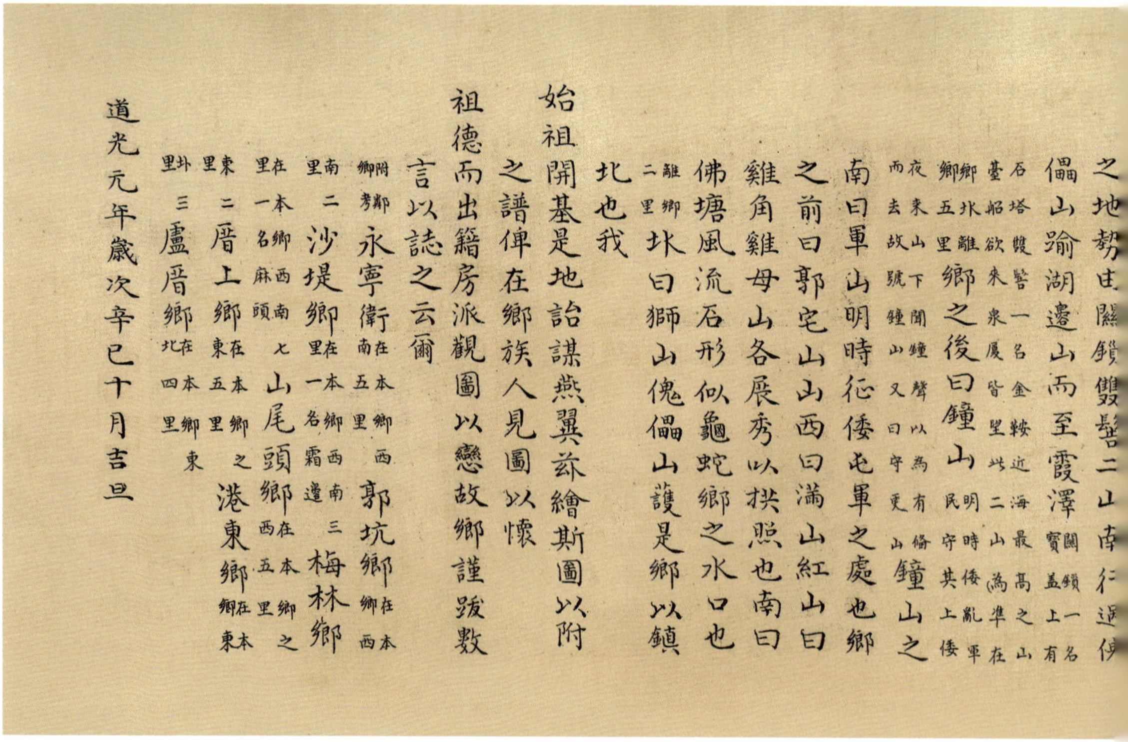
之地勢由隘鎖雙髻二山南行逕俠
偪山踰湖邊山而至霞澤關鎖一名寶蓋上有石塔雙髻一名金鞍近海最高之山臺船欲來泉厦皆望此二山為準在鄉北離鄉五里
鄉之後曰鐘山明時倭亂軍民守共上倭夜來山下聞鐘聲以為有備而去故號鐘山又曰守更山鐘山之
南曰軍山明時征倭屯軍之處也鄉
之前曰郭宅山山西曰滿山紅山曰
雞角雞母山各展秀以拱照也南曰
佛塘風流石形似龜蛇鄉之水口也
離鄉二里坵曰獅山傀儡山護是鄉以鎮
北也我
始祖開基是地詒謀燕翼爰繪斯圖以附
之譜俾在鄉族人見圖以懷
祖德而出籍房派覩圖以戀故鄉謹跋數
言以誌之云爾
附鄰鄉考永寧衛在本鄉西南五里郭坑鄉在本鄉西
南二里沙堤鄉在本鄉西南三里一名霜邊梅林鄉
在本鄉西南七里一名麻頭山尾頭鄉在本鄉之西五里
東二里厝上鄉在本鄉之東五里港東鄉在本鄉東
北三里盧厝鄉在本鄉東北四里
道光元年歲次辛巳十月吉旦

清道光元年绘制的《霞泽乡地图》。（李国宏 供图）
Xiaze Township Map drawn in 1821 of the Qing Dynasty. (Courtesy of Li Guohong)

Lin Zhensong (1731—1799), born in Yongning (now Yongning Town, Shishi City), was a prominent figure in the trade between Fujian and Taiwan during the Qing Dynasty. He started his business in salt retail and established Rimao Hang in Lugang, Taiwan. Yang Yanjie, a researcher at Fujian Academy of Social Sciences, conducted a special investigation into the remains of Rimao Hang in Taiwan and published *Yongning and Taiwan: Lin Rimao and His Family Culture*. Taiwan scholars Zhang Bingnan and Ye Dapei have also introduced the history of Lin Zhensong's family in their works *Cultivation History of Lugang* and *History of Lugang's Development* respectively.

The late historian Zhang Xun's collection of ancient maritime maps from the Qing Dynasty prominently features "Gusao Pagoda" and identifies it as a navigational landmark for ships entering Quanzhou Port. This corroborates the description in the maritime work *The Rules and Methods of Navigation*, compiled in the late Ming and early Qing Dynasty, indicating that the restored Gusao Pagoda continued to serve as a navigational beacon for Quanzhou Port. *Xiaze Township Map* drawn in 1821 also marks "Gusao Pagoda". During that time, the imperial court had officially opened trade between Quanzhou Prefecture's Hanjiang Port and Changhua County's Lugang in Taiwan. The map specifically notes that merchant ships from Taiwan used Gusao Pagoda as a navigational landmark when entering Quanzhou Port.

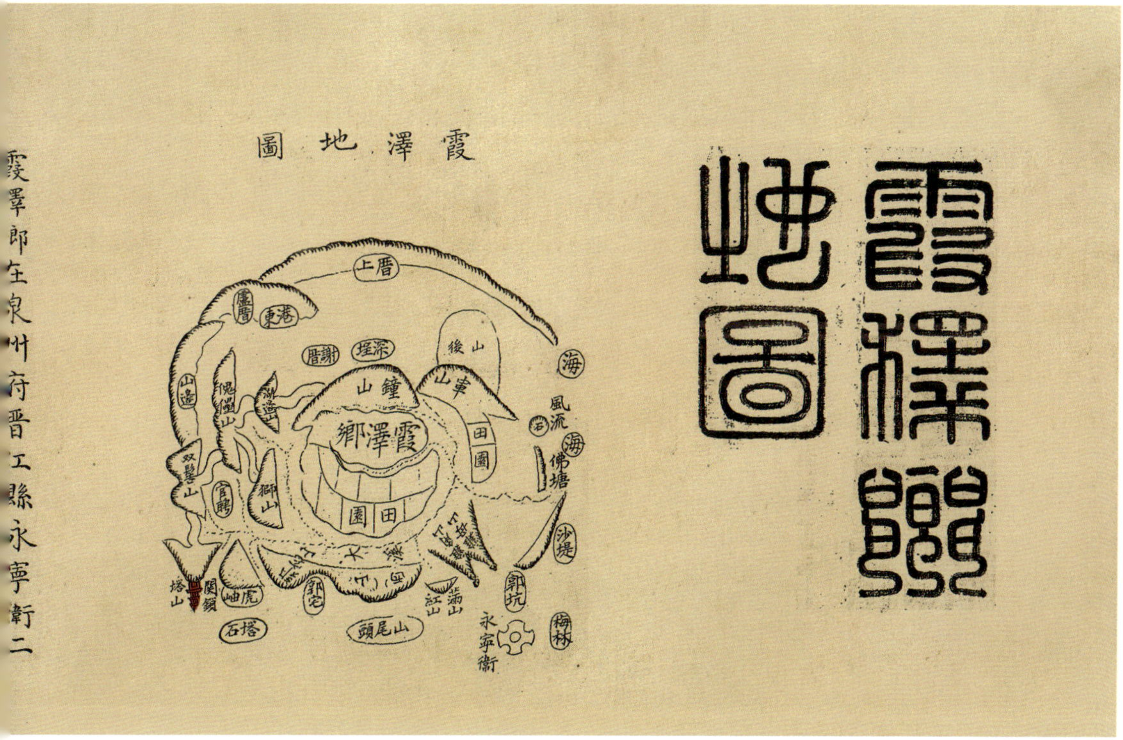

西方来客眼中的姑嫂塔

1843 年 9 月底，台湾海峡的一场风暴迫使英国人罗伯特 · 福琼乘坐的船只驶入泉州深沪湾避风。在水手们忙于修理船舶的间隙，福琼登上宝盖山顶的姑嫂塔，成为第一个实地考察姑嫂塔的西方来客。后来福琼在《两访中国茶乡》中记录："那座宝塔，就耸立在最高的山峰上，给海边过往的船只提供参照坐标。"他还翔实地描述这座航标塔的建筑特征："它的主体部分因为当初建设得很牢固，现在还算大体完整。几尊石像或者神像，圆屋顶，夹层墙，中间一部旋转而上的楼梯，通向每一层的外廊，风穿廊而过，发出呜咽的悲鸣。这座塔也就仅此而已。察看了全塔，我又站在塔上向四下眺望，视野非常开阔，可以看到数十里以外。"

从深沪湾远眺姑嫂塔。（林国雄 摄）
The view of Gusao Pagoda from Shenhu Bay. (Photo by Lin Guoxiong)

Gusao Pagoda in the Eyes of Western Visitors

In the late September of 1843, a storm in Taiwan Strait forced Robert Fortune, a British visitor, to seek shelter in Quanzhou's Shenhu Bay. While the sailors were busy repairing the ship, Fortune decided to climb to the top of Baogai Mountain and visit Gusao Pagoda, thus becoming the first Western visitor to witness its grandeur firsthand. In his work, *Two Visits to the Tea Countries of China and the British Tea Plantations in the Himalaya,* Fortune made note of the pagoda's significance as a reference point for passing ships along the coast. Furthermore, he provided a detailed description of the pagoda's architectural features, mentioning its sturdy construction, stone statues, round roof, partition walls, spiral staircases and the haunting sound of the wind passing through its corridors. After exploring the entire pagoda, Fortune stood atop and marveled at the expansive view that stretched for dozens of miles.

罗伯特·福琼画像。（李国宏 供图）
The portrait of Robert Fortune. (Courtesy of Li Guohong)

福琼发现，泉州湾是“外国船只停靠的一个码头”，泉州人“是中国最好、最有敬业精神的水手，无论哪个港口，都有他们的身影”。类似的情景也曾出现在哥伦比亚商人唐可·阿尔梅洛的笔下。此人于1856年乘坐“埃蒙特”号快船从福州前往厦门，曾在泉州港短暂停靠。从他的游记中可以看出，泉州港船舶众多，保持着与台湾及东南亚等地的商业和航运往来，也是当时鸦片贸易的主要走私港。他在《穿过鸦片的硝烟》中写道：“中途我们仅在一个叫作晋江的城市稍事停留，此地也是个港口城市。尽管它不是对外通商的口岸，码头上依然停靠着众多船舶，放眼望去，港湾里樯帆如林，大多奔着稻米、樟脑和其他物产而来。而今它也成了鸦片买卖的主要集散地之一，同外国人有着巨额的商业交易。怡和洋行和颠地洋行在这里都有接送商品的船队。”

1860年5月6日，法国远征军军医阿道尔夫·阿尔芒乘船从厦门前往上海，途经台湾海峡，清晰地看见姑嫂塔，并在他的书信集《出征中国和交趾支那来信》中留下记录：“星期天晚上海面平静了些，空气清凉，二十摄氏度，景象却有些凄凉。山顶有座宝塔，山脚下是一片带港湾的小海滩，搭着些村镇渔民的破屋窝棚。”

塔影悠悠。（陈英杰 摄）
The lingering shadow of Gusao Pagoda. (Photo by Chen Yingjie)

Fortune also discovered that Quanzhou Bay served as "a port for foreign ships to anchor", and he praised the people of Quanzhou as "the best and the most dedicated sailors in China, with their presence seen in every port". Another visitor, Colombian merchant Nicolás Tanco Armero, had a similar experience. In 1856, he traveled from Fuzhou to Xiamen on the steamer "El Monte" and made a brief stop in Quanzhou Port. According to his travelogue, it is evident that Quanzhou Port had a bustling maritime scene, maintaining commercial and shipping connections with regions like Taiwan and other places in Southeast Asia. It was also a major hub for the illicit opium trade during that time. In his work titled *Travel from New Granada to China and from China to France*, Armero wrote, "Along the way, we only made a brief stop in a city called Jinjiang, which is also a port city. Although it is not a trading port, there are still many ships docked at the pier. Looking out, we can see that the harbor is filled with masts and sails, most of them carrying rice, camphor and other goods. Nowadays, it has also become one of the main centers for opium trade, with significant commercial transactions with foreigners. Jardine Matheson and Dent & Co. have their fleets of ships transporting goods here."

On May 6, 1860, Adolphe Armand, a French Expeditionary Force physician, set sail from Xiamen to Shanghai, passing through Taiwan Strait. As he gazed upon the landscape, he couldn't help but notice Gusao Pagoda standing proudly atop the mountain. In in his collection of letters entitled *Letters from the Expedition to China and Cochinchina: Excerpt from the Medical Gazette of Paris*, he vividly described the scene: "On Sunday evening, the sea was calm, the air cool with a temperature of 20 degrees Celsius, but the scene was somewhat desolate. A pagoda adorned the mountain peak, while at its foot lay a small beach with a harbor, surrounded by dilapidated huts of villages and fishermen."

1860 年 11 月 30 日，英国军医查尔斯 · 亚历山大 · 戈登以皇家陆军医务部医院事务副总监的身份随同英国远征军来华，乘船途经台湾海峡时，看见宝盖山顶的航标姑嫂塔，并在其观察报告《一个英国军医的中国观察实录》中对宝塔的形状做了详细的描述：“进入我们视线的第一个建筑物是一座中式小宝塔，我们大概在中午经过其附近。宝塔建于一处高地，分为几层，如果大家不厌其烦地看过这些特征明显的塔楼图片的话，肯定对这个风格并不陌生。宝塔还有一个更加别具一格的特征，即每一层的八个塔檐都往上翘，而这在中国建筑中极其普遍。”

透过这些西方访客的视角，可以看出即使在航海新技术得以运用的近代，姑嫂塔依然是船舶进出泉州湾的航标。另外，在绘制于 19 世纪中期的《七省沿海全图》等中国古代航海图中，也清晰地标有大坠岛、小坠岛、六胜塔、姑嫂塔、晋江、洛阳江、洛阳桥等重要地理标志，反映了泉州港完善的港口设施体系一直得到维护和利用。

On November 30, 1860, Charles Alexander Gordon, a British military surgeon, arrived in China as the deputy inspector-general of the hospital services of the Royal Army Medical Corps, accompanying the British Expeditionary Force. During his journey through Taiwan Strait, he too caught sight of Gusao Pagoda, which served as a guiding light for ships navigating the waters. In his detailed observational report titled *The Recollections of a British Army Medical Man in China*, he described the pagoda's structure: "The first building that came into view was a small Chinese pagoda. It was situated on an elevation, with familiar terraces resembling those depicted in characteristic tower illustrations if you have seen them many times. To further accentuate its unique appearance, each of the eight angles of its terraces curved upwards, a distinct feature of Chinese architecture."

Through the accounts of these Western visitors, it becomes evident that even in the modern era, with the advent of advanced navigation technologies, Gusao Pagoda continued to serve as a prominent landmark for ships entering and leaving Quanzhou Bay. Furthermore, ancient Chinese maritime maps, such as *The Complete Map of the Seven Coastal Provinces* from the mid-19th century, clearly marked significant landmarks of Quanzhou such as Dazhui Island, Xiaozhui Island, Liusheng Pagoda, Gusao Pagoda, Jinjiang River, Luoyang River and Luoyang Bridge. This demonstrates the well-preserved and utilized infrastructure system of Quanzhou Port.

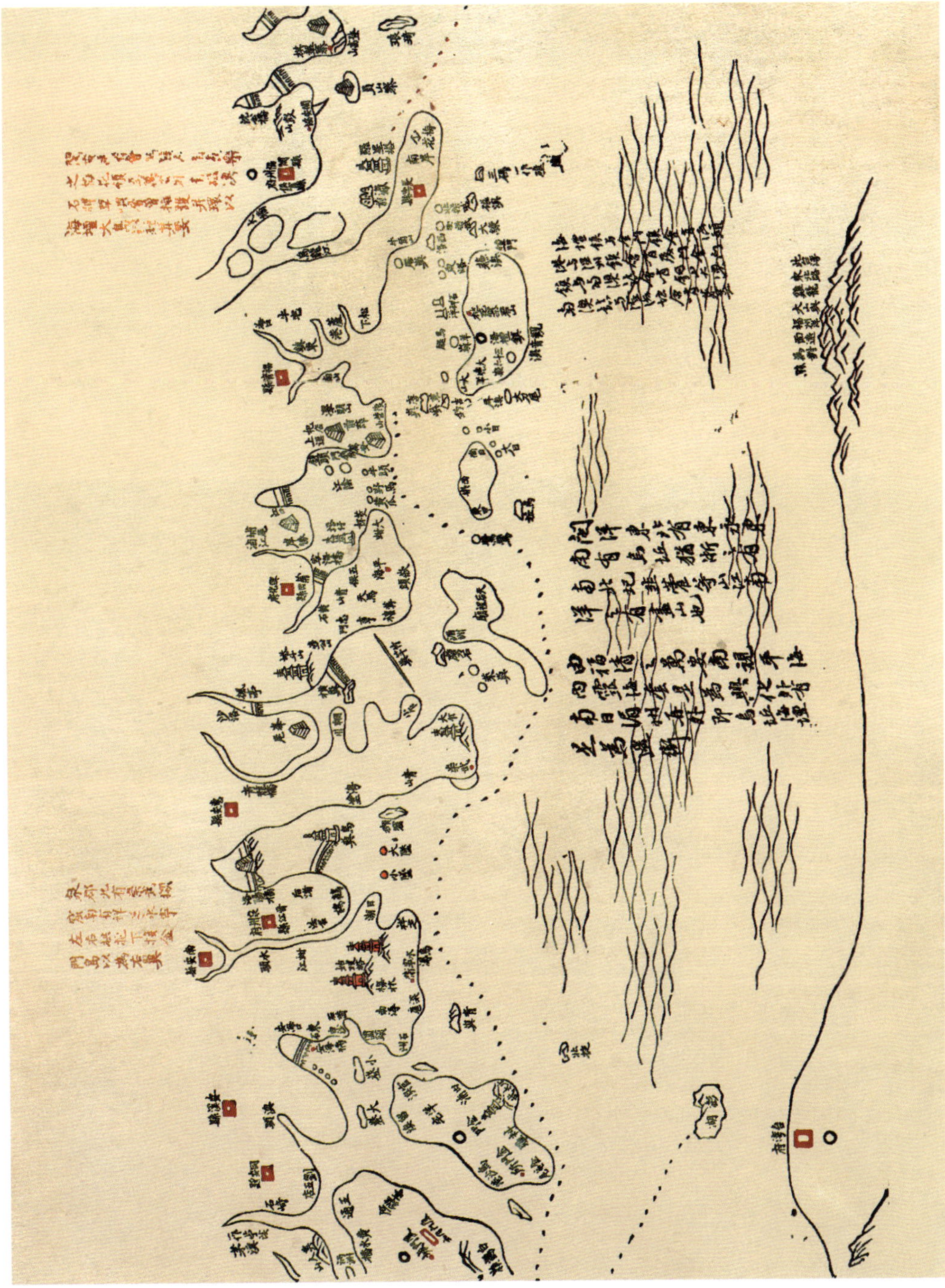

清代《七省沿海全图》。（李国宏 供图）
The Complete Map of the Seven Coastal Provinces drawn in the Qing Dynasty. (Courtesy of Li Guohong)

六胜塔：精美的石头会唱歌

六胜塔俯瞰泉州湾出海口，正对大坠岛与小坠岛之间的岱屿门主航道。南宋吴自牧《梦粱录》记载，中国商船从泉州港口出发，通过岱屿门航道，便可“放洋过海，泛往外国也”。六胜塔指引商船通过岱屿门主航道进出泉州港，万寿塔解决商船通过台湾海峡进入泉州港的导航需求，两座航标塔遥相呼应，构成古代泉州港独特又完善的导航体系。

俯瞰泉州湾的六胜塔，远处为泉州湾跨海大桥。（陈文丕 摄）
Liusheng Pagoda at the entrance of Quanzhou Bay, with Quanzhou Bay Cross-Sea Bridge in the distance. (Photo by Chen Wenpi)

Liusheng Pagoda: A Marvelous Architectural Legacy

Liusheng Pagoda, situated at the entrance of Quanzhou Bay, overlooks the main shipping lane named Daiyumen between Dazhui Island and Xiaozhui Island. According to Wu Zimu's records about Quanzhou, Chinese merchant ships departing from Quanzhou Port were able to sail to foreign lands by passing through the Daiyumen Channel. Liusheng Pagoda served as a guide for these ships, ensuring they safely entered and left Quanzhou Port through Daiyumen main shipping lane. On the other hand, Wanshou Pagoda catered to the navigation needs of merchant ships entering Quanzhou Port via Taiwan Strait. Together, these two landmarks formed a comprehensive and unique navigation system for ancient Quanzhou Port.

六胜之缘

北宋政和初年，蚶江石湖金钗山东岳寺高僧祖慧、宗什见此地扼守泉州湾出海口，“层峦耸秀，万壑争流，极山海之奇观，神灵之幽宅也”，且风光气势类似建有阿育王寺的浙江明州阿育王山，为了弘扬佛法、庇护乡里、祈求过往船只顺风顺水，遂与石湖乡绅薛公素一道募资兴建六胜塔。“六胜”之名从印度佛教的“六胜缘”而来。佛典《阿毗达摩俱舍论》记载，小乘教派有“舍多寿行”（在世舍福延寿）和“留多命行”（寿终永生享福）两种修行方式。“六胜”是修得“留多命行”必须具备的六个最佳条件，即人胜、解脱胜、修习胜、福田胜、依止胜、转业胜。祖慧、宗什应是修行小乘教派的高僧，为了成就阿罗汉果、祈求上升大自在天宫而修建了这座雄伟的六胜宝塔。

六胜塔与东岳寺。（黄国炎 摄）
Liusheng Pagoda and Dongyue Temple. (Photo by Huang Guoyan)

The Origin of Liusheng

During the period from 1111 to 1113, the Buddhist monks, Zuhui and Zongshi, residing in Dongyue Temple on Jinchai Mountain in Shihu, Hanjiang, the estuary of Quanzhou Bay, were captivated by the natural beauty of the area. They regarded it as a sacred place with breathtaking mountains and flowing streams, reminiscent of the famous Ayuwang Mountain in Mingzhou, Zhejiang, where Ayuwang Temple was located. Motivated to promote Buddhism, protect the local community and ensure the safe passage of ships, the two monks, along with Xue Gongsu, a local scholar, raised funds to construct Liusheng Pagoda. The name "Liusheng" is derived from the concept of "Six Paramitas" or "Six Perfections" in Indian Buddhism. According to the Buddhist text *Abhidharmakosha*, there are two ways of practice in the Hinayana school, which involve cultivating blessings and longevity in the current life and attaining eternal life and blessings after death. "Liusheng" refers to the six optimal conditions necessary for achieving the practice of "preserving multiple lives", namely victories over oneself, in liberation, in practice, in blessings, in reliance and in transformation. Zuhui and Zongshi, likely practitioners of the Hinayana school, built this magnificent pagoda so as to fulfill their aspirations of becoming Arhats, a high spiritual realization in Buddhism representing complete liberation from the cycle of birth and death to attain a state of ultimate liberation, and ascending to the realm of the Great Brahma Heaven, one of the heavenly realms where beings experience a high degree of bliss and happiness.

人们常常将六胜塔与泉州开元寺东西塔相提并论，如明代何乔远盛赞“其壮丽不减城中开元寺塔也”，学界也大多认为六胜塔借鉴了泉州东西塔的建筑技艺。但六胜塔的建造沿革表明，该塔始建于北宋政和初年，而开元寺西塔由砖塔改建为石塔始于南宋绍定元年（1228），竣工于嘉熙元年（1237），前后历时十年。东塔建造过程更是历经十二年，迟至淳祐十年（1250）才全部完工。如此说来，倒有可能是东西塔改建之时曾经借鉴北宋六胜塔的建造技艺。

南宋景炎二年（1277），宋端宗受元军所迫，流亡闽南，又为“导元倾宋”的官商蒲寿庚所阻，未能进入泉州城，一度避居石湖，后经石湖港出海，逃亡广东。石湖遂遭到元军洗劫，六胜塔亦未能幸免，被拆毁大半。元朝初年，泉州港海外贸易勃兴。元世祖至元二十三年（1286），重修六胜塔。元顺帝至元二年（1336），蚶江海商凌恢甫捐资重建，十二月兴工，至元五年（1339）三月完工，前后耗时两年零四个月。因此，要说六胜塔借鉴东西塔的建筑技艺，应该是在凌恢甫重建之时。

跨越近千年时光的六胜塔。（陈英杰 摄）
Liusheng Pagoda of nearly a millennium of history. (Photo by Chen Yingjie)

Liusheng Pagoda is often compared with the East and West Pagodas of Kaiyuan Temple in Quanzhou. The Ming Dynasty scholar He Qiaoyuan praised Liusheng Pagoda, saying that "Its magnificence was no less than that of the two pagodas in Kaiyuan Temple." Many scholars also believe that Liusheng Pagoda drew inspiration from the architectural techniques of the East and West Pagodas. However, the construction history of Liusheng Pagoda indicates that it was first built between 1111 and 1113. On the other hand, the conversion of the West Pagoda of Kaiyuan Temple from a brick pagoda to a stone pagoda began in 1228 and was completed in 1237, taking a total of ten years. The construction of the East Pagoda took even longer, lasting twelve years and was completed in 1250. Therefore, it is possible that during the renovation of the East and West Pagodas, they borrowed construction techniques from Liusheng Pagoda of the Northern Song Dynasty (960—1127).

In 1277, Emperor Duanzong was forced to flee to Southern Fujian due to the invasion of the Yuan army. However, he was blocked by Pu Shougeng, an official and merchant in Quanzhou who supported Yuan, and was unable to enter the city. He had to take refuge in Shihu for a while and eventually escaped to Guangdong by sea through Shihu Port. As a result, Shihu was plundered by the Yuan army, and Liusheng Pagoda was also partially demolished. In the early years of the Yuan Dynasty (1271—1368), overseas trade in Quanzhou flourished. In 1286, Liusheng Pagoda was rebuilt. In 1336, Ling Huifu, a sea merchant from Hanjiang, donated funds for the reconstruction of the pagoda. Construction began in lunar December of 1336 and was completed in lunar March 1339, taking a total of two years and four months. Therefore, if we were to say Liusheng Pagoda borrowed architectural techniques from the East and West Pagodas, it would likely be during the reconstruction period by Ling Huifu.

六胜塔是中国唯一依据印度佛教小乘教派“六胜缘”义理直接命名为“六胜”的佛塔，是宋元时期印度佛教文化与泉州本土文化交融并蓄的历史见证。独特的地理位置使得六胜塔除了具备宗教建筑的意义之外，也直接服务于泉州海外贸易的实际需求，成为泉州港主航道的航标塔，这也是六胜塔有别于东西塔的重要文化价值。凌恢甫重建六胜塔时经济实力雄厚，使六胜塔得以充分吸收传统建筑的精华，多方位采取抗震防风的技术手段，成熟驾驭仿木建筑特点，最终成为中国元代仿木楼阁式空心石塔建筑的典范。

Liusheng Pagoda is the only Buddhist pagoda in China named directly after the concept of "Six Paramitas" from the Hinayana school of Indian Buddhism. It is a historical witness to the integration of Indian Buddhist culture and local culture in Quanzhou during the Song and Yuan dynasties. Its unique geographical location not only gave it religious significance but also served the practical needs of Quanzhou's overseas trade, making it a landmark pagoda on the main shipping route of Quanzhou Port. This is an important cultural value that sets Liusheng Pagoda apart from the East and West Pagodas. When Ling Huifu reconstructed Liusheng Pagoda, he had strong economic resources, allowing the pagoda to fully incorporate the essence of traditional architecture. Various techniques were employed to enhance its seismic resistance and windproof capabilities, and the characteristics of imitating wooden architecture were skillfully incorporated. As a result, Liusheng Pagoda became a model of hollow stone pagodas in the style of imitating wooden pavilions of the Yuan Dynasty.

六胜塔，仿木楼阁式空心石塔建筑的典范。（陈英杰 摄）
Liusheng Pagoda, a model of hollow stone pagodas in the style of imitating wooden pavilions. (Photo by Chen Yingjie)

六胜塔建筑奇观

六胜塔最突出的建筑特色体现在三个方面：其一，实现了建筑艺术性与结构稳定性的完美结合；其二，集中体现了宋元时期仿木楼阁式石塔建筑的精华；其三，显示了师古而不泥古、因地制宜、独具匠心的泉州工匠精神。

六胜塔塔基牢固，准确地选择地下大片完整的花岗岩作为基础，有效避免出现砂基液化现象。基座采用一大一小相互叠加的双须弥座形式，内收外展，节奏明朗，富有层次感。在双须弥座的围护下，塔体重心向下，有利于防风抗震。相较于东西塔只设置一层须弥座，六胜塔这种双须弥座的做法显得独具匠心。须弥座束腰、华板、上枋均雕刻瑞兽和缠枝花卉，富有艺术性。石塔须弥座的流行与中国建筑重视基台的传统有关，须弥座不仅保证了石塔的坚固稳定，而且增强了艺术上庄严雄伟的气势。

六胜塔平面呈八边形，这是中国古代石塔建筑的一大特点。厚重的塔体通过八个角度延伸，边缘线条曲折柔婉，塔身线条柔和飘逸。八边形的平面结构使得每一条边的立面对地基形成的压力比较均匀，整体结构更加稳定。此外，八边形塔体外壁角度较为平缓，能削弱来自各个方向的风压，有利于抵御强风袭击。

六胜塔的须弥座结构。（李国宏 供图）
The Sumeru pedestal of Liusheng Pagoda. (Courtesy of Li Guohong)

Liusheng Pagoda: An Architectural Marvel

Liusheng Pagoda exhibits three prominent architectural features. Firstly, it seamlessly combines artistic design with structural stability, creating a harmonious and secure structure. Secondly, it is the epitome of stone pagodas that imitate the style of wooden pavilions in the Song and Yuan dynasties, capturing their essence and charm. Lastly, it reflects the creativity and adaptability of Quanzhou craftsmen, who were able to draw inspiration from ancient traditions while adding their own unique touch.

The foundation of Liusheng Pagoda is exceptionally solid and secure. Built on a large area of intact granite underground, it effectively prevents any liquefaction of the sandy base. The base of the pagoda is designed with two tiers of Sumeru pedestals, one large and one small, creating a visually appealing layered effect. The curvature of the pedestals adds to their beauty. Compared with the single-tiered Sumeru pedestals of the East and West Pagodas, this unique double-tiered pedestal design not only enhances the pagoda's stability but also showcases the ingenuity of its creators. The pedestals are exquisitely carved with auspicious beasts and intertwining floral patterns, displaying their artistic value. This design is rooted in the traditional emphasis on foundations in Chinese architecture, ensuring both solidity and grandeur.

The plan of Liusheng Pagoda features the octagonal shape commonly seen in ancient Chinese stone pagodas. The pagoda's body extends gracefully from each of its eight angles, with soft and elegant edges. The octagonal floor plan distributes the pressure evenly on the foundation, resulting in a more stable structure. Additionally, the gentle angles of the pagoda help to reduce wind pressure from different directions, making it more resistant to strong winds. This thoughtful design ensures both stability and beauty.

六胜塔塔身采用丁顺砌筑法，最大限度降低砌体剪应力的破坏。塔身逐层收分，重心向内收缩，增加抗震等级。各层门龛错位安置，避免开口集中在同一条垂直线上。塔身压力沿着八条边线的垂直面平均分散，既增强了稳定性，也使得塔体外形富有韵律感。塔盖采用攒尖顶，以塔心柱顶端作为塔盖的尖顶位置。塔顶置石质金刚宝箧式塔刹，便于抵抗风雨侵蚀。

六胜塔第一层每个转角都有一根粗壮的石柱作为支撑，柱础采用素身覆盆式，通过增加受力面积来减轻上层建筑压力对地基的重压。塔体第二层至第五层的石柱有一个共同的特点，就是每根石柱都是由三段叠接而成。叠接而成的石柱中间有缝隙，发生地震时，这些缝隙便能起到缓冲作用，抵抗摩擦和挤压的冲力，消减地震能量，不至于发生塔柱断裂、塔体倒塌的情况。“三段式接柱法”具有抗震减压的实际效果，是古代仿木石塔建筑的一项技术创新。

此外，六胜塔每层的斗拱结构与排列顺序相同，有着整齐的节奏感，显示出成熟的仿木结构建造技艺。石质斗拱的柔韧性不如木斗拱，但这些石斗拱仍具有较强的抗震能力，可以把地震力传递给有着良好抗震性能的大石柱，整个斗拱层犹如“整体浮筏式基础”，能够有效地缓解地震波对塔身的冲击。

排列有序的六胜塔斗拱。（陈英杰 摄）
Liusheng Pagoda's meticulously arranged arch layers. (Photo by Chen Yingjie)

Liusheng Pagoda showcases the traditional *Dingshun* (alternate headers and stretchers) masonry technique, ensuring its sturdy and stable structure. The pagoda is designed with layers that gradually shift the center of gravity inward, enhancing its seismic resistance. The door niches of each layer are strategically placed in a staggered arrangement to avoid concentration along a vertical line. The gravity pressure is thus evenly distributed along its vertical edges, giving the pagoda both stability and rhythmic appearance. The pagoda is crowned with an upturned eave roof and a stone Vajra treasure-box-style finial, providing resistance against wind and rain erosion.

The first level of the pagoda is supported by sturdy stone pillars, with plain-bodied inverted-basin-shaped column bases to reduce pressure on the foundation. From the second to the fifth level, each of the stone pillars is composed of three sections with gaps between them, acting as buffers during earthquakes and preventing fractures and collapse. This "three-section jointing method" represents a technological innovation in ancient wood-imitating stone pagoda architecture.

The arches on each level of the pagoda are meticulously arranged, showcasing the mature craftsmanship of wood-imitating construction. Although stone arches are less flexible than wooden ones, they still possess strong seismic resistance and can transfer seismic forces to the large stone pillars. The arch layer functions like a "floating raft foundation", effectively mitigating the impact of seismic waves on the pagoda.

六胜塔石柱。（陈英杰 摄）
The stone pillars of Liusheng Pagoda. (Photo by Chen Yingjie)

石塔建筑如果以塔身周长作为塔身高度，便符合圆形物体周长接近高度时最美观、最和谐的建筑理念，泉州东西塔的高度就分别与其第一层外围周长几乎相同。而六胜塔高度为 36 米，一层外围周长为 47 米，比例显得不甚协调。这是因为六胜塔濒临泉州湾，常年遭受强风袭击，为了更加有效地抵抗强风的破坏，工匠通过适当降低塔身高度来增加建筑的稳定性。虽然六胜塔的实际高度比理论高度低了十来米，但这并不影响六胜塔作为航标的功能，因为六胜塔选址精准，三面临海，视廊通透，可视性良好。古代泉州工匠遵循古法又不拘泥于程式，在建造过程中兼顾了六胜塔的结构稳定性、比例协调性和功能实用性。

If we build a pagoda with the circumference being similar to its height, it aligns with the architectural concept of achieving a visually pleasing and harmonious design. Applying this principle, the East and West Pagodas in Quanzhou have heights that are nearly equal to the outer perimeters of their first levels. However, Liusheng Pagoda stands at a height of 36 meters with a circumference of 47 meters, which seems disproportionate. This is because Liusheng Pagoda is situated near Quanzhou Bay and is constantly exposed to strong winds. To effectively withstand wind damage, craftsmen decided to lower the height of the pagoda in order to enhance its stability. Although the actual height of Liusheng Pagoda is about ten meters less than the theoretical height, it still serves its purpose as a navigational beacon. Liusheng Pagoda is strategically positioned, facing the sea on three sides, providing unobstructed sightline and excellent visibility. During the construction process, ancient Quanzhou craftsmen followed traditional methods while considering the stability, proportion and practicality of Liusheng Pagoda.

给人敦实稳重之感的六胜塔。（陈英杰 摄）

The solid and dignified Liusheng Pagoda. (Photo by Chen Yingjie)

六胜塔与东西塔一样，充分利用中国传统木结构的建筑技术，借鉴成熟的木作工艺，将坚硬笨重的石材雕凿成立柱、栌斗、跳头、楣枋、阑额、飞昂、飞檐、雀替等构件。塔檐则借鉴木建筑屋檐的翚飞式造型与装饰，结构严谨，布局均衡，具有轻盈挺秀的美感，仰望塔身，可感受到一种凌空欲飞的姿态。六胜塔在遵守《营造法式》原理的基础上吸纳了闽南民间建筑的精华，既保留木构建筑的灵动轻盈，也凸显石构建筑的雄伟浑厚，完美体现仿木楼阁式石塔的建筑美感。

六胜塔在保存宋塔建筑风格的基础上，也明显体现着元代建筑的特征，如塔身每一面两根立柱上端之间均架设圆鼓形琴面阑额，阑额两端楔入立柱卯孔，并做有出头，出头卷杀呈现元代霸王拳的样式。阑额的出头改善了柱子上部的结构，增强了石柱与阑额之间的拉力。此外，六胜塔各层转角石柱顶上置圆形仰莲式栌斗，这种栌斗符合元代建筑的特点，也有利于消减海风冲击。六胜塔雀替也独具特色。雀替的作用是缩短梁枋的跨度，增强梁头剪力。六胜塔的雀替较为繁复，具有鲜明的元代建筑风格，其中一、二层大立柱两旁的雀替雕刻着卷云图案，增加了建筑立面的艺术效果。

六胜塔立柱、栌斗、斗拱。（姜玉荣 摄）
The column, capblock and arch layer of Liusheng Pagoda. (Photo by Jiang Yurong)

Similar to the East and West Pagodas, Liusheng Pagoda extensively utilizes traditional Chinese wooden architecture techniques, drawing inspiration from well-established woodworking craftsmanship to sculpt the solid and heavy stone materials into various components such as columns, capblocks, corbels, lintels, architraves, flying brackets, cornices, sparrow braces and other elements. Inspired by the eaves of wooden architecture, the pagoda's eaves are designed in a soaring style with similar decorations, showcasing a well-structured layout, balanced arrangements, and a sense of lightness and grace. When gazing up at the pagoda, one can experience a sensation of soaring and floating in the sky. While adhering to the principles of *Treatise on Architectural Methods* written in the Northern Song Dynasty, Liusheng Pagoda also incorporates the essence of traditional folk architecture in Southern Fujian. It retains the nimble and lightweight characteristics of wooden structures while highlighting the grand and sturdy nature of stone structures, perfectly exemplifying the architectural beauty of a stone pagoda that imitates wood ones.

Liusheng Pagoda, while maintaining the architectural style of the Song Dynasty (960—1279), also incorporates distinct features of the Yuan Dynasty. One notable feature is the circular drum-shaped architraves with a bending surface similar to Chinese *Guqin* that are situated between the upper ends of each pair of columns on every side of the pagoda. These architraves are wedged into the column mortises and have protrusions that resemble the shape of a clenched fist, popular in the Yuan Dynasty. These protrusions not only enhance the structure of the upper part of the columns but also increase the tension between the columns and the architraves. Additionally, circular upturned lotus-shaped capblocks can be found at the top of the corner columns on each level of the pagoda. These capblocks, in line with the characteristics of the Yuan Dynasty architecture, serve to reduce the impact of sea winds. The sparrow braces of the pagoda serve to shorten the span of the beams and enhance their shear strength. The intricate carvings on the sparrow braces exhibit a distinct Yuan Dynasty architectural style, with swirling cloud patterns adorning the braces on the first and second levels, adding artistic effects to the facade.

六胜塔建筑细节。（成冬冬 摄）
The architectural details of Liusheng Pagoda. (Photo by Cheng Dongdong)

从塔身雕刻来看，与东西塔表现浓厚的佛教义理不同，六胜塔的雕刻从形象到排序都显得比较自由，融入更多的世俗文化色彩。当然，六胜塔的雕刻艺术也完全可以与东西塔相媲美：金刚、天王造型雄健，形态各异，手持各种法器，透露出威武之气；高僧、罗汉、菩萨造型圆润，神情自然，庄严肃穆；塔檐端坐镇塔将军，表情严峻，正视前方；浮雕线条流畅，简洁大气，整体画面饱满，比例协调，服饰飘带临风而动，高低起伏，富有艺术感染力。

六胜塔一至五层各龛浮雕。（李国宏 供图）
The relief sculptures enshrined in the door niches from the first to the fifth layer of Liusheng Pagoda. (Courtesy of Li Guohong)

In terms of the carvings on the body of the pagoda, Liusheng Pagoda differs from the East and West Pagodas, which prominently showcase Buddhist ideas. The carvings on Liusheng Pagoda have a more free-spirited style and incorporate a greater influence of secular culture. However, the artistic quality of these carvings can certainly rival those of the East and West Pagodas. The carvings depict vigorous and diverse figures such as vajras and heavenly guardians, each holding various Buddhist implements, emanating a sense of power and might. The representations of eminent monks, arhats, and bodhisattvas are plump and natural, conveying a solemn and dignified aura. At the corners of the eaves, there are commanding figures of guardian generals, characterized by stern expressions and a forward gaze. The relief sculptures feature smooth and concise lines, creating a sense of fullness in the overall composition. The proportions are harmonious, and the flowing garments and ribbons appear to be in motion, conveying a dynamic and artistic appeal.

凌恢甫之谜

六胜塔正面高悬的匾额写着“万寿塔”三个字，说起这方匾额，还有一段来历。元顺帝至元二年（1336）十二月，凌恢甫重建六胜塔，为了祈求众生平安，悬挂“万寿塔”匾额，表达良好愿望。匾额镌刻上款“檀越锦江凌恢甫立”，“檀越”说明凌恢甫是捐资人，“锦江”（蚶江雅称，在今石狮市北部）表明凌恢甫的籍贯是蚶江；下款“至元二年丙子腊月日建”，显示六胜塔重建工程始于1336年底。能重建此塔，说明凌恢甫绝非等闲之辈。可是，为了躲避元末战乱，蚶江凌家后来纷纷外迁，散居福建泉州和广东海丰、陆丰等地。由于史料散失，盛极一时的蚶江凌恢甫家族的变迁显得扑朔迷离。

明确记载凌恢甫重建六胜塔的史料见于清代蔡永蒹所撰《西山杂志》。祖慧募资建塔，有《闽书》为证；凌恢甫捐资重建，与现存六胜塔匾额题刻吻合。如此看来，《西山杂志》关于六胜塔建造沿革的描述并非道听途说。尤其是蔡永蒹在书中提供了南宋景炎二年（1277）元兵毁塔和元世祖至元二十二年（1285）修塔的史料，填补了六胜塔从“宋塔”转变为“元塔”期间的一段历史空白，具有重要的文献价值。

六胜塔上的“万寿塔”匾额。（姜玉荣 摄）
The plaque of "Wanshou Pagoda" on the front of Liusheng Pagoda. (Photo by Jiang Yurong)

The Mystery About Ling Huifu

The hanging plaque on the front of Liusheng Pagoda, which reads "Wanshou Pagoda", has an interesting backstory. Ling Huifu, a prominent maritime merchant in Quanzhou during the Yuan Dynasty, took on the task of rebuilding the pagoda in 1336. To wish for the well-being of all beings, a plaque with the inscription "Wanshou Pagoda" (*wanshou* means longevity) was hung. The right part of the plaque indicates that it was donated by Ling Huifu from Hanjiang (now the northern part of Shishi City), Quanzhou. The left part of the plaque indicates that the reconstruction of Liusheng Pagoda began in 1336. Ling Huifu's involvement in such a significant reconstruction project suggests his importance. However, due to the turmoil of the late Yuan Dynasty, the Ling family from Hanjiang gradually dispersed to different locations, including Quanzhou in Fujian, Haifeng and Lufeng in Guangdong. Due to the loss of historical records, however, it is difficult to trace the once prominent Ling family.

The reconstruction of Liusheng Pagoda by Ling Huifu is documented in *Xishan Miscellaneous Records* written by Cai Yongjian in the Qing Dynasty. The fundraising efforts by Zuhui are mentioned in *The Book of Min*. The donation made by Ling Huifu for the reconstruction aligns with the inscription on the plaque of Liusheng Pagoda. Therefore, the description of the construction history of Liusheng Pagoda in *Xishan Miscellaneous Records* is not mere hearsay. Cai Yongjian's work provides historical evidence, including the destruction of the pagoda by the Yuan army in 1277 during the Southern Song Dynasty (1127—1279) and its subsequent reconstruction in 1286. This fills the important historical blank about how "a pagoda of the Song Dynasty" was transferred to "a pagoda of the Yuan Dynasty". Such information holds significant value as a historical document.

据说，凌恢甫重建六胜塔之时，将剩余的资金用于修缮附近的东岳寺，寺中原有一方清道光十八年（1838）重修石碑，所刻碑记提及这段历史，可惜这方石碑早已不知所终。好在 1945 年，蚶江书法家林英仪曾经摘录东岳寺重修碑记。1954 年，文史专家吴文良和建筑专家张步骞、朱鸣泉实地考察六胜塔、东岳寺之时，也看到并摘录东岳寺碑记，确认凌恢甫建造六胜塔的史实。同时，吴文良考证了凌恢甫“经营蓄货起家”的身世，认定六胜塔作为泉州港航海标志的地位和作用。

蚶江民间称凌恢甫为“凌长者”。相传凌恢甫以从事香料、珍宝贸易成为富甲一方的海商。除了重建六胜塔，凌恢甫还捐资修建蚶江前垵、后垵两处码头，方便船舶停靠。乡民尊崇凌恢甫的家世德望，不敢直呼其名，尊其为“凌长者”。那么，关于凌恢甫的信息，除了《西山杂志》有零星记载之外，还能找到其他文献佐证吗？通过调查，发现清代《蚶江锦里吴氏大宗族谱》保存着一则与“凌长者”有关的史料：锦里吴氏始祖吴仁甫，字长善，号原江。元代，从泉州南安迁居蚶江，被称为“善士”。长子吴均举，字克任，号翊原，“娶凌氏，系蚶江长者讳恢甫公女”。吴均举夫妻合葬于锦里金茂山，由此可见，民间流传的“凌长者”掌故有其可信性。

六胜塔匾额以及第二至五层横梁均镌刻“檀越凌恢甫鼎建”字样和每一层修造的时间，民间也流传着“凌恢甫独资兴建六胜塔”的说法。但是，《闽书》却说六胜塔重建之时，石湖僧众礼请泉州开元寺诗僧释大圭撰写《石湖六胜塔缘》以募捐，留下“山势抱金钗，耸一柱擎天之雄观；地灵侔玉几，睹六龙回日之高标”的佳句。看来，释大圭的疏文虽然写得好，可惜募捐效果却不佳，最终还是靠凌恢甫独肩大任，完成六胜塔重建工程。“凌恢甫现象”反映了 14 世纪泉州海外交通和贸易的繁盛以及海商经济实力的雄厚。正是由于泉州海外交通及贸易的繁华，才造就了凌恢甫的惊人财富，而他也有着拳拳的反哺之心，这才花了两年多的时间去重建六胜塔，为当地的海商、渔民祈求平安。

至今，蚶江仍可见凌氏祖墓、凌府宅第旧址、壁将军雕像等遗迹，承载与凌恢甫有关的传奇故事，等待有心人继续破解“凌恢甫之谜”。

“檀越凌恢甫鼎建”题刻。（姜玉荣 摄）
The inscription of “Donated by Ling Huifu”. (Photo by Jiang Yurong)

According to historical accounts, when Ling Huifu rebuilt Liusheng Pagoda, he used the remaining funds to repair the nearby Dongyue Temple. This information was recorded on a stone tablet erected in 1838 to commemorate to reconstruction of the temple, which unfortunately has been lost. However, in 1945, a calligrapher named Lin Yingyi transcribed the inscription, preserving its contents. In 1954, cultural and historical expert Wu Wenliang, along with architectural expert Zhang Buqian and Zhu Mingquan, conducted a field investigation of Liusheng Pagoda and Dongyue Temple. They also transcribed the inscription at Dongyue Temple, confirming that Ling Huifu was responsible for rebuilding Liusheng Pagoda. Wu Wenliang further verified Ling Huifu's background as a successful merchant involved in foreign trade and identified Liusheng Pagoda as a significant maritime landmark of Quanzhou Port.

Ling Huifu, known as "Elder Ling" among the people of Hanjiang, was a wealthy sea merchant who traded spices and precious goods. In addition to rebuilding Liusheng Pagoda, he donated funds to build two docks in Hanjiang, Qian'an and Hou'an, to facilitate ship docking. Due to his family background and reputation, the local villagers held him in high regard, referring to him as "Elder Ling". While there are sporadic records in *Xishan Miscellaneous Records*, further evidence about Ling Huifu can be found in *Genealogy of the Wu Family in Hanjiang Jinli* of the Qing Dynasty. This genealogy contains historical materials related to "Elder Ling" and confirms his connection to the Wu family through marriage. The burial site of Wu Junju and his wife (Ling's daughter) on Jinmao Mountain in Jinli Village further supports the credibility of the folk legend about "Elder Ling".

The plaque of Liusheng Pagoda and the horizontal beams of its second to fifth levels all engraved with the characters meaning "Donated by Ling Huifu" and the respective construction dates of each level align with the local saying that "Ling Huifu single-handedly financed the construction of Liusheng Pagoda." However, according to *The Book of Min*, when Liusheng Pagoda was rebuilt, the monks of Shihu asked the renowned poet monk Shi Dagui of Kaiyuan Temple in Quanzhou to write a commentary to solicit funds for the construction. In this commentary, Shi Dagui wrote beautiful lines describing the majesty of the mountain and its prime location. Despite the well-written commentary, the fundraising efforts were not successful, and it was ultimately Ling Huifu who took on the responsibility and completed the reconstruction of Liusheng Pagoda. The "Ling Huifu phenomenon" reflects the prosperity of overseas trade and transport in Quanzhou during the 14th century, as well as the economic power of maritime merchants. Ling Huifu amassed his wealth through the flourishing overseas trade and commerce in Quanzhou, and he had a strong desire to repay his fortune. That's why he spent over two years rebuilding Liusheng Pagoda, praying for the safety and well-being of the local maritime merchants and fishermen.

Even today, remnants such as the ancestral tomb of the Ling family, the former site of Ling's residence and the statue of General Bi, which is said to be the door-god at the gate, can still be found in Hanjiang. They hold the legendary stories associated with Ling Huifu and are waiting to be explored by those curious about the "mystery about Ling Huifu".

蚶江壁将军雕像，相传为凌恢甫府宅遗物。（李国宏 供图）

The statue of General Bi at Hanjiang, which is said to be a relic from the residence of Ling Huifu. (Courtesy of Li Guohong)

定格六胜塔的历史地位

宋代，商船只要从泉州港出发，通过岱屿门航道，便可放洋过海，驶往外国。这些远洋海船都会配备一位“火长”，专门负责看管罗盘与指南针，以保证海上航行安全。元代，刺桐港成为官方确立的重要外贸港口。大德元年（1297），置福建平海行中书省，以泉州为治所，这是泉州行政建制史上绝无仅有的一次“最高配置”，标志着海上丝绸之路进入“泉州时代”。泉州成为“梯航万国”的国际大都会，“四海舶商，诸蕃琛贡，皆于是集乎”。发达的海外贸易培养了泉州人“以海为田”的海洋意识，“罟师估人，高帆健橹，疾榜击汰，出没于雾涛风浪中，习而安之，不惧也”。沿海民众积极参与对外贸易，不仅促进泉州经济的持续增长，也使当地形成开放包容的文化气质和乐善好施的民风民俗。万历《泉州府志》载：“晋江人文甲于诸邑，石湖、安平番舶去处，大半市易上国及诸岛夷。稍习机利，不能如山谷淳朴矣。然好礼相先，轻财能施，曷可少也。”

The Historical Significance of Liusheng Pagoda

During the Song Dynasty, Quanzhou Port was a major hub for Chinese merchant ships setting off on overseas voyages through Daiyumen Channel. Each of these ships had a “fire watcher” who was responsible for watching over the compass and ensuring safe navigation. In the Yuan Dynasty, Zayton (another name for ancient Quanzhou) Port became an officially recognized important port for foreign trade. In 1297, Fujian Pinghai Administrative Province was established, with Quanzhou as its capital. This was a groundbreaking administrative setup for Quanzhou and marked the beginning of the “Quanzhou Era” of the Maritime Silk Road. Quanzhou became an international metropolis known as the “Gateway to the World”, attracting merchants and envoys from all over. The thriving overseas trade fostered a maritime consciousness among the people of Quanzhou, who became skilled navigators unafraid of the challenges posed by winds and waves. The coastal population actively participated in foreign trade, which not only boosted Quanzhou’s economy but also created an open and inclusive cultural atmosphere, with local customs of benevolence and charity. *Local Chronicles of Quanzhou Prefecture* during the period between 1573 and 1620 states: “Jinjiang people excel in culture, and Shihu and Anping are the main destinations for foreign ships. Most of the trading is conducted with neighboring countries and islands. People there are somewhat opportunistic, who cannot be compared to those unsophisticated people from mountainous areas. Nevertheless, they prioritize etiquette, and are generous with their wealth, which should not be underestimated.”

六胜塔正对大坠岛与小坠岛，扼守岱屿门主航道。（吴文斌 摄）
Liusheng Pagoda is situated at the entrance of Quanzhou Bay and overlooks the main shipping lane named Daiyumen between Dazhui Island and Xiaozhui Island. (Photo by Wu Wenbin)

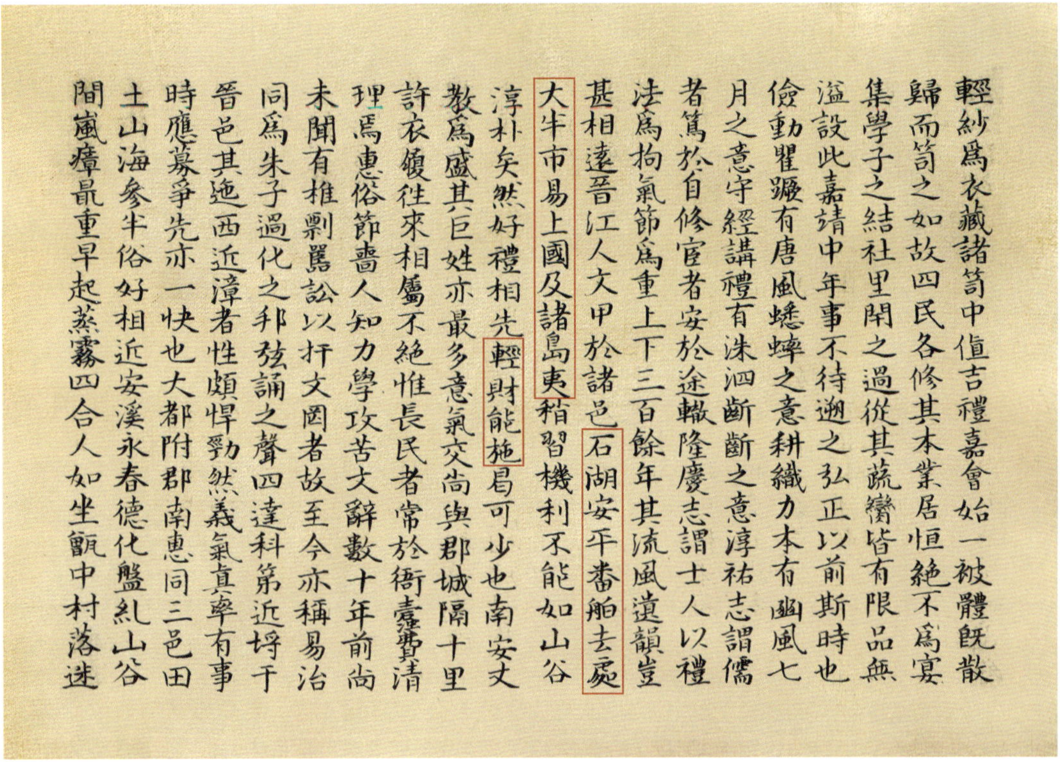
輕紗爲衣藏諸笥中值吉禮嘉會始一被體既散
歸而笥之如故四民各修其本業居恒絶不爲宴
集學子之結社里閈之過從其蔬饗皆有限品無
濫設此嘉靖中年事不待遡之弘正以前斯時也
儉動瞿瞿有唐風蟋蟀之意耕織力本有豳風七
月之意守經講禮有洙泗斷斷之意淳祐志謂儒
者篤於自修宦者安於途轍隆慶志謂士人以禮
法爲拘氣節爲重上下三百餘年其流風遺韻豈
甚相遠晉江人文甲於諸邑石湖安平番船去處
大半市易上國及諸島夷稍習機利不能如山谷
淳朴矣然好禮相先輕財能施曷可少也南安文
教爲盛其巨姓亦最多意氣交尚與郡城隔十里
許衣屨往來相屬不絶惟長民者常於衙蠹費清
理焉惠俗節嗇人知力學攻苦文辭數十年前尚
未聞有椎剽囂訟以扞文罔者故至今亦稱易治
同爲朱子過化之邦弦誦之聲四達科第近埒于
晉邑其迤西近漳者性頗悍勁然義氣直率有事
時應募爭先亦一快也大都附郡南惠同三邑田
土山海參半俗好相近安溪永春德化盤紆山谷
間嵐瘴最重早起蒸霧四合人如坐甑中村落迷

明万历版《泉州府志》中关于泉州贸易及民风的记载。（李国宏 供图）

The record about trade and folk customs in Quanzhou in *Local Chronicles of Quanzhou Prefecture* written between 1573 and 1620 during the Ming Dynasty. (Courtesy of Li Guohong)

然而，在获得巨大商业利润的同时，海商也随时会面临各种风险，更需要从宗教信仰中寻找精神上的慰藉，并通过行善积德来满足情感上的寄托。正所谓："海舶无禁，利入甚富且易，不捐之桥梁道路，则以崇侈释氏，无所爱惜，理或然欤。"由此可见，凌恢甫重建六胜塔浓缩着"刺桐梦华录"的辉煌，见证了泉州海港设施建设的成就、航海技术的发达和海外贸易的繁盛。

1981 年，石湖水域打捞出一件明代远洋船舶使用的四爪铁锚，现保存于泉州湾古船陈列馆中。该铁锚的形状与 1597 年罗懋登所撰《三宝太监西洋记通俗演义》中的铁锚图相似，见证了郑和下西洋船队经停泉州石湖港的历史事实，郑和船队经停的海湾至今仍被称为"三宝澳"。以海港石塔为航标的做法，也随着海上丝绸之路的延伸对东南亚地区港口导航设施的使用产生明显的影响。明代巩珍《西洋番国志》记载："（占城）国之东北百里有海口名新州港（今越南归仁港），岸上有一石塔，诸处船望见塔即收港。"

石湖水域打捞明代铁锚时的现场调运画面。（陈鹏鹏 摄）
The scene of transporting an iron anchor used by the Ming Dynasty ocean-going ship excavated from the waters of Shihu Port. (Photo by Chen Pengpeng)

Maritime merchants, while making immense profits, also faced risks and thus sought solace in religious beliefs. They fulfilled their emotional needs through acts of charity. As the saying goes, "Without restrictions on maritime trade, wealth can be easily gained. If the wealthy do not donate money for the maintenance of bridges or roads, they may become extravagant and release their desires without any restraint." From this, it can be seen that the reconstruction of Liusheng Pagoda by Ling Huifu encapsulates the splendor of the prosperity in Zayton, showcasing the achievements of its harbor facilities, advanced navigation technology and flourishing overseas trade.

In 1981, a four-claw iron anchor used by the Ming Dynasty ocean-going ship was excavated from the waters of Shihu Port, which is now preserved in the Museum of Quanzhou Bay Ancient Ships. Interestingly, the shape of this iron anchor matches the one depicted in Luo Maodeng's work in 1597, *Popular Stories of Sanbao Eunuch's Journey to the Western World.* This suggests that Zheng He's fleet made a stop at Shihu Port in Quanzhou during their voyages. Even today, the bay where they stopped is known as Sanbao Bay. The use of stone pagodas as navigational landmarks also had a significant influence on the use of navigation facilities in ports throughout Southeast Asia, as the maritime Silk Road extended. Gong Zhen's *Records of Foreign Countries in the Western World* written during the Ming Dynasty mentioned: "To the northeast of the country of Champa, there is a sea mouth called Xinzhou Port (today known as Qui Nhon Port in Vietnam). On the shore, there is a stone pagoda, and ships from various places would immediately enter the port upon sighting the pagoda."

明代《泉州府舆地图说》、清代《福建海岸全图》《七省沿海全图》等古地图，也无一例外地绘有六胜塔图标，反映了泉州完善的海港导航设施体系一直得到保护与利用。2001 年 11 月 8 日，中葡两国邮政主管部门联合发行的《古代帆船》特种邮票首发式在福建泉州和葡萄牙里斯本同时举行。该套邮票包含两枚，其中一枚表现的是泉州湾出土的宋代海船，背景就是六胜塔；另一枚表现的是 15 世纪的葡萄牙远航帆船，背景则是贝勒姆灯塔。方寸之中，巍然耸立的六胜塔守护着岱屿门航道，迎送着每一次的天际归帆，也凝结着刺桐港的万千风情。

明代《泉州府舆地图说》绘有孤山塔（万寿塔）、石湖塔（六胜塔）图标。（李国宏 供图）

The Geographic Map of Quanzhou Prefecture of the Ming Dynasty depicts icons of Gushan Pagoda (Wanshou Pagoda) and Shihu Pagoda (Liusheng Pagoda). (Courtesy of Li Guohong)

Ancient maps such as *The Geographic Map of Quanzhou Prefecture* of the Ming Dynasty, *The Complete Map of Fujian Coast* and *The Complete Map of the Seven Coastal Provinces* of the Qing Dynasty also depict the iconic symbol of Liusheng Pagoda, reflecting the sound harbor navigation system in Quanzhou has always been maintained and utilized. On November 8, 2001, China and Portugal held a joint ceremony to issue a set of special postage stamps featuring ancient sailing ships. One stamp showcased a Song Dynasty sea vessel unearthed from Quanzhou Bay with Liusheng Pagoda in the background, while the other depicted a 15th-century Portuguese sailing ship with the Belém Tower in the background. On the small stamp the towering Liusheng Pagoda stands as a guardian over Daiyumen Channel, welcoming and bidding farewell to every sail on the horizon, and embodying the charm of Zayton Port.

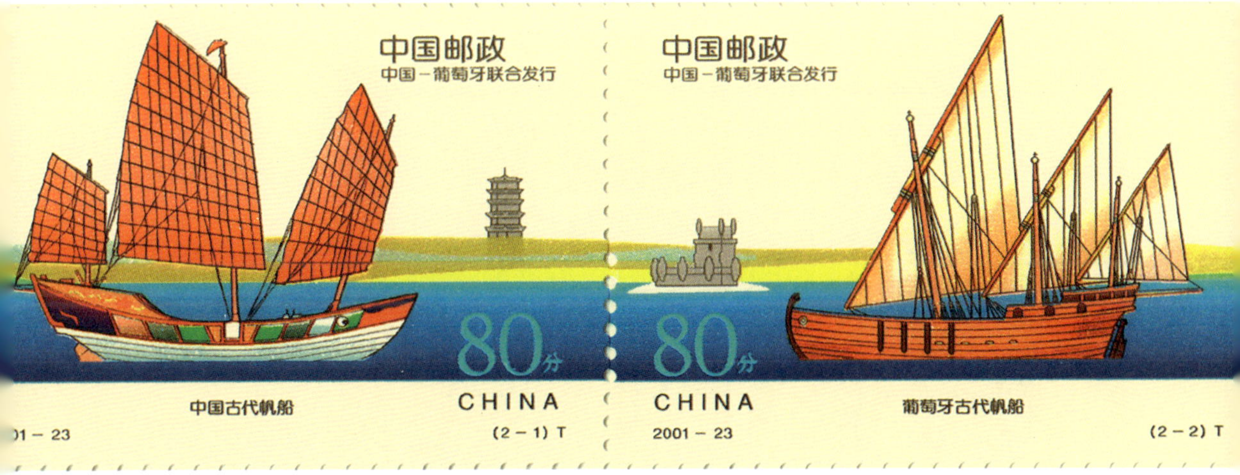

中葡两国邮政主管部门联合发行的《古代帆船》特种邮票。（李国宏 供图）

The special postage stamps of *Ancient Sailing Ships* jointly issued by the postal authorities of China and Portugal. (Courtesy of Li Guohong)

东岳大帝从山神到海神的转变

石湖东岳寺与六胜塔相邻，据传，寺庙始建于唐开元十八年（730）。寺中存有两尊宋代金刚力神浮雕，威风凛凛，堪称镇寺之宝。东岳寺供奉东岳大帝，又名泰山神，本是山神，位居五岳神之尊。后人根据《封神演义》的故事，将东岳大帝附会为“威行天下，义重四方”的忠良君子黄飞虎，尊为“天齐仁圣大帝”，总管人间吉凶祸福。

从宋代开始，泉州沿海地区供奉东岳大帝的庙宇多了一项功能，那就是祈求东岳大帝“镇压飓风”，以保佑航海平安。祖慧、宗什募建六胜塔成功之后，该塔成为海港地标，附近航道畅通，船舶往来顺利，商贸兴盛，进入泉州港的商船时常停靠石湖码头，船上商客必备办厚礼答谢东岳大帝，东岳寺因此香火鼎盛，闻名遐迩。直至清代，闽台两岸从事通商贸易的商人依然崇奉东岳大帝为航运保护神。

蚶江著名郊商欧阳捷从事蚶江与台湾鹿港之间的航运业务，“经营劳苦，创置舟楫以济不通，自是财源日进，利薮无穷”。清道光十七年（1837），当他发现“岳帝庙门庭颓坏，殿宇荒凉”之时，便捐巨资重修，“以鼎建告成之日，勒碑庙侧，凡兹邻里乡党，莫不闻风仰慕”。东岳寺现在依然保存着欧阳捷题名敬奉的石供桌。

在泉州，东岳大帝从山神转变为镇风神，最终演化成航海保护神，看似只是“职能”的转变，实际上反映了泉州港海上贸易兴盛的史实和当时航运业者现实的需求。

东岳寺宋代金刚力神雕像。（成冬冬 摄）
The Song Dynasty sculptures of Vajrapani at Dongyue Temple. (Photo by Cheng Dongdong)

The Transformation of Emperor Dongyue from a Mountain Deity to a Sea Deity

Dongyue Temple, located near Liusheng Pagoda, is believed to have been constructed in 730. The temple houses two majestic-looking sculptures of Vajrapani passed down from the Song Dynasty, which are considered invaluable treasures. Within Dongyue Temple, Emperor Dongyue, also known as the deity of Mount Tai, is enshrined. Originally a mountain god, Emperor Dongyue held a prominent position among the deities of the Five Sacred Mountains in China. Over time, Emperor Dongyue became associated with Huang Feihu, a virtuous and courageous figure known for his loyalty and righteousness. Consequently, he was revered as the "Divine Emperor of Benevolence", believed to oversee the fortunes and misfortunes of the world.

Since the Song Dynasty, the temples dedicated to Emperor Dongyue in the coastal areas of Quanzhou have served an additional purpose: praying for the Emperor's intervention in controlling typhoons to ensure safe navigation. After Zuhui and Zongshi constructed Liusheng Pagoda, it became a landmark in the harbor, ensuring smooth navigation in the nearby waterways and promoting prosperous trade. When merchant ships arrived at Quanzhou Port, they often anchored at Shihu Dock, and merchants and passengers on board would present offerings to express their gratitude to Emperor Dongyue. As a result, Dongyue Temple flourished and gained widespread renown. Even during the Qing Dynasty, merchants engaged in trade between Fujian and Taiwan continued to revere Emperor Dongyue as the guardian of maritime transportation.

Ouyang Jie, a renowned merchant from Hanjiang, was involved in the shipping business between Quanzhou's Hanjiang and Lukang in Taiwan. Through his hard work and the establishment of boats and ships to overcome obstacles, his wealth grew exponentially, and his profits were immeasurable. In 1837, when he discovered the dilapidated state of Dongyue Temple's gate and deserted halls, he generously donated a substantial sum of money for its restoration. Upon completion, a stone tablet was erected next to the temple, attracting visitors from neighboring villages and towns who came to admire his benevolence. To this day, Dongyue Temple proudly preserves the stone altar inscribed with Ouyang Jie's name as a mark of reverence.

The transformation of Emperor Dongyue in Quanzhou from a mountain deity to a wind-controlling deity, and eventually to a protector of maritime navigation, not only reflects a shift in function but also highlights the historical reality of the thriving sea trade in Quanzhou Port and the practical needs of the maritime industry participants during that era.

扬帆启航

Docks: Docking Sites for Foreign Merchant Ships

石湖码头：送你一片辽远的蓝

Shihu Dock: Facing a Vast Blue Sea

江口码头：穿越法石港的千里烟波

Estuary Docks: Amidst the Vast Waves along Fashi Port

石湖码头：送你一片辽远的蓝

石湖地处泉州湾出海口，石湖半岛延伸至海中，形成一个天然的避风港湾，地理位置得天独厚。唐开元八年（720），晋江航海家林銮在此建造石湖码头，俗称“林銮渡”。北宋元祐年间，担任过侍禁的晋江籍官员傅碓修建通济栈桥，连接林銮渡，使之成为宋元时期泉州港水陆转运的重要外港码头。石湖码头构造科学，经久耐用，是早期码头建筑中的珍品，也是古代泉州港海外贸易繁盛和多元文化融合的重要历史见证。

泉州石湖港区。（陈英杰 摄）
Shihu Port Area in Quanzhou City. (Photo by Chen Yingjie)

Shihu Dock: Facing a Vast Blue Sea

Shihu, situated at the mouth of Quanzhou Bay, boasts Shihu Peninsula that stretches out into the sea, creating a natural sheltered harbor and establishing itself as a crucial strategic location. In 720, the intrepid maritime explorer Lin Luan constructed Shihu Dock, which became widely known as "Lin Luan Ferry". During the period from 1086 to 1094, Fu Jin, an official from Jinjiang and former court censor, built Tongji Jetty, linking with Lin Luan Ferry and transforming the latter into a vital outer port for water-land transshipment within Quanzhou Port during the Song and Yuan dynasties. The construction of Shihu Dock was meticulously planned and built to last, making it a precious treasure among early dock structures. It also serves as a significant historical testament to the flourishing overseas trade and cultural blending in ancient Quanzhou Port.

林銮的“第一桶金”

有关林銮建造石湖码头的文献史料出自清嘉庆年间晋江人蔡永蒹所撰《西山杂志》。据其载，唐开元八年，东石（今泉州市晋江市东石镇）航海家林銮在石湖建造码头，开通泉州至渤泥（文莱）航线，以丝绸换取香料，取得丰厚的利润，带动泉州沿海民众参与东南亚地区的贸易，香料由此成为泉州港最大宗的进口商品，并产生了深刻的社会影响。

“林銮试舟到勃（渤）泥，往来有利。沿海畲家人俱从之往，引来蕃舟。蛮人喜彩绣，武陵多女红，故以香料易彩衣。”一个“试”字，道尽了林銮一路向海的开拓精神和走向深蓝的坚定信心。而那个“喜”字，则形象地刻画出当年泉州出口的丝绸、瓷器、金属制品以及琳琅满目的“中国制造”在海外市场上成为抢手货的情景。在平等互利的贸易往来中，渤泥盛产的龙脑、樟脑、降真香、黄蜡等名贵香料也深受中国客商的欢迎，“香料易彩衣”表明泉州与渤泥在经济贸易上的互补性。

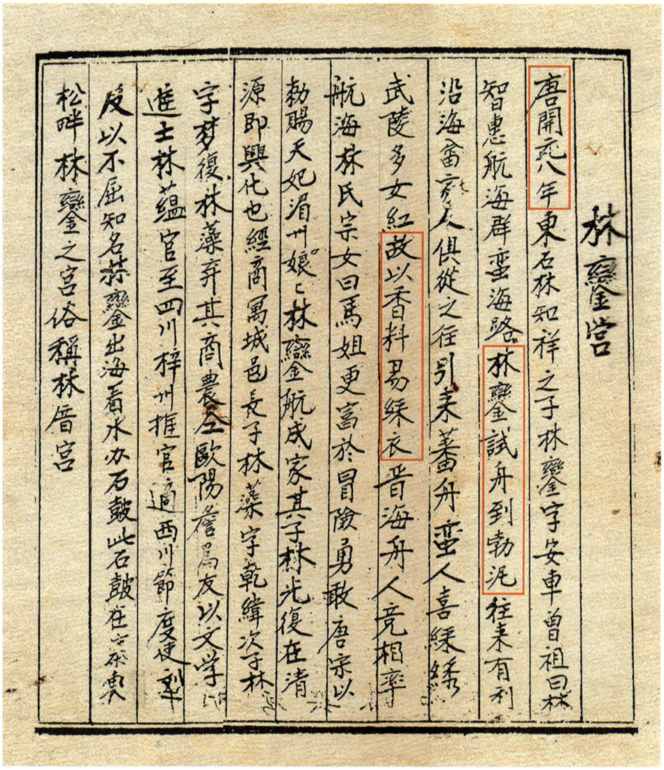
林鑾宮
唐開元八年東石林知祥之子林鑾字安東曾祖曰林
智惠航海群蛮海路林鑾試舟到勃泥往来有利
沿海畲家人俱從之往引来蕃舟蛮人喜綵繡
武陵多女紅故以香料易綵衣晋海舟人竞相率
航海林氏宗女曰馬姐更富於冒險勇敢唐宗以
勅賜天妃湄州娘娘林鑾航成家其子林光復在清
源即興化也經商羈城邑長子林藻字乾緯次子林
字芳復林藻弃其商農金歐陽詹為友以文學
進士林蘊官至四川梓州推官適西川節度使劉
反以不屈知名茶鑾出海看水办石鼓此石鼓在[illegible]
松畔林鑾之宮俗稱林厝宮

清代蔡永蒹《西山杂志》中关于林銮通航渤泥的记载。（李国宏 供图）
The record about Lin Luan's navigating Brunei in Cai Yongjian's *Xishan Miscellaneous Records* of the Qing Dynasty. (Courtesy of Li Guohong)

Lin Luan's "First Fortune"

The historical accounts of Lin Luan's construction of Shihu Dock can be found in a work entitled *Xishan Miscellaneous Records* written by Cai Yongjian, a native of Jinjiang, during the period between 1796 and 1820. According to the records, in the year 720, Lin Luan, a skilled navigator from Dongshi (now Dongshi Town, Jinjiang City, Quanzhou), built a dock in Shihu and successfully established a trade route from Quanzhou to Brunei. This route enabled the exchange of silk for spices, resulting in substantial profits. As a result, many coastal residents of Quanzhou were attracted to engage in trade with Southeast Asia, making spices the primary imported commodity at Quanzhou Port and bringing about much social impact.

As was recorded, Lin Luan tried sailing to Brunei and his voyages proved to be profitable. Members of the coastal She family were inspired by his success and also ventured to Brunei, returning with foreign vessels. These foreigners had a liking for colorful embroideries, and since Wuling (Quanzhou) had an abundance of needlework, they traded spices in exchange for vibrant clothing. The word "tried" exemplifies Lin Luan's pioneering spirit and unwavering confidence in exploring the vast ocean. The word "liking" vividly depicts the widespread popularity of Chinese products such as silk, porcelain and metal goods in overseas markets. In a mutually beneficial trade, the precious spices produced in Brunei, such as borneol, camphor, Dalbergia and yellow wax, were highly sought after by Chinese merchants. The phrase "traded spices in exchange for vibrant clothing" highlights the economic and trade complementarity between Quanzhou and Brunei.

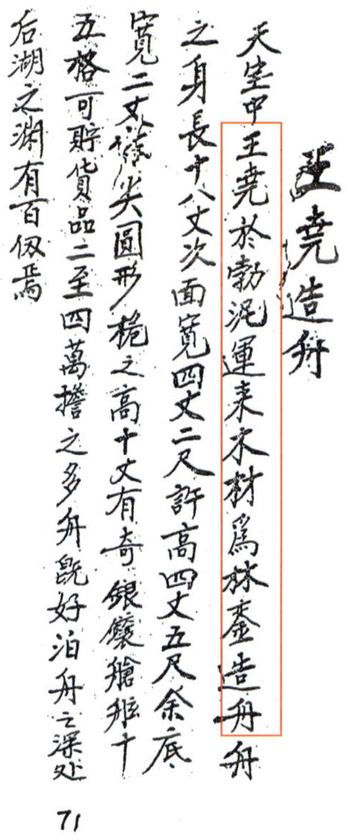
王堯造舟

天寳中王堯於勃泥運来木材爲林銮造舟舟之身長十八丈次面寬四丈二尺許高四丈五尺余底寬二丈操尖圆形桅之高十丈有奇銀鐮艙舡十五格可貯貨品二至四萬擔之多舟既好泊舟之深处后湖之湖有百仞焉

71

《西山杂志》中关于王尧为林銮造舟的记载。（林瀚 供图）

The record about Wang Yao building a boat for Lin Luan in *Xishan Miscellaneous Records*. (Courtesy of Lin Han)

林銮的付出得到应有的回报，当返航的季风来临之时，停泊石湖码头的商船运回属于林銮的“第一桶金”。他的航海故事在蔡永蒹生活的年代依然流传于晋江民间。这些早期泉州港海外贸易兴起之时的历史信息经过沉淀之后，成为晋江民间的一种乡土记忆和文本复述。泉州（丝绸）、林銮（码头）、渤泥（香料）构成林銮航海故事的核心元素，这些元素是真实存在的，也是唐代泉州航海文明的历史印迹。

2019 年 2 月，福建博物院联合石狮市博物馆，对石湖码头通济栈桥进行小范围的考古发掘，在早期堆积层中出土五代青瓷碗和北宋白瓷碗等遗物，印证了北宋元祐年间建造通济栈桥的文献记录是可靠的，同时佐证了《西山杂志》关于林銮渡建造于唐代的说法是可信的，石湖码头历史沿革的逻辑性是合理的。海外学者的研究成果也证实唐代中国商人在加里曼丹岛的活动轨迹。文莱国家博物馆名誉馆长罗伯特 · 尼科尔根据史料推测，晚唐时期来自中国的商人为了掌控樟脑贸易，选择留居加里曼丹岛东北部（今马来西亚沙巴所在地），那里曾经出现过一个中国人的聚落。1958 年，沙捞越尼亚洞曾出土唐代石制器具、陶瓷器、金属器皿、珠宝以及钱币等文物，成为唐代中国与渤泥之间有着密切友好交往关系的历史见证。

林銮古渡口。（陈英杰 摄）
The ancient Lin Luan Ferry. (Photo by Chen Yingjie)

Lin Luan's efforts paid off when the merchant ships docked at Shihu Dock, bringing him his "first fortune". The story of Lin's maritime adventures was still popular among the people of Jinjiang during Cai Yongjian's era, being a cherished part of local folklore. Quanzhou (known for silk), Lin Luan (known for building the dock), and Brunei (known for spices) are tangible elements that form the core of Lin Luan's maritime tale, serving as historical imprints of Quanzhou's maritime civilization during the Tang Dynasty (618—907).

In February 2019, Fujian Museum, in collaboration with Shishi City Museum, conducted a small-scale archaeological excavation of Tongji Jetty in Shihu. The discovery of artifacts such as celadon bowls of the Five Dynasties (907—960) and white porcelain bowls of the Northern Song Dynasty in the early layers of accumulation provided evidence that Tongji Jetty was built between 1086 and 1094, supporting the claims made in *Xishan Miscellaneous Records* regarding the construction of Lin Luan Ferry during the Tang Dynasty. Overseas scholars' research has also confirmed the presence of Chinese merchants in Kalimantan Island during the Tang Dynasty. Historical records suggest that Chinese merchants settled in the northeastern part of Kalimantan (now located in Sabah, Malaysia) in the late Tang Dynasty to control the camphor trade, as speculated by Robert Nicol, the honorary curator of Brunei National Museum. In 1958, some Tang Dynasty cultural relics such as stone tools, ceramics, metal utensils, jewelry and coins unearthed in Niah Caves, Sarawak served as historical evidence of the close and friendly relationship between Tang China and Brunei.

石湖码头出土的宋代瓷片。（李国宏 供图）

The Song Dynasty porcelain fragments excavated at Shihu Port. (Courtesy of Li Guohong)

石湖巡检寨监管番舶

潮落潮起，涛声依旧，林銮的航海传奇化作一丝丝印记，清晰地镌刻在石湖码头的礁盘上，弥漫着历史的芳香，使泉州与渤泥之间的故事至今依旧引人入胜。北宋元丰五年（1082），渤泥国遣使入贡，返程之时，渤泥使臣请求从泉州港搭乘海船回国，得到朝廷的许可。要知道泉州市舶司的设立是五年之后的元祐二年（1087），这说明在被朝廷正式确立为国际贸易港之前，泉州港已经积蓄巨大的能量，发挥重要的作用，产生重大的影响。渤泥使臣的请求得到批准，说明当时的泉州港已拥有高超的造船技术，其海外航线的便捷性与安全性也已经受到普遍的认可与信任。

航道畅通和航运安全是海外贸易得以顺利进行的基本保障，泉州港需要建立完善和行之有效的海防管理体系。北宋熙宁年间，朝廷在石湖码头附近的制高点寨石山设立石湖巡检寨。南宋乾道七年（1171），石湖寨的驻军从原有的 125 人增加至 200 人，海港防卫实力得以提升。嘉定十一年（1218），泉州太守真德秀率领观察推官李方子、晋江知县许叔用、左翼军副将丘全遍行海滨，审视情形，决定将石湖寨的水军员额由原来的 38 人扩编为 100 人，合并步军、土军在内，编制达到 325 人，并申请拨款在石湖寨新建营房 68 间。从此，石湖寨成为扼守泉州湾的重要军事据点。

石湖寨遗址。（李国宏 供图）
The former site of Shihu Patrol Fort. (Courtesy of Li Guohong)

Shihu Patrol Fort Regulating Foreign Ships

Lin Luan's epic voyage continues to captivate us with the tale of exchange between Quanzhou and Brunei. In 1082, Brunei's envoys arrived in China to pay tribute and they requested to return home via sea from Quanzhou Port. The imperial court granted their request. It is worth noting that Quanzhou Shi Bo Si (Maritime Trade Office) was officially established five years later in 1087, indicating Quanzhou Port's significant role even before its official recognition as an international trading port. The approval to the request of Brunei's envoys demonstrates that Quanzhou Port at that time possessed advanced shipbuilding technology, and the convenience and safety of its overseas routes had been widely recognized.

To ensure smooth waterways and maritime safety for overseas trade, a sound and robust maritime defense management system was established in Quanzhou Port. The court built Shihu Patrol Fort on the high point of Stone Mountain near Shihu Dock between 1068 and 1077. In 1171, the garrison of Shihu Patrol Fort was increased to 200 troops, enhancing the defense strength of the seaport. In 1218, accomplished by some local officials, Quanzhou Prefect Zhen Dexiu led an inspection along the coast, resulting in the expansion of naval personnel and the construction of new barracks in Shihu Patrol Fort. From then on, Shihu Patrol Fort became a vital military stronghold guarding Quanzhou Bay.

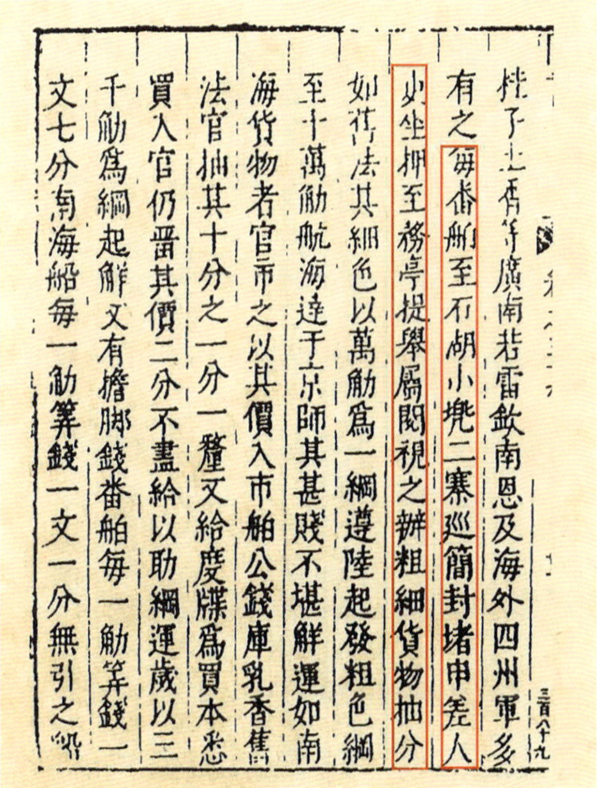
桂了土香符廣南若雷欽南恩及海外四州軍多
有之每番舶至石湖小兜二寨巡簡封堵申差人
少坐押至務亭提舉厲閱視之辨粗細貨物抽分
如祥法其細色以萬觔爲一綱遵陸起發粗色綱
至十萬觔航海達于京師其甚賤不堪解運如南
海貨物者官市之以其價入市舶公錢庫乳香售
法官抽其十分之一分一釐又給度牒爲買本悉
買入官仍畱其價二分不盡給以助綱運歲以三
千觔爲綱起觧又有擔脚錢番舶每一觔筭錢一
文七分南海船每一觔筭錢一文一分無引之船
三百八十九

明代何乔远《闽书》中关于石湖巡检寨监管番舶的记载。（李国宏 供图）

The record about Shihu Patrol Fort regulating foreign merchant ships in He Qiaoyuan's work *The Book of Min* written in the Ming Dynasty. (Courtesy of Li Guohong)

宋代海外贸易管理条例规定，外国商船进入泉州港之后，必须先停泊在石湖码头附近海域，由石湖巡检寨和惠安小兜巡检寨派员登船，核检封仓，然后由差吏随船顺着晋江护送至都务亭，再由泉州市舶司官员根据条例检验货物和人员手续，征收关税，统购货物。完成上述通关流程之后，其他货物准许进入市场交易。宋代巡检司的职能大致包括训练甲兵、巡逻州邑、擒捕盗贼，并由所在州县守令节制。石湖巡检寨兼有“封堵番舶”的职责，这是其与众不同的功能，是由泉州港海外贸易管理的实际需求所决定的。就这样，石湖码头连同石湖巡检寨登上历史舞台，成为宋代泉州港海外贸易管理体系中的一个重要环节。

再来看一下前面提到的都务亭。其实，它可以理解为古代的征税机构。北宋熙宁八年（1075），都税务设立，位于泉州城内镇雅坊街东侧。都税务下辖两处外务，一处位于临漳门外石笋桥边，一处位于南门外辛公亭，故又称都务亭。南宋嘉定十年（1217），位于辛公亭的外务船舶停靠点改为泉州左翼军船厂，泉州太守真德秀将辛公亭外务迁移到浯浦天妃宫（今泉州天后宫）之前。

综上，石湖码头是满载香料和珍宝的外国商船进入泉州港的第一个停靠站，设在石湖的巡检寨不仅是海防据点，也承担着监管外贸商船的职能。

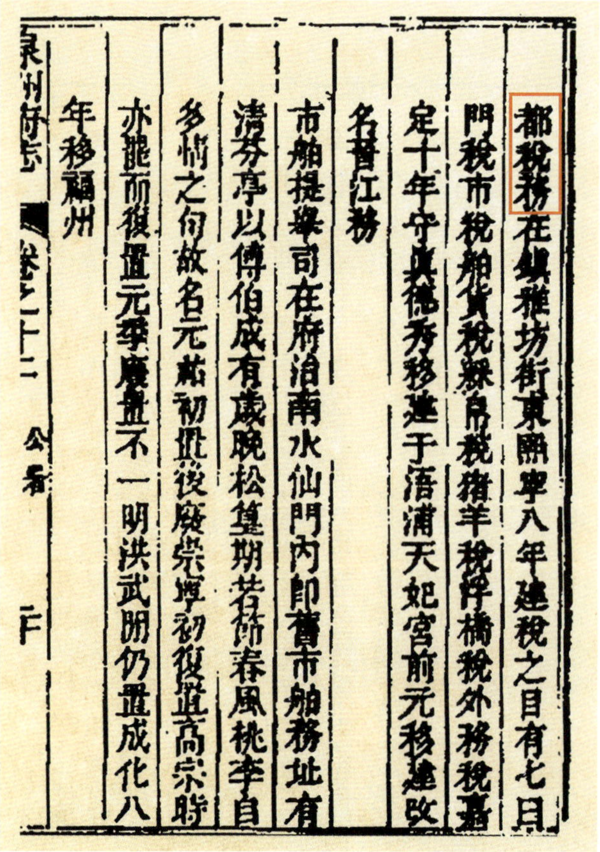
都稅務在鎮雅坊街東熙寧八年建稅之目有七曰
門稅市稅船貨稅絲帛稅豬羊稅浮橋稅外務稅嘉
定十年守真德秀移建于浯浦天妃宮前元移建改
名晉江務
市舶提舉司在府治南水仙門內即舊市舶務址有
清芬亭以傅伯成有歲晚松篁期若節春風桃李自
多情之句故名元祐初置後廢崇寧初復置高宗時
亦罷而復置元季廢置不一明洪武初仍置成化八
年移福州
泉州府志 卷之二十二 公署

清代乾隆版《泉州府志》中关于都税务的记载。（李国宏 供图）
The record about the tax institution named Dushuiwu in the Qianlong edition of *Local Chronicles of Quanzhou Prefecture*. (Courtesy of Li Guohong)

According to the regulations on the management of overseas trade in the Song Dynasty, foreign merchant ships entering Quanzhou Port were required to first anchor in the waters near Shihu Dock. Officials from Shihu Patrol Fort and Xiaodou Patrol Fort (in today's Chongwu, Hui'an) would then be sent to board the ships to inspect and seal the cargo holds, and lastly the ships would be escorted along Jinjiang River by officials to Duwu Pavilion, where officials of Quanzhou Maritime Trade Office would inspect the cargo and documentation, collect tariffs, and purchase goods in bulk. Once the customs clearance process was completed, other goods were allowed to enter the market for trading. The Song Dynasty patrol forts had various functions, including training soldiers, patrolling cities and towns, and capturing thieves, all under the control of local prefects and county officials. Shihu Patrol Fort, however, had the unique responsibility of "blocking foreign ships", which was essential for managing overseas trade in Quanzhou Port. Therefore, Shihu Dock, together with Shihu Patrol Fort, boarded the stage of history and played a crucial role in the overseas trade management system of Quanzhou Port during the Song Dynasty.

Let's take a look at Duwu Pavilion mentioned above. In essence, it can be regarded as an ancient tax office. In 1075, a tax institution named Dushuiwu was established on the eastern side of Zhenyafang Street in the city of Quanzhou. It had two subordinate branches, one near Shisun Bridge outside Linzhang Gate and the other near Xin Gong Pavilion outside Nanmen Gate, hence the name Duwu Pavilion. In 1217, the docking site for external ships at Xin Gong Pavilion was transformed to Quanzhou's Left Wing Naval Shipyard, and the external office of Xin Gong Pavilion was relocated to Wupu Tianfei Temple, which is now known as Tianhou Temple or the Palace of Goddess Mazu in Quanzhou.

In a word, Shihu Dock served as the initial docking site for foreign merchant ships carrying valuable spices and treasures entering Quanzhou Port. The Patrol Fort in Shihu not only functioned as a coastal defense stronghold but also played an important role in regulating the activities of foreign merchant ships.

如“瓷”动人

石湖码头通济栈桥出土的青瓷罐、青瓷小口瓶等遗物为南宋磁灶窑典型产品，青瓷罐上的模印牡丹纹亦是南宋时期泉州地区常见的瓷器纹样。出土遗物中，宋元时期磁灶窑的产品占据了较大比重，这与石湖码头所处位置接近晋江磁灶窑的实际情况相符。除此之外，遗物中有一定数量的安溪窑、同安窑、云霄窑、龙泉窑等窑口产品，则是区域贸易流通的客观反映。

南宋赵汝适《诸蕃志》记载，从泉州港出口的瓷器成为渤泥最受欢迎的舶来品之一。1995 到 1999 年间，在距离文莱首都斯里巴加湾市约 5 千米处的特鲁桑古邦遗址发现 3,000 余件来自中国宋元时期的瓷器，其中一些代表性器物无论是在釉色、图案压制技法上，还是在器型上，都与当时泉州同安窑、南安窑、德化窑、瓷灶窑生产的产品一致。此外，在距斯里巴加湾市约 20 千米处的甜桔子河遗址也发现数量众多的中国瓷器，属于宋代的典型器物，如青釉褐彩小罐、青釉龙纹军持、黑釉执壶、小口瓶、绿釉军持、素胎香薰等，均为晋江磁灶窑产品。而且这些磁灶窑产品与泉州府后山宋代市舶司仓库故址出土的同类外销瓷的形制高度相似，说明自唐宋以来，泉州与渤泥之间长期保持着友好关系和贸易往来。如此看来，林銮首航渤泥的创举厥功至伟。

泉州府后山遗址出土的宋代磁灶窑产品。（傅恩凤 供图）
Cizao Kilns artifacts of the Song Dynasty unearthed from the site of Houshan of Quanzhou Prefecture. (Courtesy of Fu Enfeng)

Attractive Porcelain

Tongji Jetty in Shihu Dock has unearthed fascinating artifacts, including celadon jars and small-mouthed bottles, which are typical products of the renowned Cizao Kilns during the Southern Song Dynasty. Notably, the pressed peony pattern on the celadon jar is a common porcelain design from Quanzhou during the same era. The fact that products made by Cizao Kilns during the Song and Yuan dynasties occupy a large proportion aligns with the proximity of Shihu Dock to Jinjiang Cizao Kilns. Additionally, the discovery of a certain amount of products from Anxi Kilns, Tong'an Kilns, Yunxiao Kilns, Longquan Kilns and other kilns in the relics further reflects regional trade exchanges.

According to Zhao Rukuo's *Records of Foreign Countries* written in the Southern Song Dynasty, Quanzhou Port's porcelain exports became highly sought-after goods in Brunei. Remarkably, between 1995 and 1999, over 3,000 pieces of porcelain from Song-Yuan China were unearthed at the Terusan Kupang archaeological site, located just 5 kilometers away from Brunei's capital city, Bandar Seri Begawan. Some representative ones exhibit glaze colors, pattern pressing techniques and vessel shapes consistent with those produced by Tong'an Kilns, Nan'an Kilns, Dehua Kilns and Cizao Kilns in Quanzhou during that time. Furthermore, at the Tangerine River site, approximately 20 kilometers away from Bandar Seri Begawan, a multitude of Chinese porcelain were discovered. Those typical ones of the Song Dynasty, including celadon-glazed brown-colored small jars, celadon-glazed dragon-patterned kendis, black-glazed teapots, small-mouthed bottles, green-glazed kendis, and plain-bodied incense burners, are all identified as products of Jinjiang Cizao Kilns. Interestingly, these Cizao Kilns artifacts bear striking resemblance to the exported porcelain excavated at the former site of the Song Dynasty Quanzhou Maritime Trade Office warehouse in Houshan. This signifies the enduring and amicable relationship as well as trade contacts between Quanzhou and Brunei since the Tang and Song dynasties. Lin Luan's pioneering voyage to Brunei deserves immense recognition for fostering this remarkable achievement.

泉州美食的舌尖诱惑

宋代泉州商人从石湖码头出发前往渤泥做生意时，必须随船带一两位手艺高超的厨师，因为当时的渤泥王室喜欢吃中国菜。商船靠岸后，商人们除了向国王和大臣敬献礼物，每天还要献上各式各样的美食给国王享用。差不多一个多月以后，国王才派官员来确定货物价格，允许这些商人到市场上自由交易。泉州商船返航时，渤泥国王会摆酒设宴，欢送客商，并回赠礼品。泉州美食竟然能助推中外贸易的顺利进行，创造和谐融洽的营商环境，是不是浪漫而又突破想象力？

即使是到了元代，当旅行家汪大渊从泉州港出洋抵达渤泥时，依然享受着礼遇。那时，在渤泥的中国商人就算是在外面喝醉了也不用担心，当地人会友善地将他们安全地送回住所。泉州港悠久的航海历史培养了泉州人勇于开拓、善于创造的性格特点，造就他们开放、尊重、分享、合作的文化传统，也使相遇相知、互惠互利的美好愿景得以实现。石湖码头见证泉州人走向深蓝、拥抱世界、拥抱未来的人文情怀，它是通达四海、合作共赢的财富聚宝盆，也是万邦协和、四海一家的文化聚宝盆。

依据南宋美食家林洪《山家清供》复原的宋元海丝宴菜品展示。（李国宏 供图）

A display of the Song and Yuan dynasties Silk Road banquet dishes based on *A Homely Fare*, written by the Southern Song gastronome, Lin Hong. (Courtesy of Li Guohong)

The Temptation of Quanzhou Cuisine

During the Song Dynasty, Quanzhou merchants embarked on voyages from Shihu Port to conduct business in Brunei, and they had a unique practice. They would bring along highly skilled chefs on their ships, as the Brunei royal family had a strong affinity for Chinese cuisine. When their ships arrived, Quanzhou merchants not only presented lavish gifts to the king and ministers, but also treated them to a variety of exquisite delicacies. After about a month, officials would be sent by the king to assess the goods' prices and grant them the freedom to trade in the local market. Upon the return of these Quanzhou merchant ships, the Brunei king would host a grand feast to bid farewell to the traders and reciprocate their generosity with gifts. The role once played by Quanzhou cuisine in fostering smooth international trade, creating a harmonious and friendly business environment, is truly enchanting and goes beyond imagination.

Even during the Yuan Dynasty, when the traveler Wang Dayuan sailed from Quanzhou Port to Brunei, he received special treatment. At that time, even if Chinese merchants got intoxicated outside in Brunei, they need not worry, as the locals would kindly escort them back to their lodgings. The long-standing maritime history of Quanzhou Port has shaped the adventurous and innovative nature of its people, instilling in them an open-minded, respectful, sharing and cooperative cultural tradition. It has also paved the way for the realization of a vision centered on mutual understanding, mutual benefit and cooperation. Shihu Port stands as a testament to Quanzhou people's embrace of the vast blue sea, the world and the future. It is a treasure trove of wealth that connects the globe and fosters win-win cooperation, while also serving as a cultural gem promoting harmony among nations and a sense of global unity.

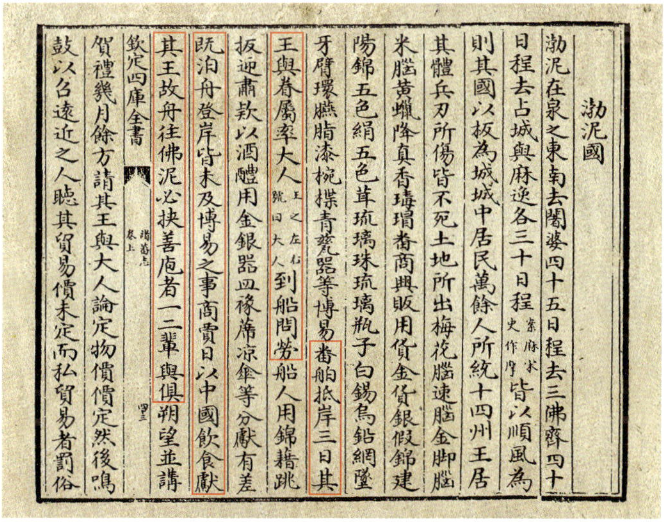
渤泥國
渤泥在泉之東南去闍婆四十五日程去三佛齊四十
日程去占城與麻逸各三十日程（案麻逸史作摩）皆以順風為
則其國以板為城城中居民萬餘人所統十四州王居
其體兵刃所傷皆不死土地所出梅花腦速腦金腳腦
米腦黃蠟降真香瑇瑁番商興販用貨金貨銀假錦建
陽錦五色絹五色茸琉璃珠琉璃瓶子白錫烏鉛網墜
牙臂環臙脂漆椀楪青甆器等博易番舶抵岸三日其
王與眷屬率大人（王之左右號曰大人）到船問勞船人用錦藉跳
板迎肅款以酒醴用金銀器皿禒席涼傘等分獻有差
既泊舟登岸皆未及博易之事商賈日以中國飲食獻
其王故舟往佛泥必挾善庖者一二輩與俱朔望並講
欽定四庫全書　諸蕃志　卷上　四三
賀禮幾月餘方請其王與大人論定物價價定然後鳴
鼓以召遠近之人聽其貿易價未定而私貿易者罰俗

宋代赵汝适《诸蕃志》中关于泉州美食风靡渤泥的记载。（李国宏 供图）

The record about the popularity of Quanzhou's cuisine in Brunei in Zhao Rukuo's *Records of Foreign Countries* written in the Song Dynasty. (Courtesy of Li Guohong)

沈有容与石湖寨城

明万历三十年（1602），安徽宣城人沈有容调任福建浯屿把总，移镇石湖寨，并负责修建石湖寨城。据明代黄国鼎《石湖爱民碑》记载，刚得知浯屿水寨要迁至石湖时，蚶江沿海百姓担心水寨守军军纪涣散、祸害民众，非常忧虑。于是，沈有容约束部属，严明纪律。他变卖公产筹款，并捐出自己多年积攒的赏银，对石湖寨旧营房进行扩建。此举不扰民、不摊派，深得蚶江百姓拥戴。沈有容镇守石湖期间，整肃军纪，关爱百姓，还指挥士卒兴建海堤，以防止海水倒灌、侵袭良田，石湖百姓亲切地将这座海堤称为“沈公堤”。

据明代陈第《舟师客问》记载，漳州、泉州沿海商人前往台湾，“往往译其语言，与贸易，以玛瑙、瓷器、布、盐、铜簪环之类，易其鹿脯、皮角”。后来，海盗与倭寇相勾结，盘踞台湾南部地区，大肆勒索商人、渔民的巨额财物，台湾北港贸易控制权自此落入倭贼手中。连台湾土著民也深受其害，不敢再在沿海平原打猎，只得迁往内地山区躲避。

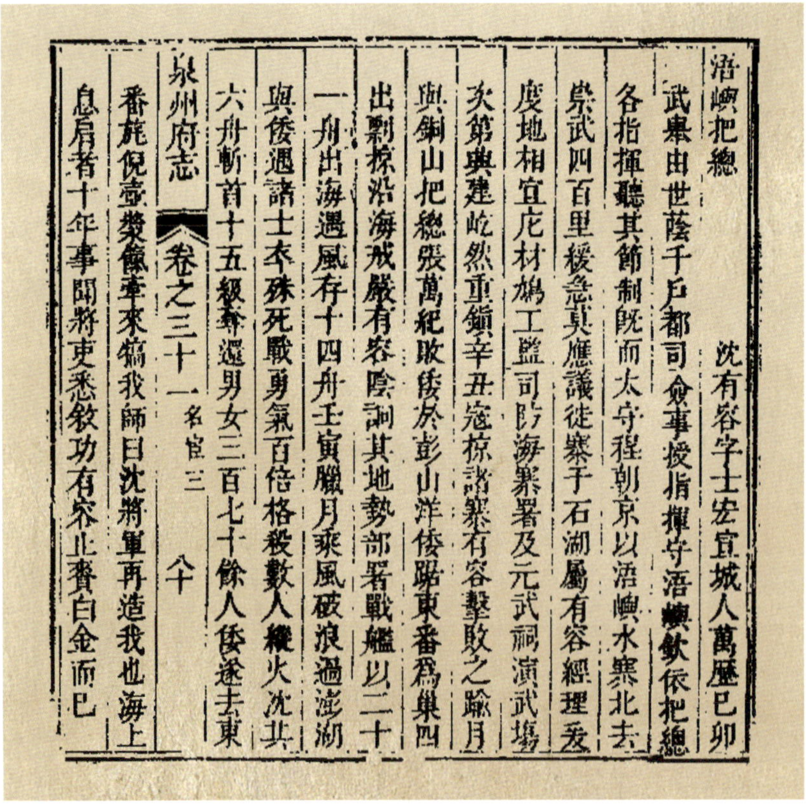
浯嶼把總　沈有容字士宏宣城人萬曆巳卯
武舉由世蔭千戶都司僉事授指揮守浯嶼欽依把總
各指揮聽其節制既而太守程朝京以浯嶼水寨北去
泉武四百里緩急莫應議徙寨于石湖屬有容經理爰
度地相宜庀材鳩工監司防海衆署及元武祠演武場
次第興建屹然重鎮辛丑寇掠諸寨有容擊敗之踰月
與銅山把總張萬紀敗倭於彭山洋倭踞東番爲巢四
出剽掠沿海戒嚴有容陰詗其地勢部署戰艦以二十
一舟出海遇風存十四舟壬寅臘月乘風破浪過澎湖
與倭遇諸士卒殊死戰勇氣百倍格殺數人縱火沈其
六舟斬首十五級奪還男女三百七十餘人倭遂去東
泉州府志　卷之三十一　名宦三　八十
番鹿倪壹斝饋牽來犒我師曰沈將軍再造我也海上
息肩者十年事聞將吏悉敘功有容止賚白金而已

清代乾隆版《泉州府志》中收录的沈有容传记。（李国宏 供图）

The biography of Sheng Yourong in the Qianlong edition of *Local Chronicles of Quanzhou Prefecture*. (Courtesy of Li Guohong)

Shen Yourong and Shihu Military Stronghold

In 1602 of the Ming Dynasty, Shen Yourong, a native of Xuancheng in Anhui Province, was appointed as the commander of Wuyu in Fujian Province and was tasked with relocating to Shihu Patrol Fort and constructing of Shihu Military Stronghold. According to the record of the *Stele of Love for the People in Shihu* by Huang Guoding in the Ming Dynasty, concerned about the potential lax military discipline and harm to the people, the coastal residents along Hanjiang River expressed their worries when they learned about the relocation of the water fortress. To address these concerns, Shen Yourong implemented strict disciplinary measures. He sold public property and donated his own rewards to expand the old barracks in Shihu Patrol Fort, earning support and admiration from Hanjiang residents. During his tenure in Shihu, Shen Yourong rectified military discipline, cared for the people and led soldiers in building a seawall to protect the fertile land from flooding. The people of Shihu thus affectionately named this seawall the "Shen Gong Dike".

According to the record of Chen Di's *Questions from a Guest of the Naval Forces* of the Ming Dynasty, coastal merchants from Zhangzhou and Quanzhou frequently engaged in trade with Taiwan, exchanging goods such as agate, porcelain, cloth, salt and copper ornaments for deer jerky and antlers. However, the situation changed when pirates collaborated with Japanese invaders and occupied the southern region of Taiwan, extorting wealth from merchants and fishermen. As a result, pirates gained control over trade in Beigang Port of Taiwan, causing great suffering to the indigenous people who were forced to give up hunting in the coastal plains and retreat to the mountainous areas.

消息传回福建，巡抚朱运昌给沈有容下达密令，让其择机出兵台湾，剿灭倭寇。由于泉州海商对台湾南部的地理、人文诸情势颇为熟悉，沈有容私下招募石湖船主郭廷，让他在前往台湾进行贸易之时，利用关系收集台湾南部的地理、气候、水文信息，绘制地图，标注可供船舶停靠的地点。如此说来，台湾南部最早的地图竟然是 400 多年前一位名叫郭廷的石湖人制作的。

做好战备后，万历三十年十二月，沈有容率领水师从石湖港出海，经由金门、澎湖，突袭盘踞在台湾南部的倭寇，攻其不备，大获全胜。多年后，右给事中彭惟城上疏议政，曾论及沈有容，称道：“沈有容在闽，能越海数日歼倭众……倭亦戒不敢掠至闽且十年，皆有容之力也。”由此可见，沈有容台湾平倭之役影响深远，为闽台之间贸易的兴盛以及北港的发展创造了极其有利的外部条件。

沈有容曾率军在台湾南部登陆，当地居民在酋长的带领下，“扶老携幼，竞以壶浆、生鹿，来犒王师，咸以手加额，德我军之扫荡安辑之也”。这是明朝中央政府在台湾宣示主权的一次重大行动，此举足以使沈有容名垂青史。福建连江人陈第随军出征，凯旋后在蚶江丰山寺寓居数月，根据亲身经历写成《东番记》《舟师客问》，成为记载明代台湾史至关重要的文献史料。

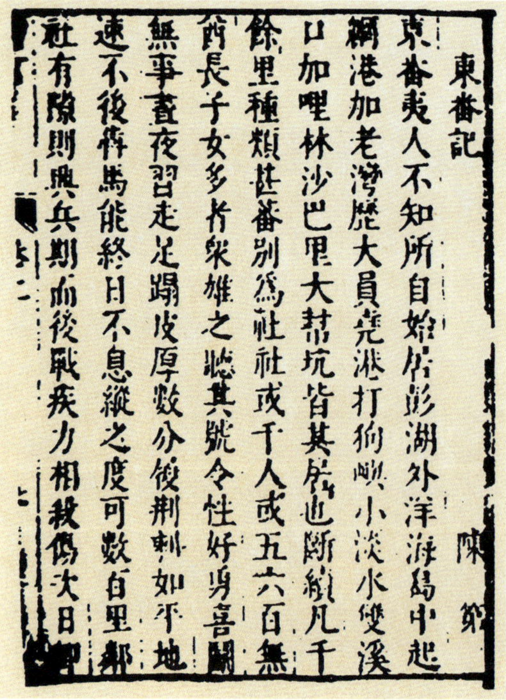
東番記　陳第
東番夷人不知所自始居彭湖外洋海島中起
魍港加老灣歷大員堯港打狗嶼小淡水雙溪
口加哩林沙巴里大幇坑皆其居也斷續凡千
餘里種類甚蕃別為社社或千人或五六百無
酋長子女多者衆雄之聽其號令性好勇喜鬬
無事晝夜習走足蹋皮厚數分履荊刺如平地
速不後犇馬能終日不息縱之度可數百里鄰
社有隙則興兵期而後戰疾力相殺傷次日即

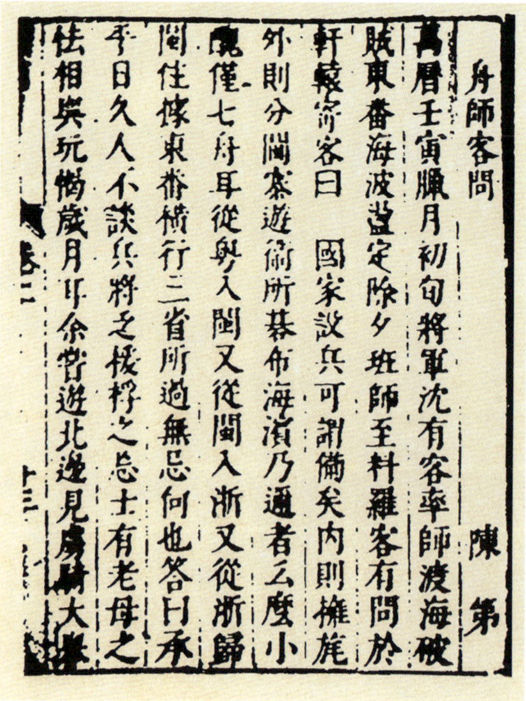
舟師客問　陳第
萬曆壬寅臘月初旬將軍沈有容率師渡海破
賊東番海波盪定除夕班師至料羅客有問於
軒轅衍客曰　國家設兵可謂備矣內則擁旄
外則分閫寨遊衛所碁布海濱乃邇者幺麼小
醜僅七舟耳從粤入閩又從閩入浙又從浙歸
閩往據東番橫行三省所過無忌何也答曰承
平日久人不談兵將乏撫綏之恩士有老母之
怯相與玩愒歲月耳余嘗遊北邊見虜騎大舉

明代《闽海赠言》中收录的陈第所撰《东番记》和《舟师客问》。（李国宏 供图）

Chen Di's *Records of Taiwan* and *Questions from a Guest of the Naval Forces* included in *Words of Praise from the Fujian Sea* compiled during the Ming Dynasty. (Courtesy of Li Guohong)

Upon hearing the news, Fujian's governor Zhu Yunchang secretly ordered Shen Yourong to lead an expedition to Taiwan and eliminate the pirates. Due to the familiarity of Quanzhou's maritime merchants with the geography and cultural situation of southern Taiwan, Shen Yourong privately recruited Guo Ting, a shipowner from Shihu, and tasked him with gathering information and creating a map of southern Taiwan, marking suitable locations for ships to anchor. Thus, it can be said that over 400 years ago, Guo Ting, a resident of Shihu, created the earliest map of southern Taiwan.

After making adequate preparations, Shen Yourong led the naval forces from Shihu Port, sailed through Jinmen and Penghu, and launched a surprise attack on the pirates entrenched in the southern part of Taiwan in lunar December 1602. Taking the pirates off guard, he achieved a complete victory. Many years later, the right censor Peng Weicheng submitted a memorial discussing politics and mentioned Shen Yourong, praising him by saying, "Shen Yourong, while in Fujian, was able to cross the sea in several days and annihilate Japanese invaders in Taiwan. Since then, Taiwan has been pacified and Japanese pirates have been deterred from plundering Fujian for over ten years, all thanks to the efforts of Shen Yourong." It can be seen that Shen Yourong's campaign to pacify Japanese invaders in Taiwan had a profound impact, creating highly favorable external conditions for the flourishing trade between Fujian and Taiwan, as well as the development of Beigang Port.

Shen Yourong led troops to land in southern Taiwan, where the local residents, under the leadership of their chieftain, "accompanied by the elderly and the young, competed to offer wine and food, and present live deer to reward the royal army. They all touched their foreheads with their hands, expressing their great gratitude for our troops' pacifying efforts." It was a significant action by the central government of the Ming Dynasty to declare sovereignty over Taiwan, which made Shen Yourong immortalized in history. Chen Di, a native of Lianjiang, Fujian, accompanied the army on the expedition and resided in Fengshan Temple in Hanjiang for several months after the victory. Based on his firsthand experience, he wrote *Records of Taiwan* and *Questions from a Guest of the Naval Forces*, which became important historical documents for recording the history of Taiwan in the Ming Dynasty.

万历三十二年（1604），荷兰东印度公司韦麻郎等率领三艘巨舰，趁明军换防之际占领澎湖马公岛。他们以互市为名，企图像葡萄牙占领澳门一样占领澎湖列岛。沈有容做好严密的战备部署，同时不顾自身安危，单舟驰往荷兰舰船，指陈利害，严正晓谕，不费一枪一弹便迫使韦麻郎退兵。韦麻郎临去之时，还请画师为沈有容画像，以示尊敬。

万历三十四年（1606），沈有容调任浙江都司参将，石湖百姓感念沈有容之功德，建生祠以怀其德政。历经沧桑变化，石湖沈公祠已难觅踪迹，但沈有容威镇海疆、台湾平倭的历史功绩早已在泉州人民心中树立起一座永不磨灭的丰碑。

In 1604, Wybrand van Warwijck and others from the Dutch East India Company led three large ships to occupy Ma Gong Island in Penghu while the Ming army was changing defense. Under the disguise of trade, they sought to occupy Penghu Islands, similar to the Portuguese occupation of Macao. Shen Yourong made careful preparations for defense and, disregarding his own safety, sailed alone to the Dutch ships. He explained the advantages and disadvantages and sternly admonished them, forcing Wybrand van Warwijck to withdraw without firing a single shot. Before departing, Wybrand van Warwijck even requested an artist to paint a portrait of Shen Yourong as a sign of respect.

In 1606, Shen Yourong was transferred to the position of deputy commander in Zhejiang Province. The people of Shihu, grateful for Shen's meritorious service, built a shrine in his honor to commemorate his virtuous governance. Over the course of time, Shen Gong Shrine has been lost amidst the changes of the world, but Shen's achievements in protecting the eastern frontier and suppressing invaders to Taiwan have already established an indelible monument in the hearts of the people of Quanzhou.

再借亭

石湖码头抵岸处有一座石碑亭，亭内竖立一方碑刻，居中“再借亭”三个大字出自明代著名书法家、泉州人张瑞图手笔。说起再借亭的由来，与明代廉吏曾樱有关。

曾樱，字仲含，号二云，江西峡江人，万历四十四年（1616）进士，历任工部主事、常州知府。明崇祯四年（1631），曾樱以右参政的身份分巡兴泉道，驻扎泉州。当时，海上武装首领郑芝龙已经接受朝廷招安，但是，流散的海盗依然与荷兰殖民者互相勾结，四处袭扰。有人建议派熟悉海盗底细的郑芝龙领兵出征，可是也有人担心郑芝龙反复无常，暗中与海盗勾结。众人相持不下之时，曾樱提出疑人不用、用人不疑，认定郑芝龙会抓住机会建功立业。他甚至用全家族一百余人的身家性命为郑芝龙做担保。郑芝龙于是出兵追剿海盗刘香，果然不负曾樱所望，大功告成。曾樱遂奏请朝廷开放海禁，允许百姓出海贸易。同时，他抑制豪强，体恤民力，将泉州治理得井井有条。曾樱为官清廉，从不收受贿赂，“海舶珍奇，唾若粪土”。据乾隆版《泉州府志》记载，曾樱在泉州为官多年，离任之时，行李中除了一包清源山茶，别无长物。

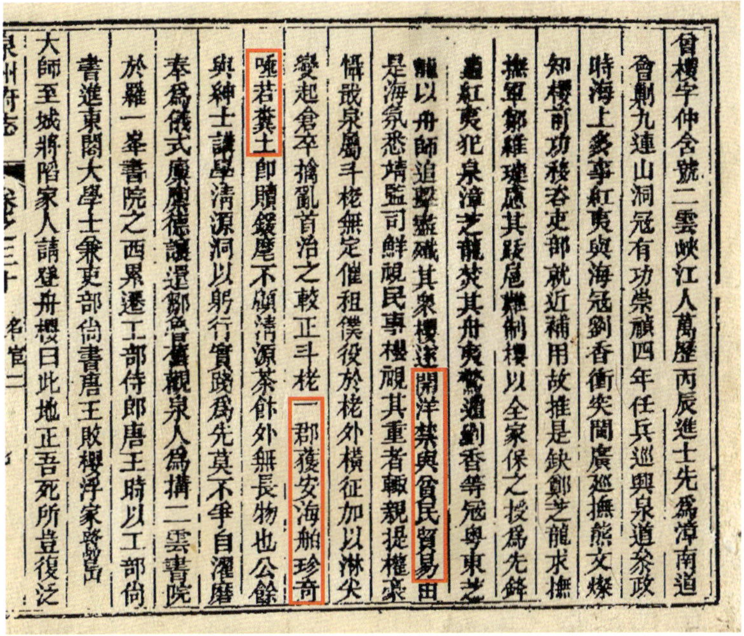

曾櫻字仲含號二雲峽江人萬曆丙辰進士先爲漳南道
僉事勦九連山洞寇有功崇禎四年任兵巡興泉道參政
時海上多事紅夷與海寇劉香衝突閩廣巡撫熊文燦
知櫻前功移咨吏部就近補用故推是缺鄭芝龍求撫
撫軍鄭雖疑其跋扈難制櫻以全家保之授爲先鋒
盡紅夷犯泉漳芝龍焚其舟夷驚遁劉香等寇粵東芝
龍以舟師追擊殲其衆櫻遂開洋禁與貧民貿易由
是海氛悉靖監司鮮親民事櫻視其重者輙親提權豪
慴戢泉屬手栳無定催租僕役於栳外橫征加以淋尖
變起倉卒擒亂首治之較正斗栳一郡獲安海船珍奇
唾若糞土卸贖鍰塵不㶊清源茶餘外無長物也公餘
與紳士講學清源洞以躬行實踐爲先莫不爭自濯磨
奉爲儀式廉聲德讓遷鄖撫觀泉人爲搆二雲書院
於羅一峯書院之西累遷工部侍郎唐王時以工部尚
書進東閣大學士兼吏部尚書唐王敗櫻浮家鷺島
大師至城將陷家人請登舟櫻曰此地正吾死所豈復泛

泉州府志 卷之三十 名宦二

清代乾隆版《泉州府志》中收录的曾樱传记。（李国宏 供图）

The biography of Zeng Ying included in the Qianlong edition of *Local Chronicles of Quanzhou Prefecture*. (Courtesy of Li Guohong)

Zaijieting Pavilion

At the landing point of Shihu Dock, there is a stone pavilion with an inscribed tablet standing inside. At the center of the tablet, there are three prominent characters that read "Zai Jie Ting" (Re-borrowing Pavilion), which were written by Zhang Ruitu, a renowned calligrapher from Quanzhou during the Ming Dynasty. As for the origin of the pavilion, there was a story about the Ming Dynasty upright official, Zeng Ying.

Zeng Ying, born in Xiajiang, Jiangxi Province, passed the imperial examination in 1616 and held positions as director of the Ministry of Works and the magistrate of Changzhou. In 1631, Zeng Ying stationed in Quanzhou as the right assistant minister to oversee Xingquan region. At that time, the maritime warlord Zheng Zhilong had already accepted the court's amnesty. However, scattered pirates continued to collude with Dutch colonizers and wreaked havoc in the area. Some suggested sending Zheng Zhilong, who was familiar with the pirates, to lead troops against them, but others worried about his fickleness and secret collusion with the pirates. Amidst the deadlock, Zeng Ying firmly believed that Zheng Zhilong would seize the opportunity to make contributions. He even pledged the lives and fortunes of over a hundred members of his own family as a guarantee for Zheng Zhilong. As expected, Zheng Zhilong led his troops to suppress the pirate Liu Xiang and achieved great success. Zeng Ying subsequently requested the court to lift the maritime restrictions, allowing people to engage in overseas trade. At the same time, he restrained the powerful and cared for the welfare of the people, effectively governing Quanzhou. Zeng Ying, known for his integrity, never accepted bribes and considered precious maritime treasures as worthless as dirt. According to the Qianlong edition of *Local Chronicles of Quanzhou Prefecture*, when Zeng Ying left his post in Quanzhou after many years of service, his luggage only contained a package of Qingyuan Mountain tea, and nothing else of value.

崇祯十年(1637),坊间传闻曾樱即将升迁外任。郑芝龙唯恐失去这位值得依靠和信赖的好官,便自作主张,暗中派人到京城活动,争取让曾樱留在福建任职。不料,消息走漏,东厂密探向崇祯报告“曾樱行贿谋求升官”。结果,曾樱被捕入京,接受审讯。消息传开,泉州百姓千余人进京为曾樱鸣冤。弄巧成拙的郑芝龙懊悔不已,出面承担责任。福建地方要员也据实上报,为曾樱洗刷冤情。崇祯皇帝看到曾樱如此受泉州百姓爱戴,特地下旨,“再借”曾樱留任泉州。于是,泉州民众在石湖竖立再借亭碑,纪念其德政。

令人感慨的是,清兵入关后挥师浙闽,郑芝龙为一己之私而降清。其子郑成功却毅然举兵抗清,曾樱时任东阁大学士兼吏部尚书,被郑成功奉为尊长,随郑成功驻扎厦门。清顺治八年(1651),郑成功出兵南澳。清军乘机突袭厦门,曾樱陷入重围。家人劝他登船避难,曾樱却将生死置之度外,笑着说:“这里就是干净的地方,死得其所,何必漂洋过海苟活于乱世?”说完,曾樱悬梁自尽。南明永历皇帝闻讯,追赠曾樱光禄大夫,赐谥“文忠”。

今天,当你行走在石湖码头之时,只见一桥横跨泉州湾,水天一色,风光迷人。夕阳映照下的再借亭依然散发着浓郁的历史气息,传颂着曾樱清正廉洁、忠烈千秋的美德。

再借亭。(成冬冬 摄)
Zaijieting Pavilion. (Photo by Cheng Dongdong)

In 1637, there were rumors spreading that Zeng Ying was about to be promoted to an external position. Zheng Zhilong, fearing to lose this reliable and trustworthy official, took matters into his own hands and secretly sent acolytes to the capital to lobby for Zeng Ying's stay in Fujian. However, the news leaked, and a spy from the Eastern Depot (the emperor's secret service during the Ming Dynasty) reported to Emperor Chongzhen that "Zeng Ying bribed to seek promotion." As a result, Zeng Ying was arrested and carted to Beijing for interrogation. The news spread, and over a thousand people from Quanzhou went to the capital to protest on behalf of Zeng Ying. Regretting his ill-conceived plan, Zheng Zhilong took responsibility and appeared before the authorities. Local officials in Fujian also reported the truth to clear Zeng Ying's name. Upon seeing how beloved Zeng Ying was by the people of Quanzhou, Emperor Chongzhen issued a decree to "re-borrow" Zeng Ying for continued service in Quanzhou. As a result, the people of Quanzhou erected a tablet inscribed with "Zaijieting Pavilion" in Shihu to commemorate his virtuous governance.

Regrettably, after the Qing army entered the central plains, Zheng Zhilong surrendered for his own personal gain. However, his son Zheng Chenggong resolutely took up arms against the Qing government. At that time, Zeng Ying served as the grand secretary of the Eastern Cabinet and minister of personnel, and he was respected by Zheng Chenggong as an elder brother. He stationed himself in Xiamen with Zheng Chenggong. In 1651, Zheng launched a military campaign in Nan'ao. Taking advantage of this, the Qing army launched a surprise attack on Xiamen, and Zeng Ying found himself trapped. His family urged him to board a ship and sought refuge, but Zeng Ying disregarded his own life and said with a smile, "This place is clean. If I die here, it will be where I belong. Why should I cross the ocean and struggle to survive in a chaotic world?" After saying this, Zeng Ying hung himself. When the Southern Ming Emperor Yongli heard the news, he appointed Zeng Ying as imperial minister of state and posthumously bestowed upon him the title of "Wenzhong" to commemorate his exceptional qualities and achievements in terms of cultural cultivation and loyalty.

Today, walking along Shihu Dock, you will see a bridge spanning Quanzhou Bay, with the water and sky blending into one, creating a charming scenery. Under the glow of the setting sun, Zaijieting Pavilion still exudes a rich historical atmosphere, commemorating the virtues of Zeng Ying—his integrity, honesty and loyalty.

江口码头：穿越法石港的千里烟波

江口码头包括文兴、美山两处沿江驳岸码头，位于泉州古城东南晋江北岸的江海交汇处，它与真武庙同为宋元泉州重要内港法石港的遗存。江口码头与地处泉州湾出海口的石湖码头一道构成泉州古代集群港的格局，反映了宋元泉州港繁荣时期的独有风貌。此外，法石港发现的宋代海船是继泉州湾后渚港海船出水之后的又一重大考古成果，为南宋时期泉州的海外交通史、造船史、航海史提供了重要的历史见证和研究资料。

明代《泉州府舆地图说》中绘有法石澳。（李国宏 供图）

The Geographic Map of Quanzhou Prefecture of the Ming Dynasty depicts Fashi Port Area. (Courtesy of Li Guohong)

Estuary Docks: Amidst the Vast Waves Along Fashi Port

Estuary Docks, including Wenxing Dock and Meishan Dock, are situated at the confluence of Jinjiang River and the sea on the northern bank of Jinjiang River in the southeast of ancient Quanzhou. These docks, along with Zhenwu Temple, are remnants of Fashi Port, which was a significant inner harbor in Quanzhou during the Song and Yuan dynasties. Estuary Docks, along with Shihu Dock located at the mouth of Quanzhou Bay, forms an ancient port cluster in Quanzhou that reflects the distinct characteristics of the prosperous Quanzhou Port during the Song and Yuan dynasties. Furthermore, the unearthing of seagoing vessels of the Song Dynasty in Fashi Port represents another noteworthy archaeological accomplishment after the excavation of the ancient ship in Houzhu Port, providing valuable historical evidence and research materials for the study of overseas transportation, shipbuilding and navigation in Quanzhou during the Southern Song Dynasty.

拍摄于 1982 年的法石港，依然有帆船行驶。（泉州海外交通史博物馆 供图）
A photograph of Fashi Port with a boat sailing taken in 1982. (Courtesy of Quanzhou Maritime Museum)

法石风云

法石港处在晋江下游北岸的山地丘陵边缘，是最靠近泉州古城的沿江高地。这里背山面江，又有陆上通道与泉州城、后渚港相连。得天独厚的水陆交通条件使法石一带成为泉州城郊人烟辐辏之地，也是古城水路运输与陆路运输的转换枢纽。

南宋淳熙十三年（1186），泉州左翼军统制韩俊奏请设置法石寨，调拨水军 150 人驻扎，免其调遣。法石寨就设于法石港石头山，地势险要，居高临下，俯瞰江口码头，便于居中调度，成为泉州湾出海口与州城沿江要道的重要据点。

南宋嘉定十一年（1218），海寇赵希却袭击泉州围头湾。泉州太守真德秀及时调兵遣将，一举击溃海寇，擒获赵希却。随后真德秀提请在围头湾设立宝盖寨，调拨原本驻扎于城南宝林寨的 120 名水军驻守围头，并将法石寨水军编制增加至 200 人。

真德秀画像。（李国宏 供图）
The portrait of Zhen Dexiu. (Courtesy of Li Guohong)

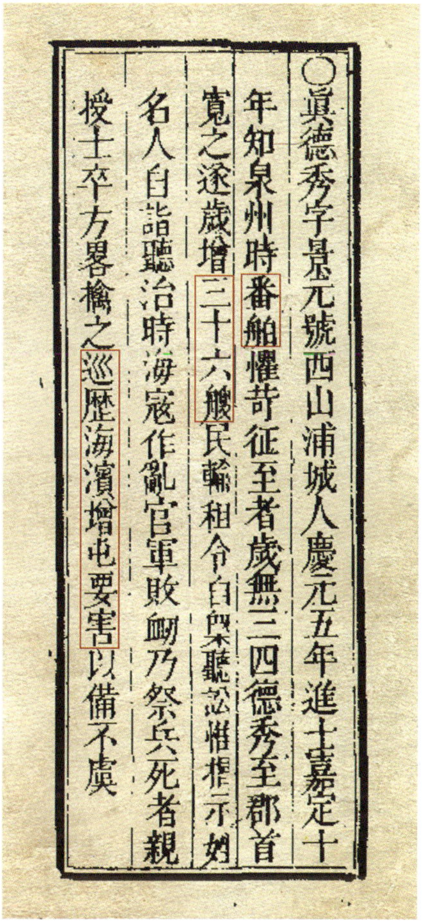

○真德秀字景元號西山浦城人慶元五年進士嘉定十
年知泉州時番舶憚苛征至者歲無三四德秀至郡首
寬之遂歲增三十六艘民輸租令自槩聽訟惟揭示姓
名人自詣聽治時海寇作亂官軍敗衄乃祭兵死者親
授士卒方畧擒之巡歷海濱增屯要害以備不虞

清代乾隆版《泉州府志》中关于真德秀整饬泉州港海防的记载。（李国宏 供图）

The record about Zhen Dexiu organizing the maritime defense of Quanzhou Port in the Qianlong edition of *Local Chronicles of Quanzhou Prefecture*. (Courtesy of Li Guohong)

The History of Fashi Port

Fashi Port, located on the edge of the mountainous region near the northern bank of the lower reaches of Jinjiang River, holds a significant position as the closest highland to the ancient Quanzhou along the river. It is geographically supported by mountains and faces the river, with a land passage connecting it to Quanzhou City and Houzhu Port. The distinctive water and land transportation conditions rendered Fashi Port a crucial hub for the suburban population of Quanzhou and a pivotal transition point between the waterway and land transportation in ancient time.

In 1186 of the Southern Song Dynasty, Han Jun, commander of the left-wing army in Quanzhou, proposed the establishment of Fashi Fort and the allocation of 150 naval troops to be stationed there, exempting them from being deployed elsewhere. Positioned on the Stone Mountain of Fashi Port, the fort possessed a strategic location and commanding views that overlooked Estuary Docks, facilitating central coordination and control. Fashi Fort played a vital role as a stronghold for Quanzhou Bay's sea exit and the artery to Quanzhou along the river.

In 1218 of the Southern Song Dynasty, the pirate Zhao Xique launched an audacious attack on Quanzhou's Weitou Bay. In response, Zhen Dexiu, prefect of Quanzhou, swiftly mobilized troops and dispatched skilled generals to confront the pirates. Their efforts paid off as they successfully defeated the pirates and apprehended Zhao Xique. Subsequently, Zhen Dexiu proposed the establishment of Baogai Fort at Weitou Bay and reassigned 120 naval soldiers, originally stationed at Baolin Fort in the south of the city, to be stationed at Weitou, and the naval forces at Fashi Fort were also increased to 200 soldiers.

鉴于法石寨“水面广阔，寨临其上，内足以捍州城，外足以扼航道”，真德秀又将泉州左翼水军的指挥机关从城南宝林寨移置法石寨，由抓捕海盗立功的准备将廖彦通代理法石寨正将，并调拨新打造的三艘战船停泊法石港，用于海上巡哨。水寨官兵每个月出海巡逻一次，执行任务的官兵姓名、巡逻日记必须真实记录，每两年对官兵进行综合考评，作为奖罚的依据。如有抓获海盗者，按照条例给予奖赏。

另据《闽书》记载，法石港石头山“上有真武殿，宋时望祭海神之所，下为石头市，居民鳞次”。于是，法石港成为外贸船舶停靠点和祭祀海神的重要场所，法石寨也演变为泉州沿海水寨的指挥中心。

法石港真武庙，宋代泉州官方祭祀海神的重要场所。（李国宏 供图）
Zhenwu Temple in Fashi Fort was an important place for the official worship of the sea god during the Song Dynasty. (Courtesy of Li Guohong)

Recognizing the strategic advantages of Fashi Fort, which boasted a commanding view of the wide water surface and had the capability to defend the city and control the waterway, Zhen Dexiu decided to relocate the command headquarters of the left-wing naval forces in Quanzhou from Baolin Fort to Fashi Fort. He appointed the accomplished pirate-capturer Liao Yantong as the acting commander of Fashi Fort. To enhance maritime security, three newly-constructed warships were assigned to anchor at Fashi Port for regular patrols. These patrols were conducted on a monthly basis, with detailed records kept of the officers and soldiers involved, as well as their patrol logs. Every two years, a comprehensive assessment of the officers and soldiers would take place, serving as the basis for rewards and punishments. In the event of pirate captures, rewards would be granted in accordance with regulations.

According to *The Book of Min*, atop the stone hill of Fashi Port stood Zhenwu Temple, a place of worship for the sea god during the Song Dynasty. At the foot of the mountain, the lively Stone Market bustled with residents. Consequently, Fashi Port became a crucial docking point for foreign trade ships and a significant hub for worshiping the sea god. Over time, Fashi Fort evolved into the command center for Quanzhou's coastal water forts.

阿拉伯人墓葬遗迹

法石地处航运交通要道，成为宋元时期外国客商停泊、聚集的处所，甚至吸引了来自阿拉伯地区的外商在此居住。1959 年，泉州海外交通史博物馆考古调查人员在法石美山村及毗邻的云麓禅寺附近陆续发现了 7 座具有伊斯兰风格的塔式墓盖石。其中一座墓盖石由花岗岩雕琢而成，分为五层，中间镂空，底层间雕如意云纹，顶石截面呈半圆形，其余各面无纹饰。

1974 年，在法石一处名为柳公砌的遗址发现泉州郭姓回族始祖郭德广的墓碑石，现由泉州海外交通史博物馆珍藏。碑额正中阴刻一行波斯文，译文为“伊本 · 库斯 · 德广贡 · 纳姆”。右上角阴刻小篆“惠”“百奇”，左上角阴刻“晋”“坡庭”，中间竖刻楷书“元郭氏世祖坟茔”。根据郭氏谱牒记载，郭德广于元至大年间来到法石定居，后人至第三代郭仲远才由法石迁居今惠安县百崎回族乡，再从百崎分支至今石狮市蚶江镇石湖村、宝盖镇前坑村和永宁镇郭坑村。

法石美山村附近发现的元代伊斯兰风格墓盖石图示。（李国宏 供图）
The illustration of the Yuan Dynasty tower-shaped tombstone with Islamic-style designs discovered near Meishan Village of Fashi. (Courtesy of Li Guohong)

Tomb Relics of Some Arabians

Due to its strategic location along the maritime trade route, Fashi Port became a hub for foreign merchants during the Song and Yuan dynasties. It even attracted Arab traders to settle there. In 1959, during archaeological investigations by Quanzhou Maritime Museum, researchers discovered seven tower-shaped tombstones with Islamic-style designs in Meishan Village of Fashi and near the adjacent Yunlu Temple. One of these tombstones, carved from granite, consists of five layers with a hollow center. The lower layer is adorned with cloud patterns, while the top cross-section has a semi-circular shape and the remaining sides are unadorned.

In 1974, the tombstone of Guo Deguang, the founding ancestor of the Guo family from the Hui ethnic group in Quanzhou was found, which is now preserved in Quanzhou Maritime Museum. The incised Persian inscription in the center of the tombstone reads "Ibn Khusu De Guang Gong Nam" in translation. The upper right corner is incised with the seal script characters "Hui" and "Baiqi", while the upper left corner is incised with the characters "Jin" and "Poting". In the middle, there is an inscription in regular script that reads "The ancestral tomb of Yuan Guo family". According to the genealogical records of the Guo family, Guo Deguang settled in Fashi between 1308 and 1311 during the Yuan Dynasty. It was not until Guo Zhongyuan of the third generation that the family moved from Fashi to today's Baiqi Township of Hui'an County. From there, they branched out to Shihu Village in Hanjiang Town, Qiankeng Village in Baogai Town and Guokeng Village in Yongning Town, all located in today's Shishi City.

郭德广墓碑石。（成冬冬 摄）
The tombstone of Guo Deguang.
(Photo by Cheng Dongdong)

宋元碇石

古代行船，停泊时将碇石沉于水中，借以稳定船身，其作用如后世的船锚。因此，开船称为“启碇”，停船称为“下碇”。1975 年 4 月，法石海滩出土一块宋元时期的碇石，现保存于泉州海外交通史博物馆。该碇石长 232 厘米，中段宽 29 厘米，厚 17 厘米，两侧对称开凿尺寸为 29×16×1 厘米的凹槽，材质为花岗岩。其形制与日本佐贺县唐津市近海发现的一块元代碇石相似，且出土地层发现大量宋元时期的划花青瓷和白瓷片，可推断该碇石属于宋元遗物。

宋元时期中国拥有发达的造船和航海技术，碇石的使用较为普遍。宋代航海活动家徐竞所撰《宣和奉使高丽图经》记载：“船首两颊柱，中有车轮，上绾藤索，其大如椽，长五百尺，下垂矴（碇）石，石两旁夹以二木钩。”1974 年发掘泉州湾后渚港宋代海船时，发现了升降石锚的绞车构件，船舱内还有一件墨书“丘碇水记”的木签，证实这艘船舶使用的也是碇石。明清时期，由于碇泊工具的逐步改进，海船普遍使用铁制锚具。

泉州湾宋代海船绞关木。（泉州海外交通史博物馆 供图）
The ship winch of the Song Dynasty discovered in Quanzhou Bay. (Courtesy of Quanzhou Maritime Museum)

石湖港水域发现的明代船锚。（李国宏 供图）
The Ming Dynasty iron anchor discovered in the waters of Shihu Port. (Courtesy of Li Guohong)

Anchor Stones of the Song and Yuan Dynasties

In ancient times, when ships were anchored, anchor stones were submerged in the water to stabilize the vessels, serving a similar function to anchors in later periods. Therefore, setting sailing was referred to as "weighing the anchor", and anchoring the ship was called "dropping the anchor". In April 1975, an anchor stone of the Song and Yuan periods was unearthed at Fashi beach, which is now preserved in Quanzhou Maritime Museum. The anchor stone, made of granite, measures 232 cm in length, 29 cm in width at the middle section, and 17 centimeters in thickness. It features symmetrical grooves on both sides, measuring 29x16x1 centimeters. Its design is similar to an anchor stone discovered in the offshore area of Tangjin City, Saga Prefecture, Japan, dating back to the Yuan Dynasty. In addition, a large number of carved blue and white porcelain fragments of the Song and Yuan periods were found in the same archaeological layer, indicating that this anchor stone is an artifact from the Song and Yuan periods.

During the Song and Yuan dynasties, China had advanced shipbuilding and navigation technologies, and the use of anchor stones was widespread. Xu Jing, a maritime explorer in the Song Dynasty, recorded in his *Illustrated Account of the Xuanhe (1119—1125) Embassy to Kory*, "The bow of the ship has two side pillars as large as a beam and nearly 167 meters long, with a wheel in the middle and a rope is tied on top. The anchor stone hangs down with two wooden hooks on both sides." When the Song Dynasty ship was excavated in Houzhu Port in Quanzhou Bay in 1974, components of a winch for raising and lowering stone anchors were discovered, and inside the cabin, a wooden sign with the ink inscription "Record of Water Depths for Anchoring" was found, which testifies to the use of stone anchors on this ship. During the Ming and Qing dynasties (1368—1912), due to gradual improvements in anchoring tools, iron anchors became widely used on seagoing ships.

法石宋代沉船遗址

1982 年，中国科学院自然科学史研究所、泉州市文物管理委员会、泉州海外交通史博物馆联合对法石沉船进行发掘，清理出古船后部的四个舱位，出土了一些船舶构件和遗物。由于船体中部和前部尚叠压在建筑物之下，同时考虑到出土遗物的处置保护问题，经国家有关部门同意后，就地回填。此次考古发现，这艘船为装置有龙骨的尖底船，其形制与宋代文献《宣和奉使高丽图经》《太平寰宇记》中记载的泉州建造的福船形制一样，判断属于中型宋代远洋货船。沉船沉积层发现的瓷器均出自南宋时期，船上发现的小口瓶为宋代晋江磁灶窑系产品，划花青瓷为宋代泉州同安汀溪窑系产品。沉积层没有来自其他年代的掺杂物，为其所属年代是宋代的判断提供了佐证。

Site of the Song Dynasty Shipwreck in Fashi

In 1982, the Institute for the History of Natural Sciences, CAS, Quanzhou Cultural Relics Management Committee and Quanzhou Maritime Museum jointly excavated Fashi shipwreck. Four compartments at the rear of the ancient ship were cleared, and various ship components and artifacts were unearthed. Due to the fact that the middle and front sections of the ship were still buried under buildings and considering the preservation of the excavated artifacts, the site was backfilled in situ with the approval of relevant national authorities. This archaeological discovery reveals that the ship is a sharp-bottomed vessel with kneels, similar in shape to the "Fu-Chuan" made in Quanzhou and documented in the Song Dynasty work *Illustrated Account of the Xuanhe (1119—1125) Embassy to Kory* and *Universal Geography of the Taiping Era (976—983)*. It is believed to be a medium-sized Song Dynasty ocean-going cargo ship. The porcelain found in the shipwreck sediment layer all dates back to the Southern Song Dynasty. The small-mouthed bottles discovered on the ship are products of Jinjiang Cizao Kilns, and the carved blue porcelain is from Tingxi Kilns in Tong'an, Quanzhou. The absence of artifacts from other eras in the sediment layer provides evidence supporting its dating to the Song Dynasty.

1982 年法石宋代沉船考古发掘现场。（成冬冬 摄）
The archaeological excavation scene of the Song Dynasty shipwreck in Fashi in 1982. (Photo by Cheng Dongdong)

法石宋船与后渚宋船相比，前者底板为单层厚实松木结构，后者底板则由两层较薄木板合成。二者均为尖底船形，便于劈浪，且稳定性较好。鉴于尖底船板弧形弯曲度较大，建造技术难度较高，而法石宋船采用单层厚实松木一次成型制造，证实宋代泉州海船建造技术在不断提高。

法石宋船在细部处理上也更科学。一是在船底板接合工艺方面，法石宋船每列底板之间均用高低榫接合，以形成一级台阶，而后渚古船底板每三列才有一处高低榫搭接；为便于上下行走和堆放货物，法石宋船船底内壁台阶被加工成倒角，后渚古船则用加钉木条使台阶直角形成坡面。二是在隔板与底板衔接工艺方面，除用方钉钉合外，法石宋船还用木钩钉加强它们之间的联结，打入船壳板的木钩钉可能还起着肋骨的作用，以此取代了后渚宋船铁钩钉加肋骨的传统加固方式。三是在隔舱板拼接方面，与后渚宋船采用同口接（即平接）加宽铁钩钉夹合不同，法石宋船用的是四面削尖的直角方榫接合，并以锹钉加固。这种搭接方式，现在有人称之为“鱼鳞式”或“错装甲法”结构，其优点是板间联结紧密严实，整体强度高，不易漏水。

法石宋船还确证了竹帆的存在。后渚宋船曾出土六角形竹编，其为船篷还是船帆引起过争议。而在法石宋船上发现了较大面积的系有绳索的竹编，从其厚度和折叠状况看，应该是船上的竹帆残存，而不是作为遮盖用的船篷。结合《宣和奉使高丽图经》有关布帆与利篷的记载，可以确证宋元时期福建海船上竹帆的存在。

法石宋船上出土的木桶、瓷片及小口陶瓶。（成冬冬 摄）
The wooden barrel porcelain fragments and small-mouthed pottery bottles unearthed from the Song Dynasty shipwreck in Fashi. (Photo by Cheng Dongdong)

Compared with Houzhu Song Dynasty ship, Fashi Song Dynasty ship has a single-layer solid pine wood structure for its bottom board, while the latter is composed of two layers of thinner wood boards. Both are sharp-bottomed, which is good for splitting waves and stability. Given the fact that a larger curvature is needed for the sharp-bottomed ship and the construction technique is more difficult, Fashi ship, which is molded with a single layer of solid pine wood in one time, testifies to the great improvement of shipbuilding technology in Quanzhou during the Song Dynasty.

Fashi ship also demonstrates more scientific details in its construction. Firstly, in terms of the joining technique for the bottom boards, Fashi ship uses high and low tenons between each row of bottom boards to create a stepped effect, while Houzhu ship only has high and low tenons every three rows. To facilitate walking and cargo stacking, the inner wall steps of Fashi ship's bottom are chamfered, while Houzhu ship uses nailed wooden strips to create a sloping surface. Secondly, for the connection between bulkheads and the bottom boards, in addition to square nails, Fashi ship also uses wooden hook nails. The wooden hook nails driven into the hull planks may have also acted as ribs, replacing the traditional reinforcement method of iron hook nails and ribs used in Houzhu ship. Thirdly, in terms of the joining of compartment boards, Fashi ship uses four-sided pointed right-angle mortise and tenon joints, reinforced with shovel nails, instead of the flat-lap joints with widened iron hook nails used in Houzhu ship. This type of joint is now referred to as a "fish scale" or "overlapping armor" structure, which has the advantages of tight and solid interconnection between the boards, high overall intensity, and resistance to water leakage.

Fashi ship also testifies to the existence of bamboo sails. There has been a debate over whether the hexagonal bamboo weaving found on Houzhu ship is a sail or a canopy. However, on Fashi ship, a larger area of woven bamboo attached with ropes was found, which, based on its shape and folding condition, is believed to be the remnant of bamboo sails rather than canopy coverings. This, combined with the records about cloth sails and awnings in *Illustrated Account of the Xuanhe (1119—1125) Embassy to Kory*, testifies to the presence of bamboo sails on Fujian sea vessels during the Song and Yuan dynasties.

芬芳记忆

宋元时期的泉州港不仅是海上丝绸之路的起点，也是最大的香料进口港。根据《宋史》和《宋会要辑稿》记载，从北宋乾德元年至太平兴国二年的 14 年间，泉州地方长官陈洪进就向朝廷进贡了各种名贵香料共计 17 万斤。其中，977 年，仅陈洪进向朝廷进贡的乳香一项，就多达 74,000 斤。1127 年至 1161 年，从三佛齐（位于今苏门答腊岛）转运至广州和泉州的香料数量，成为评价这两个外贸港口繁荣程度的重要指标。海外香料的进口及使用对泉州社会经济的发展及生活习俗的变化都产生过深远的影响。南宋赵汝适所撰《诸蕃志》记载：“（降真香）气劲而远，能辟邪气。泉人岁除，家无贫富，皆爇之如燔柴，然其直甚廉。以三佛齐者为上，以其气味清远也。”

宋末元初，阿拉伯穆斯林海商蒲寿庚执掌泉州港海外贸易管理权，势力庞大，炙手可热，与其兄蒲寿晟一起移居法石。蒲寿庚在法石宝觉山上建造天风海涛楼，以眺望船舶进出港，也称“望海楼”，又以蒲寿庚号海云，别称“海云楼”。楼下建有一碧万顷亭，登之可临海观涛，天风徐徐，帆影点点，甚是惬意。蒲寿晟也在法石建云麓别墅，悠游林下。其《题海云楼下一碧万顷亭》诗云：“倚阑心目净，万顷一磨铜。欲画画不得，托言言更穷。阴晴山远近，日夜水西东。此意知谁会，鸥边独钓翁。”

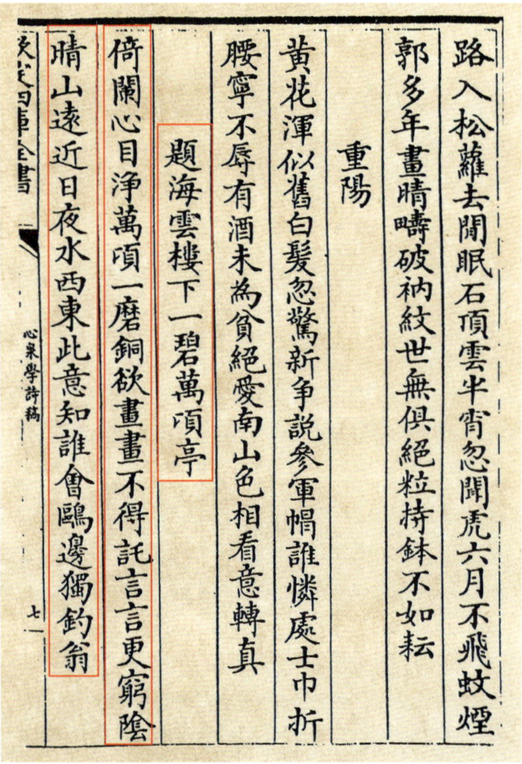
欽定四庫全書

路入松蘿去閑眠石頂雲半宵忽聞虎六月不飛蚊煙
郭多年晝晴疇破衲紋世無俱絕粒持鉢不如耘
重陽
黃花渾似舊白髮忽驚新爭說參軍帽誰憐處士巾折
腰寧不辱有酒未為貧絕愛南山色相看意轉真
題海雲樓下一碧萬頃亭
倚闌心目淨萬頃一磨銅欲畫畫不得託言言更窮陰
晴山遠近日夜水西東此意知誰會鷗邊獨釣翁

心泉學詩稿 七

元代蒲寿晟《心泉学诗稿》。（李国宏 供图）
A page of Pu Shousheng's poetry. (Courtesy of Li Guohong)

A Fragrant Memory

During the Song and Yuan dynasties, Quanzhou Port was not only the starting point of the Maritime Silk Road, but also the largest spice import port. According to *History of Song* and *Collected Statutes of the Song Dynasty*, during the 14 years from 963 to 977, Chen Hongjin, a local official of Quanzhou alone, offered a total of 170,000 catties of various precious spices to the imperial court. In 977, Chen Hongjin offered a tribute of 74,000 catties of frankincense to the government. From 1127 to 1161, the quantity of spices transported from Samboja (located on the island of Samboja today) to Guangzhou and Quanzhou became an important indicator for evaluating the prosperity of these two foreign trade ports. The import and use of foreign spices have had a profound impact on the development of Quanzhou's social economy and changes in lifestyle and customs. *Records of Foreign Countries* written by Zhao Rukuo in the Southern Song Dynasty states that, "The fragrance of Dalbergia is strong and far-reaching, capable of dispelling pathogenic *qi* (factors). Every year when the New Year is approaching, all families in Quanzhou, poor and rich, would burn Dalbergia, treating it like burning firewood, for it is very affordable. The one from Samboja is considered the best due to its fresh and distant aroma."

In about 1279, Pu Shougeng, an Arab Muslim maritime merchant, wielded power in overseas trade in Quanzhou Port. With immense power and popularity, Pu Shougeng and his brother Pu Shousheng moved to Fashi. Pu Shougeng built the Sea Wind and Wave Tower on Mount Baojue in Fashi to overlook the incoming and outgoing ships, also known as Seaview Tower or Sea and Cloud Tower which is named after the courtesy name of Pu Shougeng, Haiyun. Below the tower, there was a pavilion called Pavilion of Boundless Ripples, where one could enjoy the view of the sea waves, gentle breezes, and the sight of sails dotting the horizon, creating a pleasant atmosphere. Pu Shousheng also built a villa called Yunlu Villa in Fashi, where he enjoyed leisurely walks in the wood. In his poem entitled *The Pavilion of Boundless Ripples Below the Sea and Cloud Tower,* he depicts such leisure time.

蒲寿庚兄弟还在法石开辟花园，大量栽种来自海外的香花，如茉莉花、素馨花、含笑花等。明初，法石蒲氏改姓卜，但依旧保留着种植香花的传统和用香料、香花敬奉祖先的习俗。这些都与蒲寿庚家族来自阿拉伯地区、长期经营香料业有关。而法石港附近的蟳埔村，女性至今仍保留着"簪花围"的习俗。这是一种蟳埔女特有的盘发和用鲜花装饰发髻的方式。她们用麻绳将花苞或花蕾串成花环，用其装饰盘好的发髻，由内向外盘绕两三圈，一环比一环大，再在耳鬓插上芳香四溢的含笑花，"但使新花艳，得间美人髻"的意境顿时显现眼前。

清顺治三年（1646），蒲寿庚的后代蒲世茂由晋江东石迁居永春卓埔后溪寨（今永春县达埔镇汉口村），成为永春蒲氏开基祖，并将蒲氏家族的传统制香技艺带到永春。蒲世茂的第七世孙蒲树礼更是把祖传的庆兰堂制香铺打造成为永春汉口神香的第一品牌。1907 年，蒲树礼在后溪寨创立神香批发商铺。1930 年，在永春县城五里街开设蒲庆兰香室。1935 年，在泉州伍堡街创办庆兰堂分店。蒲家香品畅销闽南、台湾、香港等地及东南亚地区，庆兰香室步入鼎盛时期。

一缕蒲香，弥漫着异域芬芳，随着香料之路飘到闽南，历经蒲庆兰香室精心研制，又沿着海上丝绸之路远销南洋，泉州香文化就这样承载着中西文化交流的历史记忆。

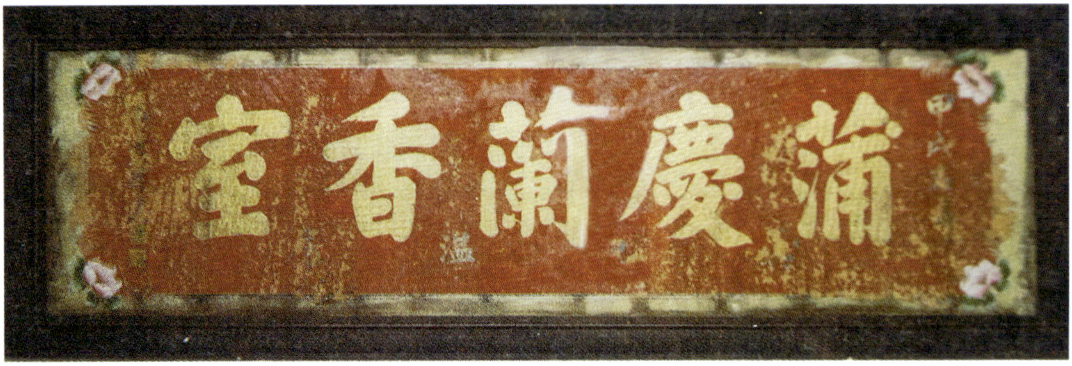

蒲庆兰香室匾额。（李国宏 供图）
The signboard of Pu Qinglan Incense Chamber. (Courtesy of Li Guohong)

The Pu brothers also established gardens in Fashi and planted a large variety of flowers from overseas, such as jasmine, frangipani and michelia. In the early Ming Dynasty, the Pu family changed their surname to Bu, but they still retained the tradition of cultivating fragrant flowers and the custom of using incense and flowers to pay respects to their ancestors. This tradition is related to the Pu family's Arabian origin and their long-term operation in the spice trade. Near Fashi Port, there is a village called Xunpu where women still practice the custom of "wearing flower wreaths" today. It is a unique way for women in Xunpu to style their hair by adorning their buns with fresh flowers. They string flower buds or blossoms into garlands with hemp ropes and use them to decorate their hair, coiling them from the inside out in two or three rounds, with each round larger than the inner one. They also insert fragrant hibiscus flowers near their temples. This creates a picturesque scene, reminiscent of the poetic imagery of "the new flowers adding beauty to a beautiful bun".

In 1646, Pu Shimao, a descendant of Pu Shougeng, moved from Dongshi, Jinjiang to Houxi Village, Zhuopu, Yongchun (now Hankou Village, Dapu Town, Yongchun County), becoming the founding ancestor of the Pu family in Yongchun and bringing the traditional incense-making techniques to Yongchun. Pu Shuli, Pu Shimao's seventh-generation descendant, transformed the ancestral incense workshop of Qinglan Chamber into the leading brand of Hankou incense industry in Yongchun. In 1907, Pu Shuli established a wholesale incense shop in Houxi Village. In 1930, he opened Pu Qinglan Incense Chamber on Wuli Street in Yongchun. In 1935, a branch of Qinglan Chamber was established on Wubao Street in Quanzhou. Pu family's incense products became popular in Southern Fujian, Taiwan, Hong Kong and Southeast Asian regions, and Qinglan Chamber entered its heyday.

A trace of Pu incense, carrying the exotic fragrance, wafted its way to Southern Fujian along the Spice Route. Meticulously crafted by Pu Qinglan Incense Chamber, it then has traveled further along the Maritime Silk Road, reaching the markets of Southeast Asia. Quanzhou's incense culture thus carries the historical memory of cultural exchanges between the East and the West.

文兴古渡

文兴码头位于今泉州市丰泽区法石社区文兴村南部。码头始建于宋代，是古泉州沿江集群商业码头之一。现存主体为宋代原物，两侧驳岸历代均有修缮。文兴码头呈南北走向，从江岸自上而下延伸至江底，为石构斜坡阶梯式驳岸码头，用花岗岩错缝砌筑，长 34 米，宽 3.5 米。由于江底为软基，码头基础均以松木桩加固。文兴码头考古发掘的出土遗物主要有建筑构件、铁器和瓷器。其中属于宋元时期的遗物有筒瓦、莲花纹瓦当、龙泉青瓷片、白釉瓷瓶等。

The Ancient Wenxing Dock

Wenxing Dock is located in the southern part of the present Wenxing Village, Fashi Community, Fengze District, Quanzhou City. The dock, first built in the Song Dynasty, is one of the ancient Quanzhou's cluster of commercial docks along the river. The main structure that remains today is from the Song Dynasty, with repairs made to the embankments on both sides throughout the dynasties. Wenxing Dock runs in a north-south direction, extending from the riverbank to the riverbed with stone-constructed sloping stepped embankments. It is built with granite masonry, measuring 34 meters in length and 3.5 meters in width. Due to the soft riverbed, the foundation of the dock is reinforced with pine wood piles. Excavations at Wenxing Dock have unearthed various artifacts, including architectural components, ironware and porcelain. Among the artifacts from the Song and Yuan dynasties are tube tiles, lotus-patterned eave tiles, Longquan celadon fragments and white-glazed porcelain bottles.

文兴古渡。（李国宏 供图）
The ancient Wenxin Dock. (Courtesy of Li Guohong)

码头上矗立一座宋代宝箧印经塔，寄托着修建者镇守防卫、护佑商旅的愿望。关于这座局部残损的宝塔，还有一个“失而复得”的故事。20 世纪 70 年代，由于江底泥沙淤积，码头渐渐失去原有的繁华景象。在风雨和潮水的冲击下，宝塔悄然坍塌，构件散失。1986 年，一位村民下水游泳时，碰到江底的一块大石头，潜入水中一看，石头上似乎刻着图案，连忙叫人帮忙打捞上岸，结果让众人大吃一惊。这块沉入江中的石头，竟然就是宝箧印经塔原来的构件——四面观音雕像。或许是机缘巧合，不久之后，文兴村一户人家整修房屋，意外在杂物堆中发现一块四面分别阴刻“佛”“法”“僧”“宝”字样的方形石头。定神一看，正好是原先安放在四面观音雕像下面的那块塔身构件。于是，村民根据记忆中这座古塔的样式，将其重新竖立在码头上。其实，重新立起来的不只是一座宝塔，更是一份沉甸甸的文化自信。在岁月的侵蚀下，宝塔上佛像的轮廓已经有些模糊，但是，他们深邃的眼神，依然注视着江上来来往往的船只。潮起潮落中，真武庙的晨钟暮鼓穿越法石港的千里烟波，和着阵阵涛声，依然轻轻地敲打在人们的心坎上。

宝塔上的“佛”“法”字样。（陈英杰 摄）
The characters "Fo" (Buddha) and "Fa" (Dharma) on the pagoda. (Photo by Chen Yingjie)

Standing on the dock is a treasure-box style pagoda built during the Song Dynasty to deposit Buddhist texts, which embodies the wish of the builder to guard and protect the merchants and travelers. There is a story about this partially damaged treasure pagoda, which involves a "lost and found" incident. In the 1970s, due to sedimentation in the riverbed, the dock gradually lost its former prosperity. Under the impact of winds, rain and tides, the pagoda quietly collapsed, and its components scattered. In 1986, a villager encountered a large stone while swimming in the river. Upon closer inspection, the stone seemed to be engraved with patterns. The villager quickly called for help to salvage it ashore. This stone, which had sunk into the river, turned out to be one of the components of the original pagoda—a sculpture carved with the face of Guanyin (the God of Mercy) on all four sides. Perhaps by a stroke of luck, not long after, a household in Wenxing Village was renovating their house and unexpectedly discovered a square stone among a pile of debris, which was engraved with four characters, "Fo" (Buddha), "Fa" (Dharma), "Seng" (Monk) and "Bao" (Treasure), on its four sides. Upon closer examination, it turned out to be the missing component that was originally placed beneath the sculpture with Guanyin faces. Following their memories of the original appearance of the ancient pagoda, the villagers re-erected it on the dock. In fact, what was reestablished was not just a pagoda but also a profound cultural confidence. Over the years, the contours of Guanyin on the pagoda have become somewhat blurred, but their profound gaze still watches over the passing ships on the river. Amidst the ebb and flow, the morning bell and evening drum of Zhenwu Temple still penetrate the misty waves along Fashi Port, harmonizing with the sound of the tides, gently resonating in people's hearts.

宝塔上的观音雕像。（陈英杰 摄）
The sculpture of Guanyin on the pagoda. (Photo by Chen Yingjie)

美山帆影

美山码头位于今法石社区美山村，地处文兴码头下游，较文兴码头处水深，故码头造型为边坡较陡的墩台，便于高潮位时大船停靠。墩台自下而上保留了不同时期增筑的痕迹，最下层的墩台南北长约 20 米、宽约 15 米，最上层的墩台南北长约 10 米、宽约 8 米。墩台南端砌石阶，东西两侧为陡坡。墩台下方东西两侧各叠压一条斜坡状台阶，便于低潮位时使用。

美山码头早期墩台的台基是由下而上渐次内收，所形成的外侧壁面呈倾斜状，其东、西、北三面现今仍残存一定高度的壁面。东侧壁面坡度 30 度，南北残长 16.25—19.9 米，东西残宽 0.4—4.65 米，残高 2.25 米。壁面全部用条石做一丁一顺交替叠砌，未见用胶结材料做填充勾缝现象。西侧壁基底至基面砌筑收分为 0.7 米，侧沿坡度为 74 度。西侧壁面用料与东侧壁面基本相同，不同之处是间用少量不规整的块石，从基面石缝观察，可见有用少量胶结物做勾缝处理。北侧壁仅见转角部位，其砌筑方式与西侧壁相同，基底至基面砌筑收分为 0.4 米。

美山码头的墩台侧壁。（李国宏 供图）
The wall surface of Meishan Dock's platform. (Courtesy of Li Guohong)

Sails in Meishan

Meishan Dock is located in the present Meishan Village of Fashi Community. It is situated downstream of Wenxing Dock and has a deeper water depth compared with Wenxing Dock. Therefore, the dock is designed with steep slopes for the platform to facilitate the docking of large ships during high tide. The platform retains traces of construction from different periods, with the bottom layer measuring approximately 20 meters long and 15 meters wide in the north-south direction, and the top layer measuring approximately 10 meters long and 8 meters wide in the north-south direction. The southern end of the platform is built with stone steps, and steep slopes are on the east and west sides. Below the platform, there are inclined steps on both the east and west sides, which are stacked to facilitate use during low tide.

The early-stage foundation of Meishan Dock's platform is gradually inwardly tapered, resulting in the inclined outer wall surfaces that are still partially preserved on the east, west and north sides. The eastern wall has a slope of 30 degrees, with remaining lengths of 16.25—19.9 meters north-south, remaining widths of 0.4—4.65 meters east-west and a remaining height of 2.25 meters. The wall surfaces are constructed with alternating layers of stones, with no evidence of jointing materials used for filling the gaps. The western wall has a base-to-surface construction taper of 0.7 meters, with a slope of 74 degrees along the edge. The materials used for the western wall are similar to those used for the eastern wall, with a difference being the occasional use of irregular stone blocks, and some evidence of jointing materials used for gap filling can be observed from the stone joints on the base surface. The northern wall is only partially visible at the corner, and its construction method is similar to that of the western wall, with a base-to-surface construction taper of 0.4 meters.

美山码头地层出土文物主要有明清时期的青花瓷和彩瓷残片，器型包括碗、盘、碟、杯等，以碗类居多，证实美山码头沿用至明清时期，是晋江沿岸重要的驳岸码头设施。

1961 年 9 月，泉州海外交通史博物馆组织考古调查，曾在美山村发现古代造船遗址和一处尚在使用的船坞。该船坞残长 50 米，宽度 6—10 米不等，深度约为 2 米，涨潮时可通晋江。调查人员看见船坞中停泊着两艘小型商船，据美山村民介绍，该船坞一直是船舶停靠、避风、修造的处所。当时，法石周边包括美山村在内的村庄，都保留着手工制作竹帆的行当，俗称“打帆”，有 400 多名从业人员。制作好的竹帆除了自用之外，还供应晋江沿海深沪、永宁、梅林、港边、石湖、蚶江等地船户使用。

美山渡。（陈英杰 摄）
Meishan Ferry. (Photo by Chen Yingjie)

Meishan Dock has yielded cultural relics mainly from the Ming and Qing dynasties, including fragments of blue and colored porcelain, with a variety of utensils such as bowls, plates, dishes and cups, bowls being the most common. This proves that Meishan Dock was in use until the Ming and Qing dynasties and served as an important dock along Jinjiang coast.

In September 1961, Quanzhou Maritime Museum organized an archaeological survey and discovered an ancient shipbuilding site and a still-in-use dock in Meishan Village. The dock has a remaining length of 50 meters, a width ranging from 6 to 10 meters and a depth of approximately 2 meters, allowing access to Jinjiang River during high tide. During the survey, two small merchant ships were seen moored in the dock. According to local villagers, the dock has long been used as a place for ship docking, shelter and repairs. At that time, the surrounding areas of Fashi, including Meishan Village, still maintained the traditional craft of handcrafting bamboo sails, commonly known as "*dafan*" (making sails), with over 400 practitioners. The bamboo sails produced were not only used by themselves but also supplied to ship owners in coastal areas such as Shenhu, Yongning, Meilin, Gangbian, Shihu and Hanjiang along Jinjiang River.

拍摄于 1982 年的法石船坞。（陈鹏鹏 摄）
A photograph of Fashi's shipyard taken in 1982. (Photo by Chen Pengpeng)

温陵城郭枕江开

从 10 世纪到 14 世纪，有众多阿拉伯和欧洲旅行家抵达泉州，并且记录下关于泉州港的信息，证实泉州是 10 到 14 世纪印度洋和西太平洋航运与贸易体系中具有重要代表性的港口城市。1240 年，出生于格林纳达的阿拉伯旅行家伊本·赛义德前往麦加朝圣，后来抵达巴格达，抄录了众多图书馆的珍贵资料，其中关于泉州港的描述值得关注：“在这第九段之内，第一条就是泉州江，其江出口处就是泉州港，那些前往中国的商人对此是十分熟悉的。凡是来自中国海的船舶都要进入该港，一直向前推进到上游 15 英里的地方。”这是阿拉伯人关于泉州港地理信息较早的文献记录。在此之前，穆斯林中介商伊德里西曾在亚丁湾发现了满载胡椒、沉香、芦荟、玳瑁、象牙、黑檀、藤、瓷器、皮鞍等货物的中国商船。这些来自泉州和广州的商船不仅是运送货物的工具，也是信息传播的载体。

宋元时期，为了满足不同种类船舶的停靠需求，晋江沿岸建设了各种类型的码头，解决贸易物资的仓储需求。同时，通过桥梁与驿道，串联起完善的商贸联通网络。

来自意大利的犹太商人雅各·德安科纳于 1271 年游历泉州，在他的著作《光明之城》中描绘了泉州沿江码头的情景，包括仓储设施等情况。

反映泉州市舶司官员在码头迎候外国商船靠岸的石雕。（成冬冬 摄）
The stone carving depicting Quanzhou's Maritime Trade Office officials welcoming foreign merchant ships at the dock. (Photo by Cheng Dongdong)

Quanzhou, Leaning Against the River and Embracing the Sea

From the 10th century to the 14th century, numerous Arabian and European travelers arrived in Quanzhou and recorded their observations about Quanzhou Port, which demonstrate its status as an important representative port city in the Indian Ocean and Western Pacific shipping and trading system during that period. In 1240, the Arabian traveler Ibn Said, born in Grenada, went to Mecca for pilgrimage and later arrived in Baghdad, where he transcribed valuable information from various libraries. Among them, the description about Quanzhou Port is worth noting: "Within this ninth section is Quanzhou River, and its outlet is Quanzhou Port, which is well known to merchants traveling to China. All ships coming from the China Sea must enter this port and proceed upstream for 15 miles." This is an early geographical record about Quanzhou Port by the Arabs. Prior to this, the Muslim intermediary Al-Idrisi discovered Chinese merchant ships in the Gulf of Aden loaded with goods such as pepper, Dalbergia, aloe vera, tortoise shells, ivories, ebony, rattan, porcelain and leather saddles. These merchant ships from Quanzhou and Guangzhou were not only vehicles for transporting goods, but also carriers of disseminating information.

During the Song and Yuan dynasties, various types of docks were built along Jinjiang River to meet the docking needs of different kinds of ships, as well as addressing the needs of warehousing trade goods. Additionally, a well-connected network of commercial trade was established with bridges and post roads.

During his travel to Quanzhou in 1271, Jacob d'Ancona, a Jewish merchant from Italy, described in his work *The City of Light* the scene of riverside docks in Quanzhou, including storage facilities and other situations.

“这是一个很大的港口，甚至比辛迦兰（广州）还大，商船从中国海进入这里。它的周围高山环绕，那些高山使它成了一个躲避风暴的港口……因此这儿有成批的商人沿江（晋江）上下，如果一个人没有亲眼看到这一情景，简直无法相信。在江堤边上有许多装着铁门的大仓库，大印度以及其他地方的商人以此来确保他们货物的安全。不过其中最大的是萨拉森人与犹太商人的仓库，像个修道院，商人可以把自己的货物藏在里面。这中间，既有那些他们想要出售的货物，也包括那些他们所购买的货物。”

连接泉州港与古刺桐城的晋江，成为名副其实的“黄金水道”。“温陵向南通海舶，贩宝诸番共为客。”遥想当年，有多少泉州客商走下沿江码头，扬帆出海。繁盛的海外贸易带来丰厚的回报，刺激着更多的人带着梦想和勇气，毅然走向充满诱惑和风险的海域，使宋元泉州的贸易线路不断延伸。繁华的商贸景象背后，海商及其家人的生活也出现了与祖祖辈辈不一样的变化。元至正十五年（1355），一位思亲的“闽中女”向诗人刘仁本诉说：“当时郎着浅番衣，浅番路近便回归。谁知却入深番去，浪逐鸳鸯远水飞。”为了打听丈夫的消息，“闽中女”想尽了各种办法：“海南番舶尽回乡，不见侬家薄幸郎。欲向船头问消息，荔枝树下买槟榔。”可是，这一等足足等了十年：“象犀珠翠海南香，万里归来水路长。薄幸又从何处去？十年海外不思乡。”只留下“闽中女”手捧“织成欲寄番船去”的寒衣，“日日江头来候潮”。此情此景，伴随滚滚的江水，流淌着淡淡的忧伤。

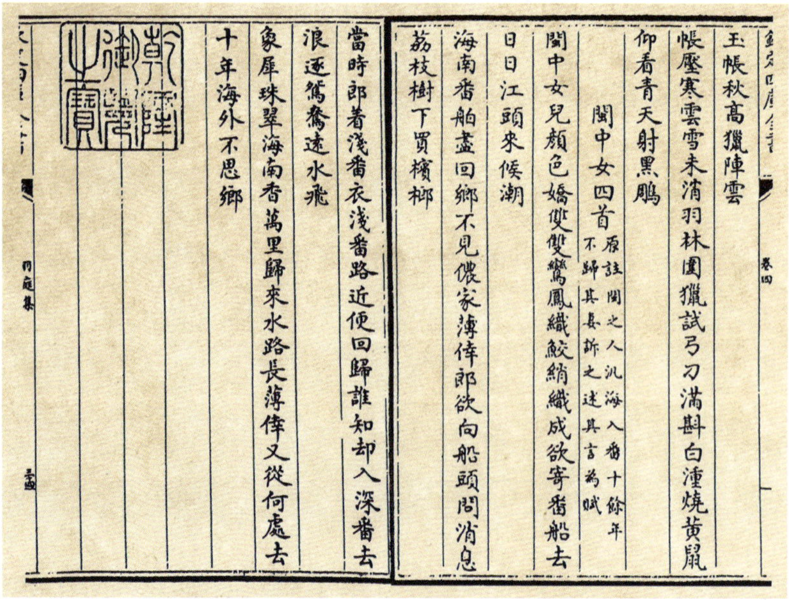
玉帳秋高獵陣雲
帳壓寒雲雪未消羽林圍獵試弓刀滿斟白湩燒黄鼠
仰看青天射黑鵰
閩中女四首 原註閩之人汎海入番十餘年不歸其妻訴之述其言為賦
閩中女兒顔色嬌雙雙鸞鳳織鮫綃織成欲寄番船去
日日江頭來候潮
海南番舶盡回鄉不見儂家薄倖郎欲向船頭問消息
荔枝樹下買檳榔
當時郎着淺番衣淺番路近便回歸誰知却入深番去
浪逐鴛鴦遠水飛
象犀珠翠海南香萬里歸来水路長薄倖又從何處去
十年海外不思鄉

元代刘仁本《羽庭集》中关于“闽中女”的记述。（李国宏 供图）
The description of “a woman from central Fujian” in Liu Renben’s *Yuting Collection* written in the Yuan Dynasty. (Courtesy of Li Guohong)

"This is a very large port, even larger than Censcalan (Guangzhou), where merchant ships enter from the China Sea. It is surrounded by high mountains, which makes it a harbor to escape storms...Therefore, there are batches of merchants moving up and down the river (Jinjiang River), and if one has not witnessed this scene with their own eyes, it is hard to believe. Along the river embankment, there are many large warehouses with iron doors, used by merchants from Greater India and other places to ensure the safety of their goods. However, the largest ones among them are the warehouses of Saracen and Jewish merchants, resembling monasteries, where merchants can hide their goods. Among them are the goods they want to sell and the goods they have purchased."

Jinjiang River, connecting Quanzhou Port and the ancient city, became a veritable "golden waterway". We may imagine numerous setting sails started from the Port along the river and ventured out to the sea. The flourishing overseas trade brought abundant returns, inspiring more people to embark on the tempting and risky sea routes, continuously expanding the trade routes of Quanzhou during the Song and Yuan dynasties. Behind the bustling commercial scene, the lives of the maritime merchants and their families underwent changes different from their ancestors. In 1355, "a woman from central Fujian" longing for her husband expressed her feelings to a poet named Liu Renben, saying, "At that time, my husband wore light-colored foreign clothes, and the route back from the foreign lands was close. Who knew he would go deeper into the foreign lands, drifting away like mandarin ducks on distant waters." In order to track down her husband, the woman tried various methods, mentioning that, "All the ships from Hainan have returned home, but my heartless husband is nowhere to be seen. I want to ask for his whereabouts at the bow of the ship, pretending to buy betel nuts under the lichi tree." However, she had been waiting for ten years, asking that, "Ivory, rhinoceros horns, jewelries and incense have been brought back after the long journey by water. Where has my heartless husband gone? Ten years overseas, not thinking of home." She only left behind a warm garment in her hands, lamenting "woven garment ready to be sent to the foreign ship", and "waiting for the tide at the river every day". Such a scene, accompanied by the rolling river water, carries a faint sadness.

马可·波罗的足迹

在当年那些抵达泉州的商人和旅行家中，最出名者可能就是意大利旅行家马可·波罗。在他的眼中，刺桐港充满着浪漫主义的气息："这个地方风光秀丽，居民崇信佛教。一切生活必需品非常丰富。这里的居民，民性和平，喜爱舒适安逸，爱好自由。"他更以商人的敏感记录了泉州的税收状况，揭示了刺桐港的"繁荣密码"："刺桐是世界上最大的港口之一，大批商人云集这里，货物堆积如山，的确难以想象。每一个商人，必须付出自己投资总额百分之十的税收，所以，大汗从这个地方获得了巨额的收入。商人们租船运货，对于上等商品，须付该货百分之三十的运费，胡椒却须付百分之四十四的运费。对于檀香木、其他药材以及一般商品，运费是百分之四十。据商人们计算，他们的花费，包括关税、运费在内，总共达到货物价值的一半。然而，就是从这余下的一半中，他们也能取得很大的利润，所以他们常常能够用更多的货物，回销到原来的市场。"

Marco Polo's Footprints

Among the merchants and travelers who arrived in Quanzhou, the most famous one may be the Italian traveler Marco Polo. In his eyes, Zayton Port was full of romanticism: "This place is beautiful, and the residents are devoted to Buddhism. There is a great abundance here of all provision for every necessity of man's life. It is a charming country, and the people are very quiet, and fond of an easy life." He further recorded the tax system in Quanzhou, with a sensitive mind as a businessman, revealing the "prosperity code" of Zayton Port: "It is one of the two greatest havens in the world for commerce. There are a large number of merchants gathering and goods piling up like mountains, which is indeed unimaginable. The Great Khan derives a very large revenue from the duties paid in this city and haven; for you must know that on all the merchandize imported, including precious stones and pearls, he levies a duty of ten per cent, or in other words, takes tithe of everything. Then again the ship's charge for freight on small wares is 30 per cent, on pepper 44 per cent, and on lignaloes, sandalwood and other bulky goods, 40 per cent, so that between freight and the Khan's duties the merchant has to pay a good half the value of his investment (though on the other half he makes such a profit that he is always glad to come back with a new supply of merchandize)."

音乐短剧《市井十洲人》展现了宋元泉州市井生活的热闹和刺桐港千帆竞发、百舸争流的繁荣景象。（陈英杰 摄）

The short musical drama *Accounts by Four Foreign Merchants in the Marketplace* portraits the lively daily life in Quanzhou and the bustling scene of Zayton Port with thousands of sails and boats pouring in during the Song-Yuan period. (Photo by Chen Yingjie)

马可·波罗的描述令人惊讶，不过泉州所拥有的丰富的历史文化遗产足以证实他的叙述是真实存在过的“泉州国际化贸易时代”。在这里，人们看到泉州的繁荣与安定，国家取得富足的税收，商人、货运物流及服务业赚取丰厚的利润；而随着货物的回销，产地与市场的差别也变得模糊，因为它们都在商品互通中得益。以泉州港为枢纽的国际化贸易网络中，似乎所有的参与者都是商业冒险游戏的赢家。这种互利互惠、合作共赢的商业模式，即使是在当下的国际贸易中也是可遇不可求的奢望，却真实地在泉州存在过。它的核心是“普惠”的价值观，就是让所有积极主动的参与者都有均等的机会获得自己的利益。

有趣的是，马可·波罗的名气也一直在文兴码头附近的村民中世代相传。从法石真武庙通往文兴码头的石头街上，曾经铺砌着被来往行人踩得光滑油亮的石板，上面也留下过马可·波罗的足迹。那是 1289 年，波斯国王阿鲁浑的元妃去世，阿鲁浑派出使者来元廷求婚。元世祖忽必烈选定阔阔真为公主，远嫁波斯，马可·波罗主动请求参与护送任务。一切准备就绪后，1292 年春，马可·波罗随同元朝使臣一同护送公主前往波斯完婚。送亲船队选择从泉州港出发，马可·波罗又一次来到令他念念不忘的刺桐城。于是马可·波罗穿行过的、石头街靠近文兴码头的那条短短的巷子，就此被称为“马可·波罗巷”。巷子口有口古井，井水甘甜，滋润了马可·波罗的喉咙，也唤起他那香甜的家乡记忆。他由此踏上归乡的路途，而热情好客的泉州人，则将这口水井命名为“马可·波罗井”，期盼远方的朋友们再次归来。

Marco Polo's description might be astonishing, but Quanzhou's rich historical and cultural heritage is enough to demonstrate the existence of "Quanzhou international trade era" he described. Here, people can see the prosperity and stability of Quanzhou, the country's abundant tax revenue, and the merchants, freight logistics and service industries earning substantial profits. With the return sales of goods, the distinction between the place of origin and the market becomes blurred because they all benefit from the exchange of commodities. In the international trade network centered around Quanzhou Port, it seems that all participants are winners in the game of commercial adventure. This mutually beneficial and win-win business model, even in today's international trade, is an extravagant hope, but it truly existed in Quanzhou. Its core value is "inclusive", which means giving all proactive participants an equal opportunity to obtain their own benefits.

Interestingly, Marco Polo's fame has been passed down through generations among the villagers near Wenxing Dock. On the stone street leading from Zhenwu Temple to Wenxing Dock, there used to be smooth and shiny stone slabs that were stepped on by passers-by, including Marco Polo. In 1289, the Persian King Arghun's consort passed away, and Arghun sent envoys to the Yuan court to propose a marriage. Emperor Kublai Khan chose Kökejin as the princess and arranged for her to marry Arghun in Persia. Marco Polo actively requested to participate in the escort mission. After all preparations were made, in the spring of 1292, Marco Polo accompanied the Yuan envoys to escort the princess to Persia for the wedding. The wedding procession chose to depart from Quanzhou Port, and Marco Polo once again came to the unforgettable Zayton City. The short alley near Wenxing Dock, where Marco Polo passed through, was hence named "Marco Polo Alley". At the entrance of the alley, there is an ancient well with sweet water that quenched Marco Polo's thirst and evoked memories of his sweet hometown. From here, he embarked on his journey back home, while the hospitable people of Quanzhou named this well "Marco Polo Well", hoping for the return of their distant friends.

桥梁飞渡

Bridges: Connecting Land with Water

洛阳桥：海内第一桥

Luoyang Bridge: China’s Earliest Stone Beam Bridge

安平桥：天下无桥长此桥

Anping Bridge: China’s Longest Extant Cross-sea Stone Beam Bridge

顺济桥：诸峰返照潮声远

Shunji Bridge: A Bustling Transportation Hub

环湾向海的地理环境造就了泉州人“每岁造舟通异域”的生存模式，澎湃的泉州湾流淌着泉州人向海而生的基因，孕育着“闽在海中”的蔚蓝梦想。有水的地方，自然是离不开桥，桥上云卷云舒，桥下潮起潮落，沧海桑田，却改变不了泉州人行走天下的豪迈。“泉州桥梁甲闽中”，在泉州人的集体记忆中，最难忘怀的当数洛阳桥、安平桥与顺济桥。

The geographical environment of Quanzhou, with its bays connecting to the sea, has shaped the living conditions of its people, who have been building ships and exploring foreign lands since ancient times. The surging Quanzhou Bay embodies Quanzhou people's connection to the sea, nurturing the dream of "Fujian in the midst of the sea". Where there is water, bridges naturally exist. Clouds roll above bridges while tides rise and fall beneath them, witnessing the change of times, yet unable to diminish the boldness of Quanzhou people in exploring the world. It is said that "the bridges of Quanzhou are unrivaled in central Fujian." In the collective memory of Quanzhou people, the most unforgettable bridges are undoubtedly Luoyang Bridge, Anping Bridge and Shunji Bridge.

一桥飞架洛阳江。（陈英杰 摄）
Luoyang Bridge. (Photo by Chen Yingjie)

洛阳桥：海内第一桥

洛阳桥是宋元泉州运输网络发展的里程碑，它加强了泉州与省城福州、江浙一带及内陆的陆运联系，开启了宋元泉州的造桥热潮，推动了国家口岸水陆转运系统的建立与完善。洛阳桥是官方主导、全民合力建造大型交通设施的典范，体现了地方政府、僧侣、商民等社会各界力量对商贸活动的推动和贡献。洛阳桥是古代大型石桥建造工程的杰作，为宋元时期泉州造桥浪潮积累了宝贵的经验。

跨海飞梁叠石成

泉州市舶司设置之前，泉州港的海外贸易就已经出现了繁盛的局面。宋嘉祐八年（1063），山东濮州人杜纯担任泉州司法参军之时，便呈“泉有番舶之饶，杂货山积”之局面。然而，泉州海上交通虽然发达，陆路货运体系却受到很大的限制。泉州通往福州乃至内地，如果想绕过洛阳江，只能走山路，从泉州城北出朝天门，再从马鞍格进入河市，翻越朋山岭和白虹山，经仙游抵达福州。山路崎岖，商旅不便。如果要跨越洛阳江，在造桥之前，只能靠舟楫摆渡。然而横渡洛阳江并非易事，据宋代方勺《泊宅编》描述：“……水阔五里，上流接大溪，外即海也。每风潮交作，数日不可渡。”故而经常出现覆舟落水的事故，以至于为了祈求平安过江，人们称此渡口为“万安渡”。当然，泉州人并没有放弃在洛阳江上架桥的尝试，无论这个过程多么艰辛曲折。

Luoyang Bridge: China's Earliest Stone Beam Bridge

Luoyang Bridge, a milestone in the development of the transportation network in Song-Yuan Quanzhou, strengthened the land transportation connection between Quanzhou and the provincial capital Fuzhou, as well as the Jiangsu-Zhejiang region and the inland areas. It also initiated a bridge-building trend in Quanzhou during the Song and Yuan dynasties, and contributed to the establishment and improvement of the water-land transshipment system in this national port. Luoyang Bridge serves as a model of large-scale transportation infrastructure, driven by government initiatives and the joint efforts of the entire community, which reflects the contributions and promotion of various sectors of society, including the local government, monks and merchants, in facilitating and promoting commercial activities. Luoyang Bridge is a masterpiece of the ancient large-scale stone bridge construction, accumulating valuable experience for the bridge-building wave in Quanzhou during the Song and Yuan dynasties.

Crossing the Sea, the Flying Bridge Stands Tall

Before the establishment of Quanzhou Maritime Trade Office, overseas trade in Quanzhou Port had already flourished. In 1063 of the Northern Song Dynasty, when Du Chun, a native of Puzhou in Shandong, served as a judicial officer in Quanzhou, there was a prosperous scene of "abundance of foreign ships and a mountain of miscellaneous goods". However, while maritime transportation in Quanzhou was well-developed, the land-based cargo transportation system faced significant limitations. To travel from Quanzhou to Fuzhou and further inland, one had to take a mountainous route to bypass Luoyang River, leaving from Chaotianmen Gate, the north gate of Quanzhou, entering Heshi via Ma'ange, crossing Pengshan Ridge and Baihong Mountain, and finally reaching Fuzhou through Xianyou. The mountainous roads were rugged, which was inconvenient for merchants and travelers. If one wanted to cross Luoyang River before the construction of Luoyang Bridge, he had to rely on boats and ferries. However, crossing the wide Luoyang River was not an easy task. Accidents of overturned boats and drowning were common. To pray for a safe crossing, people called this crossing point "Wan'an Ferry" or "Perfectly Safe Ferry". Of course, Quanzhou people did not give up on their attempts to build a bridge across Luoyang River, no matter how arduous and tortuous the process was.

北宋庆历初年，泉州人李宠决心在洛阳江上修建一座浮桥，成为第一个在洛阳江抛石筑基的有志者。在江中抛石筑基，然后架设浮桥，可谓一大创举。只是，洛阳江水流湍急、风大浪高，不仅堆积的石块容易被水流和风潮冲走，浮桥也极易被狂风巨浪掀翻。看来，架设浮桥也只能是权宜之计。

北宋皇祐五年（1053）四月，泉州僧人宗已和郡人王实、卢锡倡议建筑石桥。可是，由于工程浩大、所费不菲，工程进展遭遇巨大的困难，一度陷入停顿。或许是天意，值此困境之下，蔡襄分别于北宋至和二年（1055）、嘉祐三年（1058）两度出任泉州太守，任内劝课农桑，兴修水利，轻徭薄赋，整肃吏治，恩威并举，雷厉风行。同时，他毅然承担起主持修建洛阳桥的重任。

蔡襄礼贤下士，延揽僧人义波、宗善和乡贤许忠等加入造桥团队，群策群力，破解建筑过程中的技术难题；又紧急调用府库钱款，保障工程费用。蔡襄的母亲卢夫人也带头捐资，支持造桥，泉州民间乐善好施者踊跃响应，解决了资金短缺的问题。北宋嘉祐四年十二月（1060 年 1 月），洛阳桥这座规模空前、雄伟壮观的跨海石桥终于顺利竣工。

洛阳桥东侧的蔡襄雕像。（黄国炎 摄）
The statue of Cai Xiang on the east side of Luoyang Bridge. (Photo by Huang Guoyan)

Between 1041 and 1043, a man named Li Chong from Quanzhou made a bold decision to build a floating bridge with a foundation of stacked stones on Luoyang River. This was a remarkable feat. However, Luoyang River had swift currents and strong winds, making it easy for the stacked stones to be washed away by the water and tides, and the floating bridge was also prone to being overturned by strong winds and waves. It seemed that the construction of a floating bridge was only a temporary measure.

In lunar April 1053 of the Northen Song Dynasty, Monk Zongyi, along with local residents Wang Shi and Lu Xi in Quanzhou, proposed the construction of a stone bridge. However, due to the massive scale of the project and a high cost involved, the construction faced significant difficulties and came to a halt at one point. Perhaps it was fate, but in this difficult situation, Cai Xiang was appointed as the prefect of Quanzhou respectively in 1055 and in 1058. During his tenure, Cai encouraged agricultural development, built irrigation works, reduced taxes and levies, reformed governance, and implemented both benevolence and authority with swift and decisive actions. At the same time, he took on the responsibility of overseeing the construction of Luoyang Bridge.

Cai Xiang, a virtuous and humble man, recruited two monks Yibo and Zongshan, as well as a local scholar Xu Zhong, to join the bridge construction team. They worked together to overcome technical challenges during the construction process. Cai Xiang urgently allocated funds from the government treasury to ensure the project's financial needs. Cai's mother, Madame Lu, also led by example by making a donation to support the bridge construction. Generous individuals in Quanzhou responded enthusiastically and helped solve the problem of funding shortage. In January 1060, Luoyang Bridge, a magnificent and unprecedented stone bridge spanning the sea, was successfully completed.

北宋元丰八年（1085），福建转运判官王子京离开泉州，回京述职，遂请画工绘制洛阳桥图，并赋诗其上：“接玉架开三岛势，积金冲断两潮声。泥沙浦溆时时见，风月楼台夜夜清。”洛阳桥图册呈进御览，王子京获得嘉赏，一时传为佳话。南宋诗人陈傅良有诗赞曰：“跨海为桥布石牢，那知直下压灵鳌。基连岛屿规模壮，势截渊潭气象豪。铁马著行横绝漠，玉鲸张鬣露寒涛。缣图已幸天颜照，应得元丰史笔褒。”

今天的洛阳桥有着古代人无法想象的宽阔与平整。（陈英杰 摄）
Today's wide and smooth Luoyang Bridge that people in ancient times could not have imagined. (Photo by Chen Yingjie)

In 1085, Wang Zijing, the transport judge of Fujian, left Quanzhou and returned to the capital to report his duties. He commissioned an artist to paint a picture of Luoyang Bridge and wrote a poem on it:

"The bridge connects like a jade rack, opening up the landscape of three islands.

The accumulated gold breaks through the sound of tides.

Mud and sand are seen in the estuary.

And the tower is clear in the wind and moon at night."

The painting was presented to the emperor, and Wang Zijing received high praise, which became a well-known story. The Southern Song poet Chen Fuliang recorded about that in a poem:

"Luoyang Bridge spans the sea, with stones firmly laid,

Who knew it would press down on the mighty sea turtle.

The foundation connects islands, grand in scale,

Intercepting the deep water with a magnificent aura.

Armored horses gallop across the bridge,

The cold waves beneath are like jade whales spreading their huge fins.

The embroidered picture of the bridge has luckily received the emperor's recognition,

Deserving praise from the official historiographer."

洛阳桥上“三绝”碑

北宋嘉祐五年（1060）秋，蔡襄奉诏还京，洛阳桥自然是必经之路。此时的蔡襄行走在厚重的石桥板上，步伐却是如此的轻松。他倚栏远眺，看水天一色，顿感心旷神怡。回想起造桥的日日夜夜，点点滴滴，他必定是感慨万千。几只海鸟掠过桥边的芦苇丛，清灵的鸣叫声让沉思中的蔡襄回过神来。他稍稍平复一下激动的心情，便淡定地提起笔来，一气呵成，写下传诵千古的《万安桥记》。寥寥 153 字，描述了造桥的时间，桥梁的质地、形制、尺度，建造的费用及其来源，桥梁建成后的功用，以及造桥的主要参与者等，言简意赅，清新隽永。

《万安桥记》也成为研究蔡襄书法艺术时不可错过的经典之作。苏轼曾说：“蔡君谟书，天资既高，积学深至，心手相应，变态无穷，遂为本朝第一。”明代文学家王世贞评价《万安桥记》“结法全自颜平原（颜真卿）来，唯策法用虞永兴（虞世南）耳”，甚至动情地说道：“万安天下第一桥，君谟此书雄伟遒丽，当与桥争胜。”

为了纪念蔡襄建造洛阳桥的历史功绩，泉州民众在洛阳桥南侧修建蔡襄祠，将蔡襄亲撰的《万安桥记》刻成石碑，立于祠内。工匠在镌刻碑文的时候，怀着对蔡襄的敬仰之情，一笔一画，一丝不苟，形神兼备地保留了书法作品的笔势和气韵。《万安桥记》碑刻于是以文章的精练、书法的神韵、刻工的精妙被世人称为“三绝”碑。

《万安桥记》碑。（成冬冬 摄）
The stele of *A Record of Wan'an Bridge*. (Photo by Cheng Dongdong)

The "Triple Excellence" Stele on Luoyang Bridge

In the autumn of 1060, Cai Xiang was ordered to return to the capital, and Luoyang Bridge was naturally on his way. When Cai Xiang walked on the solid stone bridge, his pace might be relaxed. Leaning on the railings, he gazed into the vast expanse of water and sky, feeling a sense of tranquility and joy. Reflecting on the countless days and nights spent constructing the bridge, he must have been filled with deep emotions. Several seabirds skimmed over the reeds by the bridge, their clear and melodious cries bringing Cai Xiang back to reality from his contemplation. Calming his excited heart, he picked up his brush and effortlessly wrote the timeless *A Record of Wan'an Bridge* in one go. With a mere 153 characters, Cai Xiang described the date of construction, the material, form and scale of the bridge, the cost and its origin, the function, and the main participants in its construction. The writing was concise, yet fresh and enduring.

A Record of Wan'an Bridge has also become a must-read classic for studying Cai Xiang's calligraphy. Su Shi, a great Northern Song Dynasty poet, once commented, "Cai's calligraphy, with his natural talent and great knowledge, his mind and hand in perfect harmony, and the endless variations, makes him the best calligrapher of this era." Wang Shizhen, a literary figure in the Ming Dynasty, praised *A Record of Wan'an Bridge* as boasting a structure comparable to that of Yan Zhenqing, and only the rising stroke being similar to that of Yu Shinan, both of whom are famous calligraphers in ancient times. He even emotionally exclaimed, "Wan'an Bridge can be deemed as the No.1 bridge in the world, and Cai's magnificent calligraphy is comparable to the bridge."

In order to commemorate the historical achievements of Cai Xiang in building Luoyang Bridge, Quanzhou people constructed Cai Xiang Shrine on the southern side of the bridge. They engraved Cai Xiang's *A Record of Wan'an Bridge* onto a stone tablet and placed it in the temple. The craftsmen, filled with reverence for Cai Xiang, meticulously preserved the brushstrokes and artistic charm of the calligraphy while engraving the text. The engraved *A Record of Wan'an Bridge* became renowned as the "Triple Excellence" Stele for its concise writing, artistic calligraphy and exquisite craftsmanship.

蔡襄在《万安桥记》中没有炫耀自己对造桥的贡献，只提了一句“太守莆阳蔡襄为之合乐宴饮而落之”。其实，恰恰是蔡襄在洛阳桥建造面临最大困难的时刻，毅然地承担责任，解决资金、技术两大难题，最终促成洛阳桥工程的顺利竣工。

“合乐宴饮而落之”，看似轻描淡写的七个字，令人感受到蔡襄的淡定与平和。“桃李不言，下自成蹊”，其实，老百姓在意的不是谁“说得好”，而是谁“干得好”。清代小说家褚人获所撰《坚瓠集》收录一则流传在泉州民间的掌故，说的就是为解造桥资金短缺的燃眉之急，蔡襄来不及请示就临时动用府库钱款，结果被别有用心的人举报了。蔡襄没有过多辩解，而是平静地写下一首《谢恩诗》，以表明自己的态度：“得饶人处且须饶，曾借龙王三日潮。十万贯钱常在世，我王恩在洛阳桥。”宋仁宗得知内情后，认可了蔡襄的做法，不做追究。洛阳桥竣工之时，泉州百姓热诚地用一首歌谣传颂蔡襄的功绩：“叠石为桥与路通，惠安之北晋江东。几时募化千家宝，一旦缘成万载功。五尺栏杆遮巨浪，两头华表镇危峰。往来无限行人口，日月齐休颂蔡公。”

蔡襄祠。（李国宏 供图）
Cai Xiang Shrine. (Courtesy of Li Guohong)

In *A Record of Wan'an Bridge*, Cai Xiang did not boast about his own contributions to the construction of the bridge. He simply mentioned, "Prefect Puyang Cai Xiang organized a joyful banquet to celebrate its completion." In fact, it was precisely during the most challenging period of Luoyang Bridge's construction that Cai Xiang courageously took on the responsibility to overcome the major obstacles of funding and technology, and ultimately facilitated the completion of the Luoyang Bridge project.

The brief description of "a joyful banquet to celebrate its completion", though seemingly casually written, reflects Cai Xiang's calm and peaceful demeanor. Just like the peach and plum trees, which do not need to advertise their beauty or fragrance, people will naturally be drawn to them and paths will be formed beneath them as a result. Actions speak louder than words. According to Chu Renhuo, a novelist of the Qing Dynasty, there was a popular anecdote circulating among Quanzhou people. It tells the story that Cai Xiang, without seeking approval beforehand, temporarily used money from the government treasury when facing a desperate shortage of funds to build the bridge, which resulted in malicious reports against him. Instead of offering excessive explanations, Cai Xiang calmly wrote a poem to express his attitude, "To spare others, one must be spared; I once borrowed three days of high tides from the Dragon King. Ten thousand *guan* of money is commonly seen, but my king's favor is on Luoyang Bridge." After learning about the truth, Emperor Renzong of the Song Dynasty approved of Cai Xiang's behavior and refrained from pursuing the matter further. When Luoyang Bridge was completed, Quanzhou people sincerely praised Cai Xiang's achievements in a folk song, "Stacked stones form a bridge, connecting the north of Hui'an to the east of Jinjiang. By raising funds from thousands of families, the bridge will last for ten thousand generations. The five-foot railings withstand huge waves, and the two towering pillars exceed towering mountains. Countless people come and go, singing praises to Lord Cai day and night."

千古万古长清风

蔡襄的母亲卢夫人家住泉州府惠安县（今泉港区后龙乡）圭峰村，蔡襄少年时代常与舅舅卢锡（洛阳桥倡建者之一）在伏虎岩攻读诗书。卢夫人以自家门外高大的松树启发蔡襄，说松树不畏寒冬腊月，依然挺拔耸立，高风亮节，勉励他将来若成器，定要忠君惠民。如此说来，蔡襄注定与松树有缘。北宋庆历六年（1046）秋，蔡襄出任福建路转运使，开始谋划在福州通往泉州、漳州的驿路上种植夹道松。在他先后担任福州、泉州太守的任上，更是大力推动植树计划，及至洛阳桥竣工之时，福州至漳州长达七百里的驿路两侧夹道松已经枝繁叶茂，形成一条名副其实的林荫大道。此举既能防止水土流失，保持生态平衡，又使过往客商在炎日酷暑之时可以免受骄阳暴晒之苦。据南宋祝穆编纂的《方舆胜览》记载，泉州士民每年到洛阳桥蔡襄祠祭拜之时，都会吟唱一首歌谣，以感念蔡襄植松的功德：“道边松，大义渡至漳泉东，问谁植之我蔡公。岁久广荫如云浓，甘棠蔽芾安可同？委蛇夭矫腾苍龙，行人六月不知暑，千古万古长清风。”

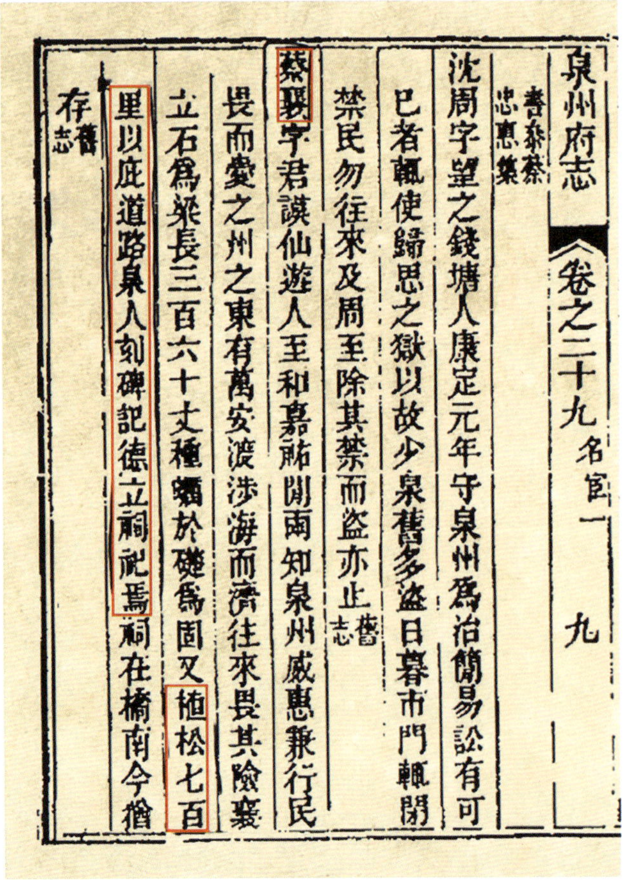
泉州府志 《卷之二十九 名宦一 九
書蔡襄忠惠集
沈周字望之錢塘人康定元年守泉州爲治簡易訟有可
已者輒使歸思之獄以故少泉舊多盜日暮市門輒閉
禁民勿往來及周至除其禁而盜亦止舊志
蔡襄字君謨仙遊人至和嘉祐閒兩知泉州威惠兼行民
畏而愛之州之東有萬安渡涉海而濟往來畏其險襄
立石爲梁長三百六十丈種蠣於礎爲固又植松七百
里以庇道路泉人刻碑記德立祠祀焉祠在橋南今猶
存舊志

清代乾隆版《泉州府志》中关于蔡襄“植松七百里以庇道路”的记载。（李国宏 供图）
The record regarding Cai Xiang's tree planting projects along the 700 *li* (350 kilometers) postal road in the Qianlong edition of *Local Chronicles of Quanzhou Prefecture*. (Courtesy of Li Guohong)

For Thousands of Years, This Refreshing Wind Blows

Cai Xiang's mother, Madame Lu, lived in Guifeng Village, Hui'an County, Quanzhou Prefecture (now Houlong Township of Quangang District). During his youth, Cai Xiang often studied with his uncle, Lu Xi, one of the builders of Luoyang Bridge, at Fuhu Rock. Madame Lu inspired Cai Xiang with the tall pine trees outside their house, stating that pine trees don't fear the harsh winter and still stand tall and upright, symbolizing integrity. She told Cai Xiang to be loyal to the emperor and benevolent to the people if he worked in the government in future. Therefore, it can be said that Cai Xiang was destined to have a connection with pine trees. In the autumn of 1046, Cai Xiang was appointed as the transport commissioner of Fujian Province and planned to plant roadside pine trees along the postal route from Fuzhou to Quanzhou and Zhangzhou. During his tenure as the prefect of Fuzhou and Quanzhou, he vigorously promoted tree planting projects. By the completion of Luoyang Bridge, the 700 *li* (350 kilometers) postal road from Fuzhou to Zhangzhou was lined with flourishing pine trees, forming a truly magnificent tree-lined avenue, which not only prevented soil erosion and maintained ecological balance, but also provided shade for travelers and merchants during the scorching sun. According to *The National Gazetteer of Southern Song Dynasty* compiled by Zhu Mu, every year when Quanzhou people paid tribute at Cai Xiang Shrine at Luoyang Bridge, they would sing a folk song to express their gratitude for Cai Xiang's contributions to tree planting. The song is as follows:

"Beside the road stand the pine trees,
Symbolizing righteousness to the east of Zhangzhou and Quanzhou.
Who planted it?
Our Lord Cai.
After years of growth, the branches spread widely,
Providing dense shade like clouds.
The merits of Lord Shao cannot compare with those of Lord Cai.
The branches twist and turn like a graceful dragon,
And even in the scorching heat of June, travelers do not feel the heat.
For thousands of years, this refreshing wind blows."

出于对松树的特别情怀，蔡襄还在泉州衙署内种植松树，修建爱松堂，又取《中庸》之境界，别称其为“中和堂”，寓意听政理事必须循规蹈矩、不偏不倚。蔡襄曾赋诗一首以明心志：“偏爱堂东砌下松，三年潇洒伴衰翁。寒声动荡潮初上，疏影孤圆月正中。清澈纱帷延昼梦，绿涵金盏带春风。自缘多病饶归思，便觉山林野意通。”

堂名“中和”，可是，在现实中要真正秉持中和之道且一以贯之，谈何容易？所以，一直以蔡襄作为楷模的南宋泉州太守王十朋在瞻仰中和堂时，有感而发：“堂前老木几经春，偏阅泉南旧守臣。尽向中和堂上坐，中和为治有何人？”

虽然蔡襄在《万安桥记》中没有炫耀自己的政绩，但是“郊野尚留棠树绿”的道旁松与“晓风十里渡瑶琼”的洛阳桥必定给蔡襄带来满满的成就感，也成为他留给后人最珍贵的文化遗产。北宋治平二年（1065）二月，蔡襄给儿孙写下一份书帖：“予素不治生产，仅有埭田二百石。予为万安桥时，母太君捐一百六十石助役。虽无以遗儿孙，然道旁松、万安渡，汝辈吃不尽饭碗也。”

正是因为蔡襄的低调与淡然，反而让君子之风万古流芳。

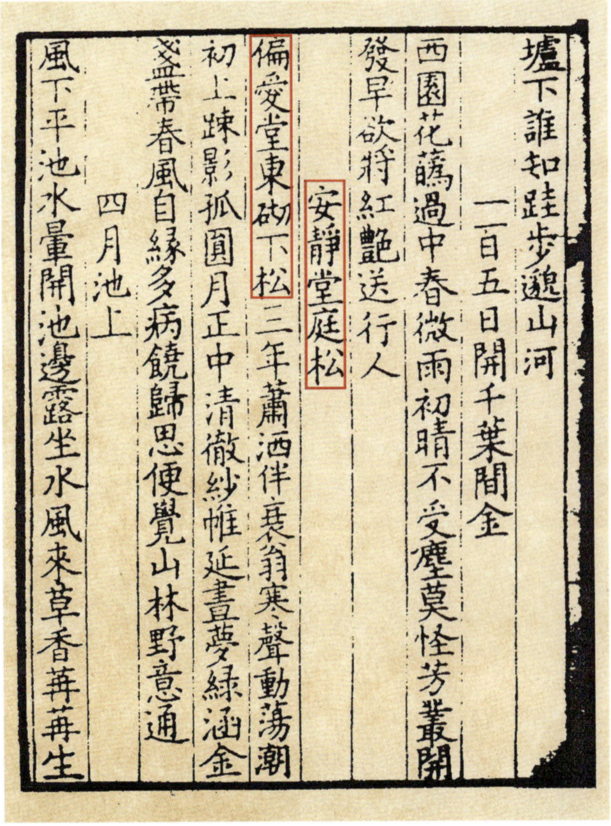
壚下誰知跬步邈山河
一百五日開千葉間金
西園花藕過中春微雨初晴不受塵莫怪芳叢開
發早欲将紅艷送行人
安静堂庭松
偏愛堂東砌下松三年蕭洒伴衰翁寒聲動蕩潮
初上疎影孤圓月正中清徹紗帷延晝夢緑涵金
盞帶春風自緣多病饒歸思便覺山林野意通
四月池上
風下平池水暈開池邊露坐水風來草香苒苒生

蔡襄诗作《安静堂庭松》。（李国宏 供图）
Cai Xiang's poem about pine trees in his courtyard. (Courtesy of Li Guohong)

Due to a special affection for pine trees, Cai Xiang planted pine trees and built "Aisong Hall" (Hall of the Love for Pine Trees) in the Quanzhou *yamen* (the government office). He also named it "Zhonghe Hall" based on the concept of "Zhong Yong" (Doctrine of the Mean), revealing the importance of governing and handling affairs in a balanced and impartial manner.

The naming of "Zhonghe" for the hall reflects Cai Xiang's ideal of practicing the Doctrine of the Mean. However, it is not easy to truly uphold and consistently follow the path of harmony in reality. Recognizing this challenge, Wang Shipeng, Quanzhou prefect of the Southern Song Dynasty, who regarded Cai Xiang as a role model, expressed his thoughts when visiting Zhonghe Hall, "In front of the hall, the old trees have experienced many springs. I specifically read about the former prefects of Quanzhou. Sitting in Zhonghe Hall, where is the person who truly embodies governance through harmony?"

Although Cai Xiang did not boast about his political achievements in *A Record of Wan'an Bridge*, the presence of the green pine trees along the roadside and the enchanting Luoyang Bridge undoubtedly brought him a sense of fulfillment and became the most cherished cultural legacy he left for future generations. In 1065 of the Northern Song Dynasty, Cai Xiang wrote a letter to his descendants, stating, "I myself have never engaged in agricultural production and only have some fields that can produce 200 *dan* (a unit of weight in ancient China) of grain. When I was in charge of constructing Wan'an Bridge, my mother, the Grand Lady, donated 160 *dan* of grain. Although I have nothing left for my descendants, the pine trees along the roadside and Wan'an Ferry will provide you with endless sustenance."

It is precisely because of his modesty and equanimity that Cai Xiang has been renowned as a man of virtue throughout the ages.

论功岂止洛阳桥

蔡襄是一位言行一致的清官，遇事总能坚持从实际出发，深谋远虑，体恤民情，兴利除弊。他对于泉州的贡献不仅仅是建造洛阳桥这一件事。

减轻赋税。庆历七年（1047），蔡襄时任福建转运使。他发现朝廷对福建征收赋税一直沿袭五代时期的制度，泉州、漳州、兴化（今莆田）三地，民众折变输米五斗，名为“身丁钱”。可是在实际征收过程中，不法官吏借机巧取豪夺，收取的米粮数量高达七斗三升，造成许多贫民流离失所。蔡襄据实向朝廷奏请，使福建地区的税赋得以减半征收。

整饬海防。嘉祐元年（1056），蔡襄出任福州太守。当时，福州、兴化、泉州、漳州地方厢军虽然有水军编制，但是水军士卒平时缺乏训练，战斗力有限，甚至出现官兵不敌海盗的尴尬情况。于是，蔡襄奏请朝廷加强福建沿海州郡的海防事务。据蔡襄《端明集》记载，设置在泉州的四县同巡检司离城七里，负责泉州沿海巡防任务，“后来无事，兵士渐次减少”。随着泉州港海外贸易的兴起，该巡检司兼有“防检商税”的职责。为此，蔡襄建议增加巡检司的兵员编制，专注于控制海上航道，同时将防卫力量延伸到船舶出入港的海口地区。

蔡襄画像。（李国宏 供图）
The portrait of Cai Xiang. (Courtesy of Li Guohong)

Cai Xiang's Other Notable Contributions

Cai Xiang was an upright official who consistently aligned his words and actions. He always approached matters from a practical standpoint, demonstrating foresight, empathy for the people and a commitment to promoting the common good while eliminating drawbacks. His contributions to Quanzhou are not limited to the construction of Luoyang Bridge.

Reducing taxes. In 1047, Cai Xiang served as Fujian transport commissioner. He found that the imperial court had been following the taxation system of the Five Dynasties, so that in Quanzhou, Zhangzhou and Xinghua (now Putian), people were required to pay five *dou* (a unit of weight in ancient China) of rice as a form of tax, known as "shen ding qian" or "personal labor tax". However, corrupt officials took advantage of the situation and seized excessive amounts of rice, with the actual collection reaching as high as more than seven *dou*, causing many poor people to be displaced. Cai Xiang reported the truth to the imperial court and successfully petitioned for a reduction in the tax burden, resulting in a halving of the tax collection in the Fujian region.

Strengthening coastal defense. In 1056, Cai Xiang was appointed as the prefect of Fuzhou. At that time, although the local armies in Fuzhou, Xinghua, Quanzhou and Zhangzhou had staff establishment for the navy, the naval soldiers lacked regular training and had limited combat capabilities. There were even embarrassing situations where the soldiers were unable to defeat pirates. Therefore, Cai Xiang requested the imperial court to enhance coastal defense in the cities and counties along Fujian coast. According to *Cai Xiang's Collected Works*, a Four-County Patrol Inspection Office, 7 *li* (3.5 kilometers) away from the city, was established to take charge of coastal patrols in Quanzhou. As the situation became peaceful, the number of soldiers gradually decreased. With the rise of overseas trade in Quanzhou Port, the patrol inspection office also took on the responsibility of "inspecting and taxing merchants". To this end, Cai Xiang proposed to increase the number of troops so that they could focus on controlling the maritime routes and extending defense forces to the coastal areas where ships entered and left the port.

北宋熙宁初年，朝廷下令将泉州四县同巡检司移至泉州湾出海口石湖村，建造巡检司寨城，设定兵员编制 125 人。由此可见，蔡襄对于泉州港海防建设的确有着先见之明。当时，驻扎泉州城的威果军配置魛鱼船，巡检司也有巡海船，蔡襄奏请朝廷拨款修造战船，酌情保留 6 至 7 艘，用于海上巡哨。他还建议安排驻扎泉州城的宣毅军兵士轮番进驻巡检司，与巡检司官兵一起，“教习舟船，谙会水势，以备差使”。

兴修水利。据明代何乔远所撰《闽书》记载，嘉祐三年（1058），蔡襄再次出任泉州太守，不料赶上泉州各地久旱无雨，农业歉收。蔡襄带领官员到南安飞阳庙祈雨，自责干旱不稔，是“郡守不德之故”，还情真意切地写下一首祈雨诗：“年年乞雨问山神，羞见耕耘陇上人。太守自知材德薄，彼苍何事罪斯民？”以此告诫僚属要关心民瘼，组织民众抗旱自救。不久恰好天降大雨，旱情解除，岁以大稔，王十朋因此称赞蔡襄“乞雨诗奇字更奇”“爱民心有彼苍知”。

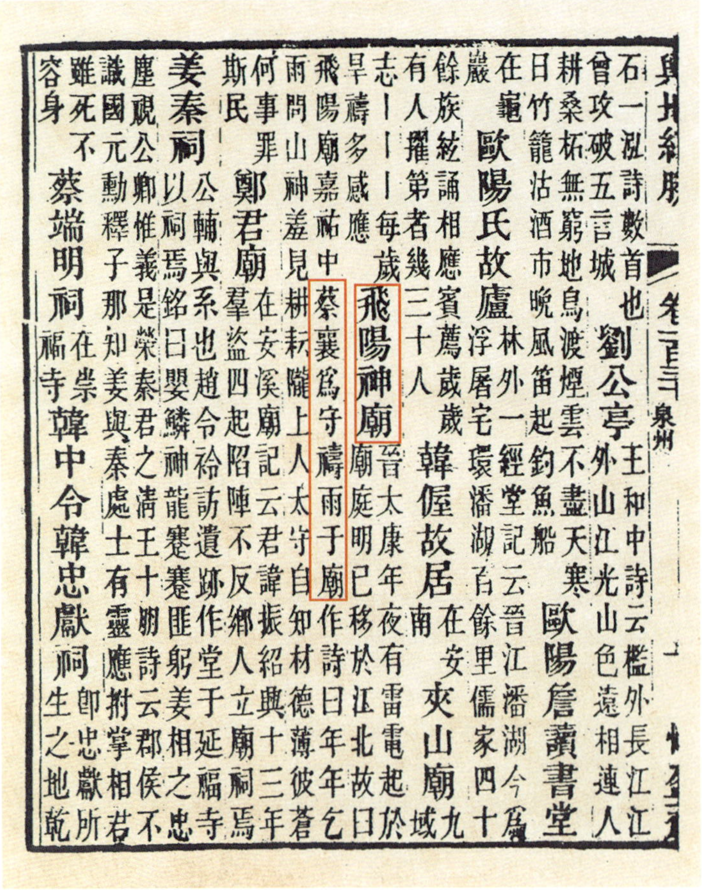
輿地紀勝 卷一百三十 泉州
石一泓詩數首也主和中詩云檻外長江江
會攻破五言城劉公亭外山江光山色遠相連人
耕桑柘無窮地鳥渡煙雲不盡天寒歐陽詹讀書堂
日竹籠沽酒市晚風笛起釣魚船
在龜林外一經堂記云晉江潘湖今爲
巖歐陽氏故廬浮屠宅環潘湖百餘里儒家四十
餘族絃誦相應賓薦歲歲韓偓故居在安夾山廟九
有人擢第者幾三十人南域
志｜｜｜｜每歲飛陽神廟晉太康年夜有雷電起於
旱禱多感應廟庭明已移於江北故日
飛陽廟嘉祐中蔡襄爲守禱雨于廟作詩曰年年乞
雨問山神羞見耕耘隴上人太守自知材德薄彼蒼
何事罪在安溪廟記云君諱振紹興十三年
斯民鄭君廟羣盜四起陷陣不反鄉人立廟祠焉
姜秦祠公輔與系也趙令衿訪遺跡作堂于延福寺
以祠焉銘曰嬰鱗神龍蹇蹇匪躬姜相之忠
塵覩公卿惟義是榮秦君之清王十朋詩云郡侯不
議國元勳釋子那知姜與秦處士有靈應捐掌相君
雖死不在崇即忠獻所
容身蔡端明祠福寺韓中令韓忠獻祠生之地乾

宋代《與地纪胜》中关于蔡襄飞阳庙祈雨的记载。（李国宏 供图）

The record about Cai Xiang's begging for rain in *Geography Records Across the Country* of the Song Dynasty. (Courtesy of Li Guohong)

Between 1068 and 1071, the imperial court ordered the Four-County Patrol Inspection Office to be moved to Shihu Village at the mouth of Quanzhou Bay, where a fortress was built. The office was staffed with 125 soldiers, which demonstrated Cai Xiang's foresight in the construction of Quanzhou Port's coastal defense. At that time, Weiguo Army stationed in Quanzhou City had Daoyu ships (a kind of medium-sized ship with a narrow bow, a wide stern and a pointed bottom, suitable for cruising on shallow sea), and the patrol inspection office had patrol boats. Cai Xiang requested the imperial court to allocate funds for the construction of warships, suggesting that 6 to 7 ships be reserved for maritime patrols. He also proposed that Xuanyi Army stationed in Quanzhou City take turns to be stationed at the patrol inspection office, familiarizing themselves with water conditions so as to be prepared for missions.

Working on water conservancy projects. According to *The Book of Min* written by He Qiaoyuan, Cai Xiang was once again appointed as the prefect of Quanzhou in 1058. However, he encountered a severe drought throughout Quanzhou which caused poor agricultural harvests. Cai Xiang led officials to Feiyang Temple in Nan'an to pray for rain, blaming himself for the drought and creating a poem earnestly pleading for rain:

"Year after year, begging for rain and asking the mountain god,
Ashamed to face the farmers toiling in the fields,
The prefect himself knows his talent and virtue are lacking,
What sin have the people committed to anger God?"

Through this poem, he reminded his subordinates to care for the people's hardships and organize them to combat the drought. Fortunately, a heavy rain fell soon after from the sky, relieving the drought, and the harvest was abundant. Wang Shipeng praised Cai Xiang that, "The poem begging for rain is extraordinary, with even more extraordinary calligraphy. His love for the people is recognized by God."

祈雨之举，表明的是一种态度；兴修水利，体现的是一种责任。位于今石狮市宝盖镇的龟湖塘，是古泉州府晋江县重要的水利工程，可灌溉农田 3,800 余亩。当时蔡襄深入实地，体察民情，发现龟湖塘周边村庄的百姓常为争夺水源而发生纠纷。加上土豪及无赖好事之徒插手搅事，沿塘百姓冤冤相报，问题久拖未决。蔡襄发动民众疏浚水塘，加固堤岸，修复水闸。同时召集龟湖塘附近吴、黄、林、蔡、苏、郑六大姓氏的族人代表，劝导众人革除陋习、和睦相处。他建议推举各姓“德行淳朴，识达时务者，轮为陂首”，共同管理龟湖塘。之后又博采众议，制定《龟湖塘规》，明确龟湖塘用水、管理、维修等 18 条细则，做到简明扼要，有据可循，赏罚分明。经过一番整治，龟湖塘焕发生机，沿塘居住的百姓衣食富足，造就“龟鉴千秋兰盆会，湖光十里稻香村”的佳话。现今，石狮市修建龟湖公园，保留龟湖塘历史遗迹，并将公园附近的一条主干道命名为“宋塘路”，以铭记蔡襄勤政爱民的美德。

龟湖公园。（李国宏 供图）
Guihu Park. (Courtesy of Li Guohong)

The act of praying for rain demonstrated a certain attitude, while the construction of water conservancy projects reflected a sense of responsibility. Guihu Lake, located in today's Baogai Town, Shishi City, was an important water conservancy project in ancient Jinjiang County, Quanzhou Prefecture, which could irrigate more than 3,800 *mu* (approximately 626 acres) of farmland. Cai Xiang, at that time, conducted on-site inspections and observed the situation of the people. He found that disputes often arose among the villagers surrounding Guihu Lake due to competition for water sources. In addition, local tyrants and troublemakers exacerbated the situation, leading to ongoing conflicts and unresolved issues. Cai Xiang mobilized the people to dredge the lake, reinforce the embankments and repair the water gates. At the same time, he convened representatives from the clans of Wu, Huang, Lin, Cai, Su and Zheng, who lived near Guihu Lake, to persuade them to abandon their bad habits and live in harmony. He suggested that individuals with good moral character and a deep understanding of current affairs be elected as leaders of the lake, jointly managing it. Subsequently, he gathered public opinions and formulated *Guihu Lake Regulations*, which clearly outlined eighteen detailed rules regarding water usage, management and maintenance, ensuring simplicity, clarity and a fair system of rewards and punishments. After the renovations, Guihu Lake flourished, and the people living along the lake enjoyed prosperity, giving rise to the saying, "Guihu Lake mirrors the prosperity of a thousand years, and the fragrance of rice fields extends for ten miles." Presently, Shishi City has built Guihu Park, preserving the historical relics of Guihu Lake. Additionally, a main road near the park has been named "Songtang Road" to commemorate Cai Xiang's diligent governance and love for the people.

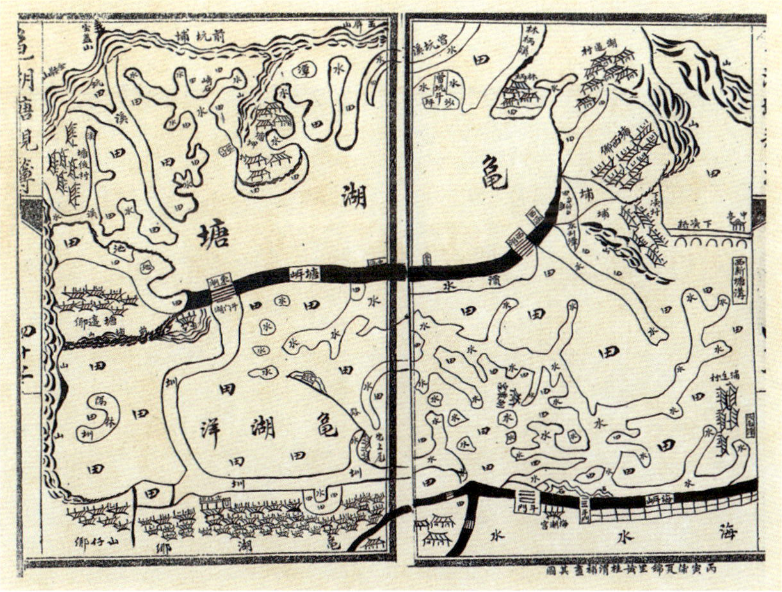

民国重刊《龟湖塘规簿》中的龟湖塘图。（李国宏 供图）

The illustration of Guihu Lake in *Guihu Lake Regulations*, reprinted during the Republican period of China. (Courtesy of Li Guohong)

撰写荔谱。蔡襄施政，常怀不扰民、不折腾的休养生息之道。为此，他在泉州衙署修建安静堂，以示退思之意。嘉祐四年（1059）八月，正是洛阳桥建筑工程即将全面告竣的时候，忙里偷闲的蔡襄就在安静堂内“顺手”完成一部划时代的作品——《荔枝谱》。书中介绍福州、兴化、泉州、漳州四地 32 个荔枝品种，内容丰富，论述翔实，尤其在讲到荔枝的栽培、生长特性、生态特征、品评和加工保鲜等方面时，具有较强的科学性。该书成为世界上第一部荔枝学专著，对国内外荔枝种植、研究和相关知识普及曾起到积极的推动作用。在国内，《荔枝谱》流传甚广，影响深远，成为荔枝学研究的里程碑。受其示范与带动，福建、广东成为中国荔枝学研究的重镇，先后出现了徐师闵、张宗闵、徐兴公、林嗣环等人编纂的荔枝谱，这些作品不仅在内容上借鉴了蔡襄的研究成果，在体例结构上也基本仿效《荔枝谱》，形成中国古代荔枝学研究的基本样态。在国外，蔡襄《荔枝谱》被译成英文、法文、拉丁文、日文等，流行于许多国家和地区，英国人李约瑟在《中国古代科技史》中称赞蔡襄的《荔枝谱》是世界上第一部果品分类学著作。

嘉祐五年（1060）三月，蔡襄在泉州安静堂用俊秀的楷书细心誊写《荔枝谱》，文法清新隽永，书法端庄浑厚，淳淡婉美，自成一体。同年秋天，蔡襄卸任回京，《荔枝谱》成为他留给泉州的一份珍贵的科技史料和艺术珍品。品读蔡襄的《荔枝谱》，总能令人浮想联翩，仿佛一幅泉州夏日田园风光就在眼前：农舍池塘边覆盖着如绿云一般的荔枝树荫，骤雨乍歇，蝉在树枝上高声吟唱，微风阵阵，一颗颗火焰般鲜红的荔枝正从浓密的翠叶间显露出来。于是，原本燥热的夏天因为荔枝而变得娇艳欲滴、甜香醉人。

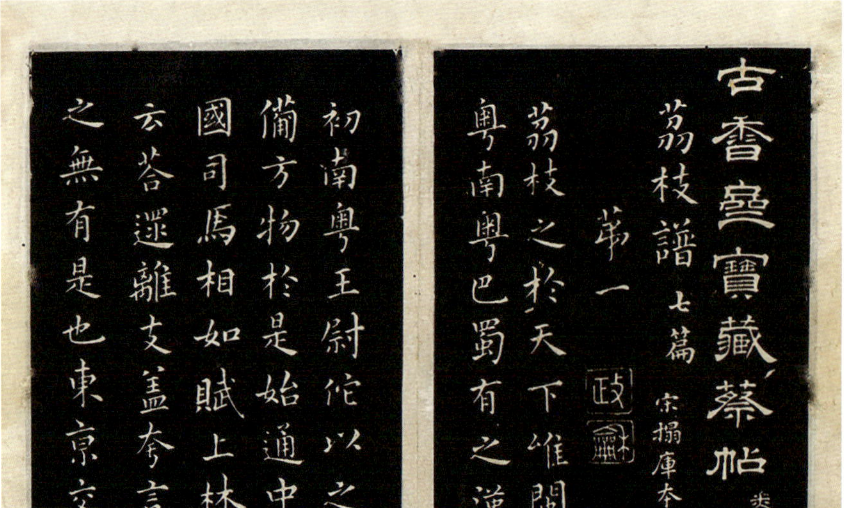

蔡襄《荔枝谱》拓本。（李国宏 供图）
The rubbings of Cai Xiang's *Lichi Manual*. (Courtesy of Li Guohong)

Composing *Lichi Manual*. In the peaceful tranquility of Anjing (Quiet) Hall in his office place, Cai Xiang embraced the philosophy of nurturing and preserving without disturbing the people during his governance. In lunar August 1058, when the construction of Luoyang Bridge in Quanzhou was nearing completion, Cai Xiang took advantage of his spare time to produce a groundbreaking work entitled *Lichi Manual*. This book introduces thirty-two varieties of lichi from Fuzhou, Xinghua, Quanzhou and Zhangzhou, providing rich and detailed descriptions. Particularly notable is its scientific approach when discussing the cultivation, growth characteristics, ecological features, evaluation, and processing and preservation of lichi. This work became the world's first specialized monograph on lichi studies, playing an active role in promoting lichi cultivation, research and knowledge dissemination both domestically and internationally. *Lichi Manual* gained wide circulation and profound influence in China, becoming a milestone in lichi research. It inspired the compilation of subsequent works on lichi by other scholars such as Xu Shimin, Zhang Zongmin, Xu Xinggong and Lin Sihuan. These works drew from Cai Xiang's research in terms of both contents and structural arrangements, hence establishing the basic framework of ancient Chinese lichi studies. Internationally, *Lichi Manual* was translated into English, French, Latin, Japanese, etc., gaining popularity in many countries and regions. Joseph Needham, a British scholar, praised it as the world's first work on pomology in his *Science and Civilisation in China*.

In lunar March 1060, Cai Xiang meticulously transcribed *Lichi Manual* in Anjing Hall of Quanzhou using elegant and refined calligraphy. The writing style was fresh and timeless, with a dignified and harmonious script that exuded a simple and graceful beauty. In the autumn of the same year, Cai Xiang retired and returned to the capital, leaving *Lichi Manual* as a precious historical and artistic treasure for Quanzhou. Reading Cai Xiang's work evokes vivid imagery, as if a painting of Quanzhou's rural scenery in the summer is unfolding before one's eyes: lichi trees, like green clouds, casting their shade by the pond near the farmhouses; the sudden rain subsiding, cicadas singing loudly on the branches; a gentle breeze rustling through the air, revealing the fiery red lichi nestled amidst the lush green leaves. Thus, the originally hot and dry summer becomes enchantingly beautiful and intoxicatingly sweet because of lichi.

洛阳桥建筑“黑科技”

根据明弘治三年(1490)刊行的《八闽通志》统计，宋代福建共建造大中型石桥梁478座，其中，泉州建造桥梁138座，包括洛阳桥、安平桥等名扬天下的大型石桥。泉州桥梁建筑以规模宏大、技术先进、影响深远在福建科技史上书写了光辉的一页，在中国和世界桥梁史上也占有重要地位，留下“闽中桥梁甲天下”“泉州桥梁甲闽中”的美誉。而洛阳桥，是其中最为杰出的代表作，称之为中国古代“黑科技”也不为过。

首创筏形基础。洛阳桥工程选址位于江海汇合处，潮浪夹击，水流湍急，无法采用传统的围堰筑堤、抽水筑基直达水底岩层的做法。洛阳桥的建筑工匠们另辟蹊径，钻研出类似现代桥梁工程称为“筏形基础”的新技术：在洛阳江江底沿着桥梁中线抛掷石块，并逐渐向两侧展开一定的宽度，形成一条横跨江底的低矮石堤，作为桥墩的基础。工匠们还把桥墩做成尖劈状，借以分散江水对墩台的冲击力，增强桥墩结构的稳定性。筏形基础的运用，对中国乃至世界桥梁建筑技术都是一个伟大的贡献，欧洲直到19世纪才开始采用这项技术。

呈尖劈状的洛阳桥桥墩。（陈英杰 摄）
Luoyang Bridge's piers with a split shape. (Photo by Chen Yingjie)

Luoyang Bridge, the Technological Innovation of Ancient China

According to *A General Gazetteer of Fujian* published in 1490, a total of 478 large and medium-sized stone bridges were built in Fujian during the Song Dynasty. Among them, 138 were built in Quanzhou, including renowned ones like Luoyang Bridge and Anping Bridge. Quanzhou's bridge construction has written a glorious chapter in the history of science and technology in Fujian with its grand scale, advanced technology and far-reaching influence. It also holds an important position in the history of bridge construction in China and the world, earning the reputation that "the bridges of central Fujian are unrivaled in the world" and "the bridges of Quanzhou are unrivaled in central Fujian". Among them, Luoyang Bridge stands out as the most outstanding masterpiece, which can be deemed as the technological innovation of ancient China.

The construction of Luoyang Bridge introduced a groundbreaking technique called the "raft-shaped foundation". The chosen location of the bridge was at the confluence of the river and the sea, where waves were strong and the water flow was turbulent. Traditional methods such as building embankments and pumping water to reach the bedrock at the bottom of the water body were not feasible. The craftsmen of Luoyang Bridge devised a new approach, similar to that of modern bridge projects, known as the raft-shaped foundation. They laid stones along the central line of the bridge on the riverbed of Luoyang River and gradually expanded it to a certain width on both sides, forming a low and wide stone embankment that crossed the riverbed. This embankment served as the foundation for the bridge piers. The craftsmen also designed the piers with a split shape to disperse the impact of the river water and enhance the stability of the pier structure. The application of the raft-shaped foundation was a significant contribution to bridge construction techniques in China and the world. It was not until the 19th century that Europe began to adopt this technology.

发明种蛎固基法。洛阳桥基础刚筑成时，石块无规则地叠压，间隙疏散，联结牢固度较差，在风浪潮汐的冲刷下，石块很容易出现漂移、陷落等问题，影响桥墩的稳定性。蔡襄在总结前人对牡蛎生物特性认识的基础上，发明了“种蛎于础以为固”的办法：把牡蛎散置于桥墩基础之上，利用牡蛎外壳吸附力强、繁殖速度快的特点，让成片成簇的牡蛎无孔不入地在石块缝隙间密集繁衍，使原本比较松散的基础牢固地胶结成为一个整体，从而达到提高桥梁基础建筑坚固性和耐久性的目的。此举开创了把生物学运用于桥梁工程的世界先例。

运用浮运架梁法。宋代泉州建造的桥梁多数为梁架式石桥，从桥基、桥墩到桥板，均采用本地花岗岩作为建筑材料。石构建筑虽然坚固耐用，但其质地沉重，给搬运、起落、就位过程带来很高的难度。尤其是要将重达数十吨甚至上百吨的石梁悬空安放在桥墩上，在没有大型起重设备的时代，似乎是一件难以企及的事情。蔡襄集思广益，发挥造桥工匠们的聪明才智，巧妙地利用洛阳江潮汐涨落规律，“激浪以涨舟，悬机以弦牵”，即借助涨潮时机，用木排将事先按规格尺寸加工好的石梁运至桥墩之间，待到落潮时，随着木排徐徐下降到预定的位置上，通过预先安置在桥墩上的木绞车把石梁牵引就位。这种充满想象力和智慧的架梁办法，在此后大型石桥梁的建筑和维修工程中被广泛运用。

浮运架梁示意图。（李国宏 供图）
The illustration of the floating-beam method. (Courtesy of Li Guohong)

Breeding oysters to reinforce the foundation of the bridge. When the foundation of Luoyang Bridge was first constructed, the stone blocks were randomly stacked with gaps between them, resulting in poor structural integrity. The stones were easily displaced or sunk due to the erosion of winds, waves, and tides, which affected the stability of the bridge piers. Based on the previous understanding of the biological characteristics of oysters, Cai Xiang invented the method of "breeding oysters on the foundation for reinforcement". By placing oysters on the foundation of bridge piers and taking advantage of their strong adhesion and fast reproduction, the loose foundation was solidified into a cohesive whole after clusters of oysters densely propagated in the gaps between the stones, which effectively improved the strength and durability of the bridge foundation. It pioneered the application of biology in bridge engineering, setting a precedent in the world.

The floating-beam method. Most of the bridges in Quanzhou during the Song Dynasty were built with stone beams, which used locally sourced granite for both the bridge foundation, piers and the bridge deck. Sturdy and durable as they were, the stone structures were heavy and posed significant challenges in terms of transportation, lifting and placement. Especially when it came to suspending stone beams weighing tens or even hundreds of tons onto the piers, it seemed like an almost impossible task in an era without large-scale lifting equipment. Cai Xiang, after putting the bridge builders' heads together, however, came up with an ingenious solution by leveraging the tidal patterns of Luoyang River. He used wooden rafts to transport pre-cut stone beams of specified dimensions between the piers during high tide. When the tide receded, the wooden rafts gradually descended to their designated positions. The stone beams were then pulled into place using wooden winches that had been pre-installed on the piers. Such a floating-beam method, embodying Cai Xiang and the bridge builders' imagination and intelligence, was subsequently widely employed in the construction and maintenance of large stone bridges.

往来利涉歌遗爱

“不谋万世者，不足谋一时；不谋全局者，不足谋一域。”蔡襄就是一位谋万世、谋全局的智者。据北宋方勺《泊宅编》记载，建造洛阳桥时，虽然采用了“种蛎固基”的新方法，但是牡蛎的繁殖需要两至三年的周期，所以桥基石缝依旧需要采取石灰勾缝的工艺，以保证桥墩结构的稳定性。于是，蔡襄别出心裁，命工匠们就地取材，利用牡蛎壳来烧制石灰，以保障工程所需。同时，他命人在洛阳桥周边建造房屋，用于出租，所得资金充公，作为烧制石灰及修缮桥梁的专用款项。他还规定每三年安排一名僧人驻守洛阳桥，来往巡查，负责督促烧制石灰、加固桥基等事务。北宋元丰七年（1084），福州人王祖道担任泉州太守时，奏请朝廷立下法令，凡是擅自挖取洛阳桥牡蛎者，一经查实，处以两年的刑罚。即便是到了明代重修洛阳桥之时，地方官员依旧沿袭宋代的成法，严禁私自采挖洛阳桥保护范围内的牡蛎。

洛阳桥桥墩上生长着密密麻麻的海蛎。（陈英杰 摄）
Numerous oysters on Luoyang Bridge's piers. (Photo by Chen Yingjie)

Facilitating the Crossing of the River

"He who does not plan for the future is not capable of planning for the present; he who does not plan for the overall situation is not capable of planning for a specific domain." Cai Xiang is such a wise man who plans for the future and the overall situation. According to *Mr. Bozhai's Historical Notes* written by Fang Shao in the Northern Song Dynasty, although a new method of "breeding oysters to reinforce the foundation of the bridge" was used in the construction of Luoyang Bridge, oyster breeding still required a cycle of two to three years. Therefore, the cracks in the bridge foundation still needed to be filled with lime mortar to ensure the stability of bridge piers. Cai Xiang came up with a unique idea and instructed the craftsmen to use oyster shells found locally to produce lime, ensuring the availability of materials for the project. At the same time, he ordered the construction of houses around Luoyang Bridge for rental purposes, and the rent was used exclusively for the production of lime and the maintenance of the bridge. He also stipulated that a monk be stationed at Luoyang Bridge every three years to patrol and supervise the production of lime and the reinforcement of the bridge foundation. In 1084 of the Northern Song Dynasty, Wang Zudao from Fuzhou served as the prefect of Quanzhou and proposed a decree to the imperial court, stating that anyone who illegally dug up oysters from Luoyang Bridge would be punished with two years of imprisonment upon investigation. Even when Luoyang Bridge was rebuilt during the Ming Dynasty, local officials still followed the practices of the Song Dynasty and strictly prohibited unauthorized excavation of oysters within the protected area of Luoyang Bridge.

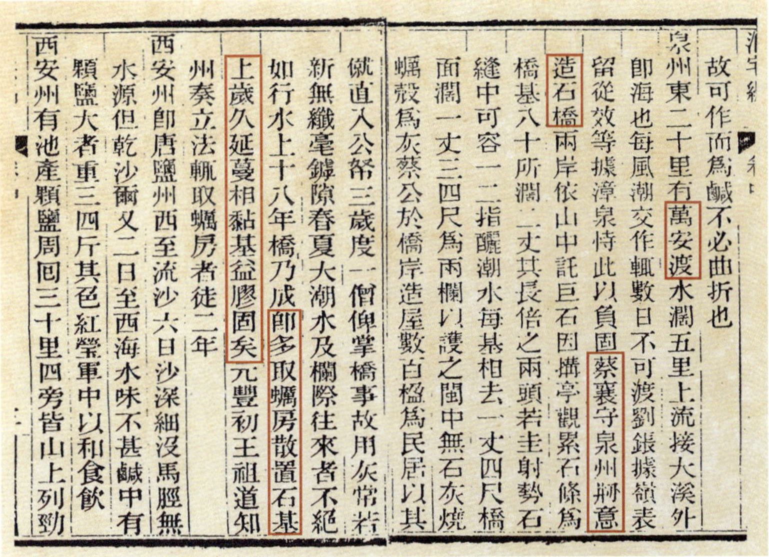
故可作而為鹹不必曲折也
泉州東二十里有萬安渡水濶五里上流接大溪外
即海也每風潮交作輒數日不可渡劉鋹據嶺表
留從效等據漳泉恃此以負固蔡襄守泉州剏意
造石橋兩岸依山中託巨石因搆亭觀累石條為
橋基八十所濶二丈其長倍之兩頭若圭射勢石
縫中可容一二指釃潮水每基相去一丈四尺橋
面濶一丈三四尺為兩欄以護之闔中無石灰燒
蠣殼為灰蔡公於橋岸造屋數百楹為民居以其
僦直入公帑三歲度一僧俾掌橋事故用灰常若
新無纖毫罅隙春夏大潮水及欄際往來者不絕
如行水上十八年橋乃成即多取蠣房散置石基
上歲久延蔓相黏基益膠固矣元豐初王祖道知
州奏立法輒取蠣房者徒二年
西安州即唐鹽州西至流沙六日沙深細沒馬脛無
水源但乾沙爾又二日至西海水味不甚鹹中有
顆鹽大者重三四斤其色紅瑩軍中以和食飲
西安州有池產顆鹽周回三十里四旁皆山上列勁

北宋方勺《泊宅编》中关于洛阳桥"种蛎固基"的记载。（李国宏 供图）

The record about breeding oysters to reinforce the foundation of Luoyang Bridge in *Mr. Bozhai's Historical Notes* of the Northern Song Dynasty. (Courtesy of Li Guohong)

洛阳桥建成之后，泉州成为“南接漳广，北通江浙”的交通枢纽，踏上洛阳桥，“一望五里排琨瑶，行人不忧沧海潮”。同时，越海跨江的洛阳桥也成为泉州重要的地理标志和文化印记。作为蔡襄的忠实粉丝，状元出身的王十朋在自己的《梅溪王先生文集》中记载，南宋乾道四年（1168）他出任泉州太守，路过莆田时，特地瞻仰蔡襄故居，徘徊顾叹而不忍离去。他深情写道，刚进入泉州地界，“则首见所谓万安桥者，与大书深刻之记争雄”。站在洛阳桥上，临渚观涛，怀古思今，王十朋的万千感慨奔涌而出，化作一首情真意切的赞歌：“北望中原万里遥，南来喜见洛阳桥。人行跨海金鳌背，亭压空江玉虹腰。功不自成因砥柱，患宜预备有风潮。蔡公力量真刚者，遗爱胜于郑国侨。”他还登上九日山，看到蔡襄诗之真迹，顿觉“凛然有生意，如见其（蔡襄）正颜色坐黄堂时也”，不禁感叹：“至今泉人称太守之贤者，必以公为首云。”

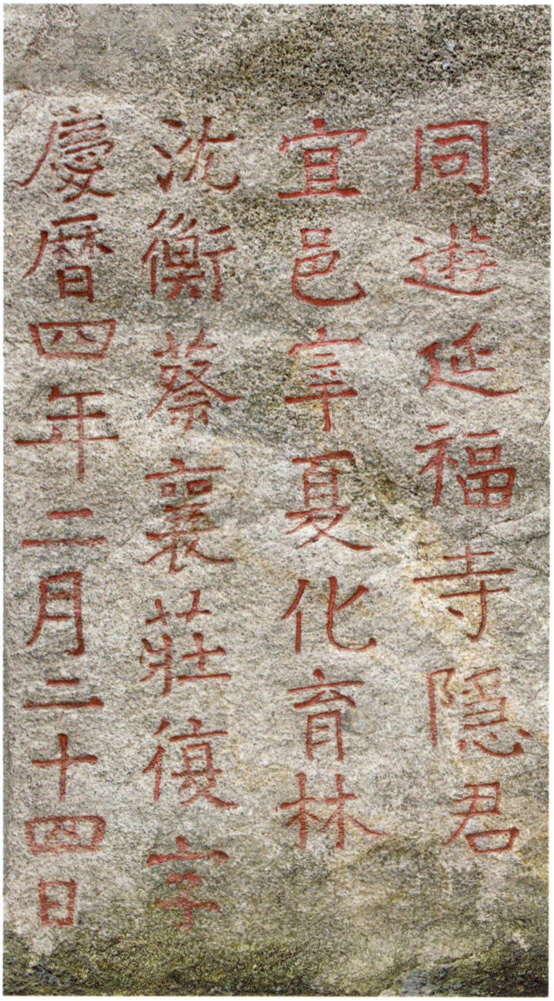

九日山蔡襄题名石刻。（何春燕 供图）
The stone inscription on Jiuri Mountain inscribed with Cai Xiang's name. (Courtesy of He Chunyan)

After the completion of Luoyang Bridge, Quanzhou became a transportation hub connecting Zhangzhou and Guangzhou in the south and Jiangsu and Zhejiang in the north. Walking on Luoyang Bridge, one could see the beautiful scenery and would not worry about the tides of the sea. At the same time, Luoyang Bridge, which spanned the sea and crossed the river, became an important geographical landmark and cultural symbol of Quanzhou. As a loyal fan of Cai Xiang, Wang Shipeng, who was a *zhuangyuan* (the top scholar in ancient Chinese imperial examinations), recorded in his collected works that in 1168 of the Southern Song Dynasty, when he served as the prefect of Quanzhou, he specifically visited Cai Xiang's former residence when passing through Putian County and lingered there, reluctant to leave. He wrote with deep affection that when he first entered Quanzhou, he saw the so-called Wan'an Bridge, which competed with the deeply engraved inscriptions on the tablet. Standing on Luoyang Bridge, overlooking the waves, he couldn't help but thought of the past and the present. Wang Shipeng's countless emotions surged and turned into a heartfelt praise:

"Looking north, the Central Plains are thousands of miles away,
And coming south, I am delighted to see Luoyang Bridge.
People walk across the sea on the back of a golden turtle,
And the pavilion presses against the river like a jade rainbow.
Achievements are not self-made,
But rely on a solid foundation,
And a foresight for the coming tides.
Lord Cai's strength is truly strong,
And his love surpasses that of Gongsun Qiao in the Zheng State."

He also climbed Jiuri Mountain and saw the calligraphy of Cai Xiang's poetry with a sense of vitality, as if he could see Cai Xiang sitting in the yellow hall with a serious expression. He couldn't help but sigh, "Even now, when people in Quanzhou praise the wise prefects, they must mention Cai Xiang first."

洛江双虹话道询

洛阳桥不仅是古代中国第一座海港大石桥，而且在营造技艺上有许多创新和突破，成为古代桥梁建筑史上的伟大创举。在蔡襄创新精神和海外贸易繁盛势头的刺激下，福建掀起一场轰轰烈烈的造桥热潮。在此期间，洛阳桥一直被模仿，却难以被超越。明代《八闽通志》就曾记载，南宋建炎三年（1129），僧人祖逊在莆田募建迎仙桥，“视洛阳桥规划创建，酾水为二十四道，榜曰龙溪”。

宋代，泉州地区建造石桥梁的位置大多跨江越海，或者顺着海岸线，与石路蜿蜒相连，重在突破港口与集市之间的交通障碍，形成水陆联动、四通八达的贸易港交通网络。因此，洛阳桥首创的筏形基础和浮运架梁技术得以长期广泛运用，屡试不爽。南宋开禧年间，僧人道询在惠安獭窟屿“率其徒操舟运石成桥”，此桥“直渡海门，长五里许”，长度甚至超过了洛阳桥和安平桥。獭窟桥的建成极大地方便了商旅往来和货物转运，促进獭窟屿经济的飞速发展。据清代洪昆所撰《獭江新考》记载：“唐、宋、元间，居民稠密，人皆事于通洋，遂为舟车输运津头，称富盛焉。”

明代《泉州府舆地图说》中绘有獭窟桥。（李国宏 供图）

The Geographic Map of Quanzhou Prefecture of the Ming Dynasty depicts Taku Islet Bridge. (Courtesy of Li Guohong)

Monk Daoxun's Contributions

Luoyang Bridge is not only the first large stone bridge built in a seaport in ancient China, but also a great innovation and breakthrough in construction techniques, making it a great feat in the history of ancient bridge architecture. Stimulated by Cai Xiang's spirit of innovation and the thriving trend of overseas trade, Fujian witnessed a bridge-building boom. During this period, Luoyang Bridge was constantly imitated but it was difficult to surpass it. *A General Gazetteer of Fujian* of the Ming Dynasty recorded that in 1129, a monk named Zuxun raised funds to build Yingxian (Welcome Immortals) Bridge in Putian. It was planned and constructed by imitating Luoyang Bridge. The river was divided into twenty-four channels, and the biggest one of them was named Longxi Crook.

During the Song Dynasty, the stone bridges built in Quanzhou mostly spanned rivers and crossed the sea, or followed the coastline, connecting with stone roads in zigzags. The focus was on overcoming transportation barriers between ports and markets, forming a well-connected trade port transportation network that integrated water and land. Therefore, the raft-shaped foundation and floating-beam technology pioneered by Luoyang Bridge were widely and successfully used. Between 1205 and 1207, Monk Daoxun led his disciples to transport stones by boat to build a bridge on Taku Islet in Hui'an. This bridge "directly crossed the sea gate and was about 2.5 kilometers long", even longer than Luoyang Bridge and Anping Bridge. The completion of Taku Islet Bridge greatly facilitated the travel of merchants and the transfer of goods, promoting the rapid economic development in Taku Islet. According to the record of Hong Kun's *New Study of Tajiang River* of the Qing Dynasty, during the Tang, Song and Yuan dynasties, the dense population and their focus on overseas trade led to the transportation of goods by boat and carriage, making the island prosperous and wealthy.

如果说獭窟桥的建造让道询在南宋泉州造桥史上崭露头角的话，那么乌屿盘光桥的落成，就是道询斩获“桥梁建筑大师”之名的高光时刻。乌屿位于洛阳桥下游，孤悬海中，原本只能通过一条简易砌筑的石路与陆地相连，每每潮怒风狂，商旅难行。南宋宝祐年间，道询募资建造盘光桥，全长四百余丈，宽一丈六尺，建筑规模超过洛阳桥。两座桥隔海相望，同样气势恢宏，被称作“洛江双虹”，为“洛阳八景”之一。

关于建造盘光桥的资金来源，流传着一则民间故事。据清代周亮工《闽小记》载，相传乌屿上有一位商人，从事海外贸易，一次驾驶船舶前往东南亚某地，遭遇风暴，船身破损不堪，只得临时在一处荒岛停靠。不料又遭蟒蛇袭击，好在这位乌屿商人最终设计杀了蟒蛇，并意外获得价值连城的明月珠。大难不死必有后福，这位乌屿商人历经千辛万苦后，终于带着财宝返回家乡。不过，邻里乡亲并不知道他竟然因为此次海外历险而获得了巨额的财富。

If the construction of Taku Islet Bridge allowed Daoxun to make a name for himself in the history of bridge construction in Quanzhou during the Southern Song Dynasty, then the completion of Panguang Bridge on Wuyu Islet was the shining moment that earned Daoxun the title of "Master of Bridge Construction". Wuyu Islet was located downstream of Luoyang Bridge, suspended in the sea, originally only connected to the mainland by a simple stone road. It was difficult for merchants and travelers to pass through during storms and high tides. Between 1253 and 1258 during the Southern Song Dynasty, Daoxun raised funds to build Panguang Bridge, which was over 400 zhang (about 1.3 kilometers) in length, 1 *zhang* and 6 *chi* (about 5.3 meters) in width, surpassing the scale of Luoyang Bridge. Equally grand, the two bridges faced each other across the sea and were known as the "Twin Rainbows over Luojiang River", one of the "Eight Scenic Spots of Luoyang".

There is a folk story about the funding source for the construction of Panguang Bridge. According to Zhou Lianggong's *Notes Made in Fujian* of the Qing Dynasty, it is said that there was a businessman on Wuyu Islet who was engaged in overseas trade. Once, he sailed to a certain place in Southeast Asia and encountered a storm. The ship was severely damaged and had to temporarily dock on a deserted island. To make things worse, he was attacked by a python, but fortunately, the Wuyu businessman managed to kill the python and unexpectedly obtained a priceless pearl. Surviving the great danger, the businessman finally returned home with his wealth after going through numerous hardships. However, his neighbors and fellow villagers were unaware that he had" obtained a huge fortune from this overseas adventure.

清代《福建沿海全图》绘有洛阳桥及乌屿盘光桥，呈现了“洛江双虹”胜景。（李国宏 供图）

The Complete Map of Fujian's Coastline of the Qing Dynasty depicts Luoyang Bridge and Panguang Bridge, showcasing the magnificent view of "Twin Rainbows over Luoyang River". (Courtesy of Li Guohong)

后来，乌屿商人想与泉州一户富豪结亲，这位富豪不知其底细，就找了个借口，推脱说："我担心女儿嫁到乌屿，渡海往来，甚是不便。如果你能够建造一座桥，并在桥上铺满金银，我就答应这门婚事。"不曾料想，乌屿商人一掷千金，专程请来道询设计建造盘光桥，最终如愿地迎娶富豪千金进门。因此，盘光桥另有一个温馨又浪漫的名字——娘子桥。

娘子桥传奇堪称宋代泉州商人海外历险故事的一个缩影，其中包含着海外航行的风险、财富的来之不易，以及人们对美好生活的憧憬等诸多信息。海外传奇故事，说的人投入，听的人入迷，无须过于计较真假。但是有一点是可以肯定的，那就是铺桥造路满足了海外贸易兴盛对完善交通体系的客观需求，而海外贸易繁盛带来的巨大社会财富，也为桥梁道路等大型城市交通设施的修建提供源源不断的资金保障，并促进泉州乐善好施社会风尚的形成。

Later, the Wuyu businessman wanted to marry the daughter of a rich family in Quanzhou. The father did not know his background and made an excuse, saying, "I am worried that my daughter will have difficulties traveling to and from Wuyu Islet by sea. If you can build a bridge and cover it with gold and silver, I will agree to this marriage." Unexpectedly, the Wuyu businessman spent a fortune to invite Daoxun to design and construct Panguang Bridge, and finally married the rich man's daughter as he wished. Therefore, Panguang Bridge has another warm and romantic name—the Lady's Bridge.

The legend of Lady's Bridge can be regarded as a microcosm of the adventures of Quanzhou merchants in the Song Dynasty, which contains much information such as the risks of overseas navigation, the hardships of earning wealth, and people's longing for a better life. Overseas legendary stories are captivating when told and listened to, and their authenticity is not a major concern. However, one thing is certain, that is, the construction of bridges and roads met the needs of thriving overseas trade, and the enormous social wealth brought by prosperous overseas trade provided a continuous source of funding for the construction of large-scale urban transportation facilities like bridges and roads, and promoted the formation of a philanthropic social trend in Quanzhou.

清代陈炯伦《沿海全图》中可清晰地看到安平桥、姑嫂塔、洛阳桥、盘光桥等塔桥构建的交通网络。(李国宏 供图)

In Chen Jionglun's *The Complete Map of the Coastline* of the Qing Dynasty, a clear depiction of the transportation network constructed by Anping Bridge, Gusao Pagoda, Luoyang Bridge and Panguang Bridge can be seen. (Courtesy of Li Guohong)

如果说蔡襄督造洛阳桥体现了官方的主导地位，那么，道询修建盘光桥则是民间力量的完美展示。可贵的是，这两种模式在泉州不是对立的，而是相辅相成的，共同维系着泉州港海外贸易的持续繁荣与相应设施的更新换代。

据乾隆版《泉州府志》记载，道询是泉州惠安人，乃白沙寺住持，得端宗赐号“灵应大师”。道询“朗悟内典，精勤戒行，宝祐中修造青龙、獭窟等桥共二百余所”。道询一生修造的两百余座桥梁中，保存至今的有惠安青龙桥和晋江清风桥，见证其造桥传奇的历史遗迹还有乌屿盘光塔、盘光亭以及浔美青莲寺《普济桥渡》《宝塔亭路》两方碑刻等。道询造桥现象堪称中国乃至世界桥梁建筑史上的奇迹，闪耀着泉州作为宋元时期世界海洋商贸中心的历史荣光。

青龙桥遗址遗迹。（黄国炎 摄）
The site and relics of Qinglong Bridge. (Photo by Huang Guoyan)

If Cai Xiang's supervision over the construction of Luoyang Bridge is said to embody the dominant position of the authorities, then Daoxun's construction of Panguang Bridge is a perfect showcase of folk power. What is valuable is that these two parties complement each other, jointly maintaining the continuous prosperity of Quanzhou Port's overseas trade and the upgrading of corresponding facilities.

According to the Qianlong edition of *Local Chronicles of Quanzhou Prefecture*, Daoxun, a native of Hui'an, Quanzhou, was the abbot of Baisha Temple and was bestowed the title "Great Master of Lingying" by Emperor Duanzong. Daoxun "thoroughly understood the scriptures, diligently practiced precepts and built over 200 bridges between 1253 and 1258, including Qinglong Bridge and Taku Islet Bridge". Among the over 200 bridges built by Daoxun, the ones that still exist today are Qinglong Bridge in Hui'an and Qingfeng Bridge in Jinjiang. Other historical relics that witness his legendary bridge-building achievements include Panguang Pagoda and Panguang Pavilion on Wuyu Islet, and the stone inscriptions at Qinglian Temple in Xunmei Community. Daoxun's bridge-building phenomenon can be regarded as a miracle in the history of bridge construction in China and even the world, shining with the historical glory of Quanzhou as an emporium of the world during the Song and Yuan dynasties.

乌屿盘光塔。（成冬冬 摄）
Panguang Pagoda on Wuyu Islet. (Photo by Cheng Dongdong)

“万安祝圣放生”碑

宋代，因帝王及高僧的倡导，各郡县先后建造放生池，并在当朝皇帝诞辰日举行祝圣放生祈福仪式。南宋乾道六年（1170），泉州太守王十朋发现贡院南侧水池“嘉莲再生，实和气致祥之地，辟而广之”，作为泉州举行祝圣放生仪式的专用场所。南宋淳熙年间，地方官认为贡院放生池比较狭小，遂将祝圣放生的场所改设在石笋桥北。南宋庆元五年（1199），泉州太守刘颖疏浚东湖，建恩波亭及东湖放生祝圣宝胜禅院，后者成为新的祝圣放生场所。南宋嘉熙二年（1238），泉州太守刘炜叔主持修缮洛阳桥，将原本位于惠安境内的定光院迁建于洛阳桥南，改称定光万安桥院，并镌刻竖立“万安祝圣放生”碑。自此，祝圣放生仪式便一直在洛阳桥举行，洛阳桥成为宋代官方祝圣放生的场所，拓展了其文化空间功能。洛阳桥的雄姿和周边壮丽的景观风貌也有助于烘托祝圣放生活动的仪式感和氛围，营造“高厚圣主恩，覆载荷汪洋”的文化意境。

“万安祝圣放生”碑。（成冬冬 摄）
The stone tablet of “Wan'an Consecration and Mercy Release”. (Photo by Cheng Dongdong)

The Stone Tablet of "*Wan'an Consecration and Mercy Release*"

During the Song Dynasty, due to the advocacy of emperors and eminent monks, various counties and prefectures successively built release ponds and held consecration and release ceremonies on the emperor's birthday. In 1170 of the Southern Song Dynasty, Wang Shipeng, the prefect of Quanzhou, discovered that the pond at the south of the Imperial Examination Hall was a place of auspiciousness and harmony, and thus expanded it as a dedicated venue for the ceremony of consecration and mercy release in Quanzhou. Between 1174 and 1189, local officials deemed the release pond in the Imperial Examination Hall to be too small and relocated the site to the north of Shisun Bridge. In 1199, Liu Ying, the prefect of Quanzhou, dredged Donghu Lake and built Enbo Pavilion and Baosheng Zen Temple for consecration and mercy release, making it the new venue for the ceremonies. In 1238, Liu Weishu, the prefect of Quanzhou, oversaw the renovation of Luoyang Bridge and moved the original Dingguang Temple from Hui'an to the south of Luoyang Bridge, renaming it Dingguang Wan'an Bridge Temple, and erected the stone tablet of "Wan'an Consecration and Mercy Release". Since then, the consecration and mercy release ceremony has been held at Luoyang Bridge, making the bridge an official venue for such ceremonies during the Song Dynasty, thus expanding its cultural function. The majestic appearance of Luoyang Bridge and the magnificent surrounding landscape also helped to enhance the ceremonial atmosphere of the consecrating and releasing activities, creating a cultural ambiance of "the grace of the virtuous sovereign covering the vast ocean".

"万安祝圣放生"碑落款中提及刘炜叔"权提举福建路市舶"，证实他担任泉州太守时兼任市舶司提举。刘炜叔，福建莆田人，曾任仓部员外郎，出守吉州（今江西省吉安市），以勤勉干练而著称。据宋代许应龙所撰《东涧集》记载，嘉熙元年（1237），朝廷认为"温陵大藩，民繁事多，蛮舶萃聚，财货浩穰"，于是任命具有"公廉练达之才"的刘炜叔担任泉州太守兼市舶司提举，期望收到"牧养阜通之绩"。

刘炜叔不负众望，勤于政务，善作善成，捐公帑数百万，整修泉州府文庙、洛阳桥、蔡襄祠等。兼任泉州市舶司提举期间，他廉洁自律，以上率下，营造良好的营商环境，外商都乐于前来泉州港做生意，泉州的外贸收入剧增。所以，"万安祝圣放生"碑既是研究宋代放生祈福习俗的实物资料，也是泉州海外交通史的重要历史见证。

The inscription of "Wan'an Consecration and Mercy Release" stone tablet mentions Liu Weishu's position as "superintendent of the Maritime Trade Office", which testifies that he held the position of both Quanzhou prefect and *Tijiu* or superintendent of the Maritime Trade Office. Liu Weishu, a native of Putian, Fujian, formerly served as a councillor in the Ministry of Granaries and was stationed in Jizhou (now Ji'an City, Jiangxi Province). He was well-known for his diligence and efficiency. According to *Mr. Dongjian's Collected Works* by Xu Yinglong, in 1237, the court believed that "Quanzhou is a major fiefdom with a multitude of things, a gathering of foreign ships and abundant wealth", and appointed Liu Weishu, who was "upright and competent", as the prefect of Quanzhou and superintendent of the Maritime Trade Office in hope of achieving "prosperity and smooth communication".

Liu Weishu lived up to the expectations of the court by diligently carrying out his political duties and accomplishing good deeds. He collected millions of public funds to renovate important cultural sites such as Quanzhou Confucian Temple and School, Luoyang Bridge and Cai Xiang Shrine. During his tenure as the superintendent of the Maritime Trade Office, he maintained high standards of integrity and discipline, leading by example and creating a favorable business environment. Foreign traders were happy to come to Quanzhou Port to do business, which significantly increased the foreign trade income for Quanzhou. Therefore, the inscription on "Wan'an Consecration and Mercy Release" stone tablet is not only a tangible material for studying the customs of mercy release for blessings in the Song Dynasty, but also an important historical witness to the history of Quanzhou's overseas transportation.

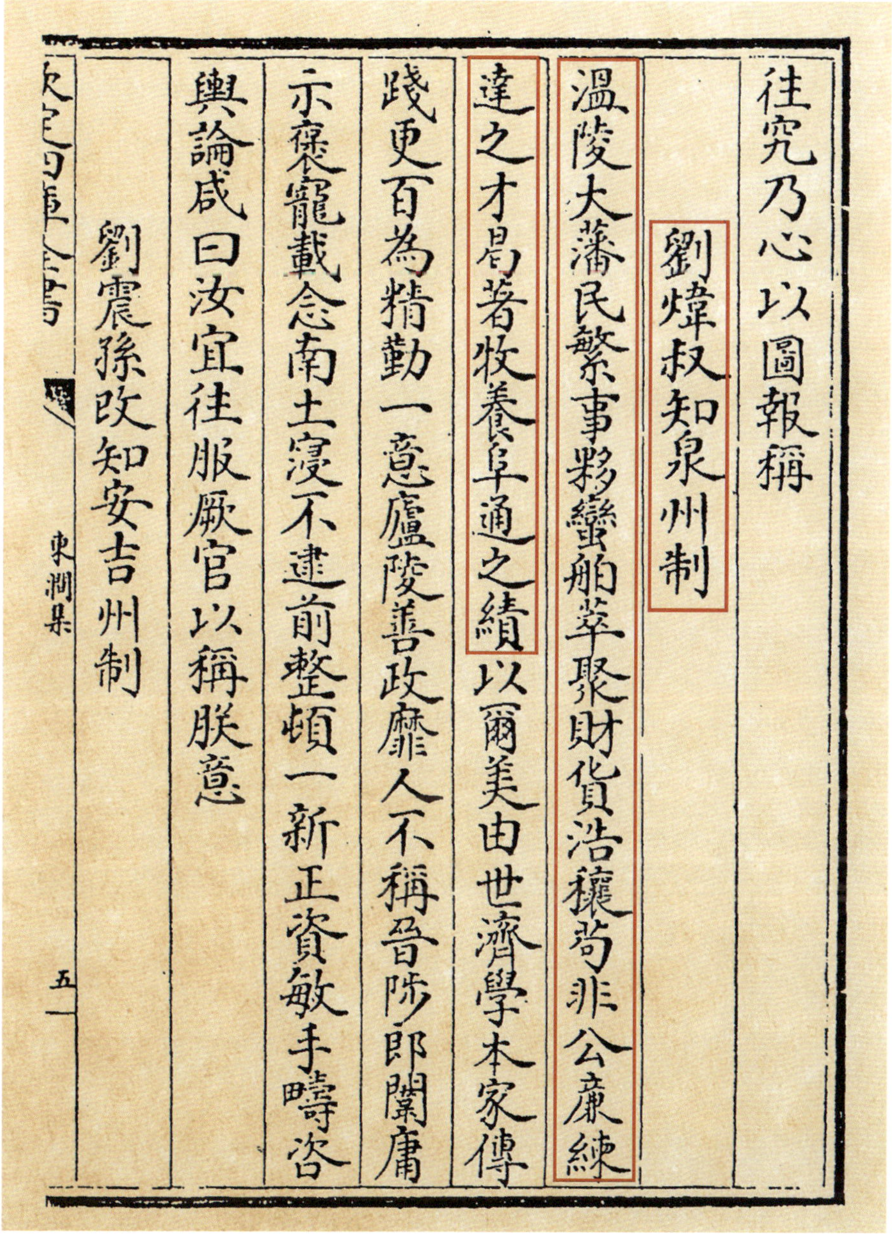
往究乃心以圖報稱
劉煒叔知泉州制
溫陵大藩民繁事夥蠻舶萃聚財貨浩穰苟非公廉練
達之才曷著牧養阜通之績以爾美由世濟學本家傳
踐更百為精勤一意廬陵善政靡人不稱晉陟郎闈庸
示褒寵載念南土寖不逮前整頓一新正資敏手疇咨
輿論咸曰汝宜往服厥官以稱朕意
劉震孫改知安吉州制

欽定四庫全書　東澗集　五

宋代许应龙《东涧集》中关于刘炜叔知泉州的记载。（李国宏 供图）

The record about Liu Weishu in Xu Yinglong's *Mr. Dongjian's Collected Works* of the Song Dynasty. (Courtesy of Li Guohong)

洛阳桥下正潮平

元至正年间，洛阳桥增设泉南佛国亭，成为观潮览胜、置酒饯别的好去处。至正十一年(1351)，翰林待制贡师泰奉旨代祀泉州天妃宫，目睹泉州港发达的海外贸易与繁华的城市风貌，写下《泉州道中》。诗中有云："千山落日丹霞北，万里孤城白水南。玉椀霜寒凝紫蔗，金丸露暖熟黄柑。海商到岸才封舶，蕃国朝天亦赐骖。满市珠玑醉歌舞，几人为尔竟沉酣。"贡师泰回朝复命时，泉州监郡偰玉立邀其在洛阳桥观潮话别，贡师泰作《泉州驿别太守偰世玉》。诗云："老夫欲起犹便睡，候吏频催却治行。万里烟云随骥足，五更风雨杂鸡声。乾坤笑我应无补，江海逢君倍有情。且解金鱼沽别酒，洛阳桥下正潮平。"

洛阳潮平。（陈英杰 摄）
The calm Luoyang River under the bridge. (Photo by Chen Yingjie)

The Tide Is Calm Under Luoyang Bridge

Between 1341 and 1368, Quannan (Quanzhou) Buddha Pavilion was added to Luoyang Bridge and became a popular place for sightseeing and farewell banquets. In 1351, Gong Shitai, the assistant consultant of Hanlin Imperial Academy, was ordered to worship at Tianfei Palace (now Tianhou Temple) in Quanzhou. Witnessing the prosperous overseas trade and bustling cityscape of Quanzhou Bay, he wrote the poem *On the Way to Quanzhou*, which says:

"The setting sun falls behind a thousand mountains in the north,
While a lonely city stands by the white waters in the south.
The frost freezes on the purple sugarcane beneath the moon,
And ripe yellow oranges are like golden pills in the dew.
Merchants from the sea can only dock their ships after arriving,
But the envoys are bestowed with horses by the emperor.
The market is full of pearls, jewels, drunken songs and dances.
How many people can enjoy such intoxication?"

When Gong Shitai returned to the court to report, Xie Yuli, the censor of Quanzhou, invited him to Luoyang Bridge to watch the tides and bid farewell. Gong Shitai wrote the poem *Farewell to Censor Xie Shiyu at Quanzhou Post*, which says:

"I want to leave but still feels like sleeping.
The waiting officials urge me repeatedly to start my journey.
The smoke and clouds follow the horse's footsteps for thousands of miles,
And the wind and rain mix with the crowing of the rooster at five in the morning.
The universe laughs at my incapability,
But meeting you, the rivers and seas double my affection.
Let's enjoy a farewell drink with the goldfish,
While the tide is calm under Luoyang Bridge."

洛阳桥的壮丽景观给贡师泰留下深刻的印象。据其门生谢肃回忆，贡师泰多次与其谈起“洛阳桥观潮时事”。明洪武十七年（1384），谢肃时任福建按察司佥事，巡视泉州府，途经洛阳桥。涛声依旧，物是人非，先师的话语却仍在耳边回荡。触景生情的谢肃口占一绝：“翰林代祀属前朝，曾说泉南看海潮。二十四年如一梦，乘骢来过洛阳桥。”步入蔡襄祠，摩挲“三绝”碑，谢肃感慨不已，认为万安桥“跨洛阳江上，潮汐吐吞，洲岛环映，可谓奇胜”，而蔡襄《万安桥记》“字体弘壮，不在唐颜太师真卿《漓滩记》下，是亦奇胜也”。于是他又赋诗一首，以赞蔡襄涉川济险之丰功伟绩。诗云：“万安桥在泉南郡，骢马来时踏淼茫。群柱直排沧海浪，夹阑横截洛阳江。荔花洲岛春风暖，榕叶亭台晓日苍。浩想蔡公能济险，转因驱石笑秦皇。”在谢肃看来，当时的泉州港依然是对外交通的重要口岸：“莫道泉南非要地，遥从海外控诸夷。云涛大舶来犀象，烽橹雄城驻虎貔。”流失了岁月，变换了沧桑，不变的是洛阳桥下奔腾向海的江水，还有泉州人直挂云帆济沧海的豪情壮志。

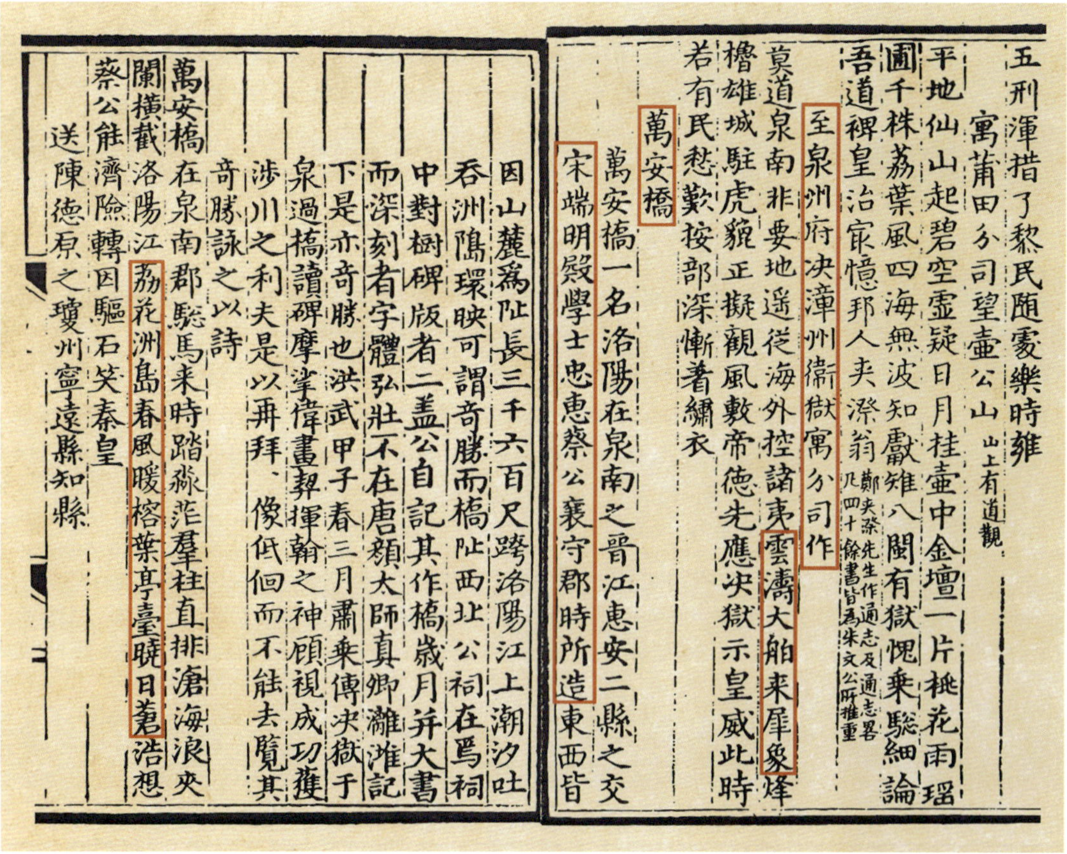
五刑渾措了黎民隨處樂時雍
寓莆田分司望壺公山 山上有道觀
平地仙山起碧空虛疑日月挂壺中金壇一片桃花雨瑶
圃千株荔葉風四海無波知獻雉八閩有獄愧乘驄細論
吾道裨皇治宦憶邦人夫潔翁 鄭夫潔先生作通志及通志畧凡四十餘書皆為朱文公所推重
至泉州府決漳州衛獄寓分司作
莫道泉南非要地遥從海外控諸夷雲濤大舶來犀象烽
櫓雄城駐虎貔正擬觀風敷帝德先應決獄示皇威此時
若有民愁歎按部深慚著繡衣
萬安橋
萬安橋一名洛陽在泉南之晉江惠安二縣之交
宋端明殿學士忠惠蔡公襄守郡時所造東西皆
因山麓爲阯長三千六百尺跨洛陽江上潮汐吐
呑洲嶼環映可謂奇勝而橋阯西北公祠在焉祠
中對樹碑版者二蓋公自記其作橋歲月并大書
而深刻者字體弘壯不在唐顔太師真卿灕灘記
下是亦奇勝也洪武甲子春三月肅乘傳決獄于
泉過橋讀碑摩挲偉畫想揮翰之神顧視成功獲
涉川之利夫是以再拜僾低佪而不能去覽其
奇勝詠之以詩
萬安橋在泉南郡驄馬来時踏淼茫羣柱直排滄海浪夾
闌横截洛陽江荔花洲島春風暖榕葉亭臺曉日蒼浩想
蔡公能濟險轉因驅石笑秦皇
送陳德原之瓊州寧遠縣知縣

元末明初谢肃《密庵诗稿》中关于泉州港及洛阳桥的记载。（李国宏 供图）
The record about Quanzhou Port and Luoyang Bridge in Xie Su's *Mr. Mi'an's Poetry* of the late Yuan and early Ming dynasties. (Courtesy of Li Guohong)

The magnificent scenery of Luoyang Bridge left a deep impression on Gong Shitai. According to his student Xie Su's recollection, Gong Shitai often talked to him about the details of watching the tides at Luoyang Bridge. In 1384, Xie Su passed by Luoyang Bridge when he inspected Quanzhou Prefecture as the assistant inspector of Fujian Province. The sound of the waves remained the same, but everything had changed. Words of the late teacher, however, still echoed in his ears. Deeply moved by the scene, Xie Su composed a quatrain:

"My teacher, a Hanlin scholar once worshiped on behalf of the emperor,
And he spoke of watching the tides in Quannan.
Twenty-four years have passed like a dream,
And it is I who ride on a bluish white horse crossing Luoyang Bridge."

Stepping into Cai Xiang Shrine and touching the "Three Excellence" Stele, Xie Su couldn't help but feel overwhelmed. He believed that Luoyang Bridge "can be called a marvel, spanning Luoyang River, with tides ebbing and flowing, surrounded by islands". He also thought that Cai Xiang's *A Record of Wan'an Bridge* had a grand and powerful style, comparable to *A Record of Litan* by Yan Zhenqing, a renowned calligrapher of the Tang Dynasty, making it a second marvel. Inspired by this, Xie Su composed another poem to recognize Cai Xiang's achievements in crossing dangerous rivers and overcoming difficulties. In Xie Su's eyes, Quanzhou Port at that time was still an important gateway for foreign trade. He acclaimed, "Don't say that Quannan is not in a strategic location. Instead, it controls the barbarians from overseas. The clouds and waves bring large ships carrying rhinoceros horns and ivories, while the beacon towers stand tall, with courageous soldiers stationed there." Despite the passage of time and the changes that have taken place, what remains unchanged is the grand aspiration of Quanzhou people, who set sail to explore the vast sea.

西川甘雨怀先贤

明嘉靖三十年（1551）夏，泉州大旱，太守方克祈雨未应，焦急万分，遂再次前往泉州府城隍庙，立下誓言："三天之内再不下雨，我就背着神像，一起跳入洛阳江，以死明志。"谁料，当夜方克梦见城隍神，告知已借来雨水以解旱情。第二天，果然甘霖普降。因方克字惟力、号西川，故泉州人将这场及时雨称为"西川甘雨"。

同年秋，福建按察使、章丘人王昺巡视泉州府，发现洛阳桥部分护栏倾斜、缺失，一些桥墩条石断裂、歪闪，便交代方克负责重修，同时重申禁令——不准私自挖取洛阳桥保护范围内的牡蛎。嘉靖三十一年（1552）五月，方克指派晋江主簿陈冕管理洛阳桥重修事务。不久，王昺调任河南右布政使，鄞县人范钦（天一阁创办人）接任福建按察使。在范钦的督促下，嘉靖三十一年八月，洛阳桥重修工程顺利竣工。

洛阳桥"西川甘雨"碑亭。（李国宏 供图）
"Rain of Xichuan" Stele Pavilion at Luoyang Bridge. (Courtesy of Li Guohong)

Rain of Xichuan in Commemoration of the Past Sage

In the summer of 1551, there was a severe drought in Quanzhou. The prefect, Fang Ke, prayed for rain but received no response, causing him great anxiety. He decided to visit the City God Temple in Quanzhou again and made a vow, "If it doesn't rain within three days, I will carry the statue of the deity and jump into Luoyang River to demonstrate my determination even in death." Unexpectedly, that night Fang Ke dreamed of the City God, who informed him that rainwater had been borrowed to alleviate the drought. The next day, it rained indeed. Quanzhou people referred to this timely rain as "Rain of Xichuan", as Fang Ke's curtesy name is "Xichuan".

In the autumn of the same year, Wang Bing, the inspector of Fujian Province and a native of Zhangqiu, conducted an inspection tour of Quanzhou Prefecture and found that some of the guardrails of Luoyang Bridge were inclined or missing, and some of the piers' stone blocks were broken or displaced. He then entrusted Fang Ke with the task of repairing the bridge and reiterated the prohibition against unauthorized digging of oysters within the protected area of Luoyang Bridge. In lunar May 1552, Fang Ke appointed Chen Mian, the chief clerk of Jinjiang, to manage the reconstruction of Luoyang Bridge. Soon, Wang Bing was transferred to the position of right assistant governor of Henan, while Fan Qin, a native of Yinxian County, also the founder of Tianyige Library, took over as the inspector of Fujian. Under Fan Qin's supervision, the reconstruction project of Luoyang Bridge was successfully completed in lunar August of the same year.

方克是安徽桐城人，曾任桐乡县令，又出守雅称为“桐城”的泉州，故自号“三桐寄主”。方克是明代泉州历史上著名的清官，史书中记载他：“廉以持身，仁以爱民，公以存心，勤以集事。兴学校，辟田畴，清户口，理赋役，除盗贼，平狱讼。”因政绩突出，升任苑马寺少卿。

明万历三年（1575），方克的族亲方梦旸担任泉州府南安县丞之时，“念先人之积诚格天，感士民之追思”，在洛阳桥中亭建造“西川甘雨”碑亭。此后，该碑亭成为泉州官方祈雨的重要场所。明崇祯三年（1630），桐乡进士姚孙榘任晋江县令，兴学重教，体恤民情，“农安耕，商安肆，士民颂之”。他曾捐资重建“西川甘雨”碑亭，以示敬仰先贤之意。

洛阳桥的每一方碑刻、每一处建筑，甚至是每一段桥板，都沉淀着泉州人的文化情结。月光菩萨慈祥的眼神，祝福着南来北往的客商；李五增修洛阳桥的豪放，抒写着流芳万古的美德；所有的赞美之词，最终都浓缩成沈汝翰笔下“海内第一桥”的爽朗大气。

洛阳桥不仅是中国古代桥梁的“状元”，也是泉州深厚历史底蕴的见证者和讲述者。“站如东西塔，卧似洛阳桥”的民谚，更是把泉州人傲立人间的志气、堂堂正正的品格表现得淋漓尽致。桥下是奔流不息的滔滔江水，桥上则总有不负韶华、勇敢前行的挺拔背影。

洛阳桥月光菩萨。（叶晓峰 摄）
The Moonlight Bodhisattva on Luoyang Bridge. (Photo by Ye Xiaofeng)

Fang Ke, a native of Tongcheng, Anhui, once served as the county magistrate of Tongxiang and was later appointed as the magistrate of Quanzhou, which was also called "Tongcheng". Therefore, he called himself "Host of the Three Tongs". Fang Ke was renowned for his integrity in the history of Quanzhou during the Ming Dynasty. Historical records describe him as "Upholding integrity, loving the people, preserving justice and being diligent in handling affairs, he promoted the establishment of schools, allocated farmland, maintained household registration, managed taxation and labor, eliminated thieves and bandits, and resolved disputes and lawsuits." Due to his outstanding performance, he was promoted to the position of assistant minister of the Imperial Stables.

In 1575 of the Ming Dynasty, when Fang Mengyang, Fang Ke's relative, served as the magistrate of Nan'an County in Quanzhou, he built the "Rain of Xichuan" Stele Pavilion in the middle of Luoyang Bridge, with the intention of honoring his ancestor's sincerity and responding to the people's remembrance. This stele pavilion then became an important place for official rain prayers in Quanzhou. In 1630 of the Ming Dynasty, Yao Sunju, a *jinshi* (the advanced scholar in ancient Chinese imperial examinations) from Tongxiang, served as the magistrate of Jinjiang county. Yao promoted education and cared for the people, which brought about prosperity in agriculture and commerce, and earned the praise of the people. He donated funds to rebuild the "Rain of Xichuan" Stele Pavilion as a sign of respect for the past sage.

Every stone inscription, every building, and even every plank of Luoyang Bridge embody the cultural sentiment of Quanzhou people. The compassionate gaze of the Moonlight Bodhisattva blesses the merchants coming and going, and the renowned merchant Li Wu's generous donation in repairing Luoyang Bridge expresses the virtue of flowing fragrance for eternity, which ultimately condense into the refreshing and majestic atmosphere of "China's earliest stone beam bridge" as depicted by Shen Ruhan.

Luoyang Bridge is not only the epitome of ancient Chinese bridges, but also a witness and narrator of Quanzhou's profound historical heritage. The folk saying of "standing like the East and West Pagodas, lying like Luoyang Bridge" vividly portrays the pride and noble character of Quanzhou people. Under the bridge flows the endless torrents of the river, while on the bridge, there are always upright figures who do not disappoint the prime of their lives and bravely move forward.

安平桥：天下无桥长此桥

安平桥位于泉州城西南方向30千米的晋江安海镇与南安水头镇交界的海湾上，因桥长五华里，俗称“五里桥”，为中国现存最长的跨海梁式石桥。安平桥是宋元时期泉州作为世界海洋商贸中心所必备的运输网络的代表性遗产要素之一，是泉州与广阔的南部沿海地区之间的陆运节点，体现了海洋贸易推动下泉州水陆转运系统的发展。

Anping Bridge: China's Longest Extant Cross-Sea Stone Beam Bridge

Anping Bridge, also known as "Wuli Bridge", is situated on the bay where Anhai Town in Jinjiang and Shuitou Town in Nan'an converge, approximately 30 kilometers southwest of Quanzhou City. This bridge holds significance as the longest stone bridge with a beam structure across the sea extant in China, spanning a length of five *li*, equivalent to around 2.5 kilometers. Anping Bridge is one of the representative heritage components reflecting the transportation network of Quanzhou as an emporium of world maritime trade during the Song and Yuan dynasties. It served as a pivotal land transportation hub connecting Quanzhou with the vast coastal region in Southern China, reflecting the development of Quanzhou's water-land transshipment system driven by maritime trade.

"天下第一长桥"——安平桥。（陈英杰 摄）

Anping Bridge, China's longest extant cross-sea stone beam bridge. (Photo by Chen Yingjie)

安平桥的“众筹”模式

安海镇位于晋江与南安的交界处，倚山濒海，与南安水头镇隔水相望。宋时，随着泉州对外交通贸易的日益繁荣，安海不但在地理位置上成为交通枢纽，亦成为日常贸易互通的货物集散地。然而，在安平桥未兴建之前，这里的行人过往、货物运输都高度依赖舟楫摆渡，甚为不便，“……飓风潮波，无时不至，船交水中，进退不可，失势下颠，漂垫相系，从古已然，大为民患”。

面对滔滔江水，安海人许下宏愿，誓将天堑变通途。南宋绍兴八年（1138），僧人祖派发愿建造石桥，安海富商黄护捐钱一万缗，僧人智渊募资一万缗，造桥工程就此开始了。可惜，工程进展到一半时，关键人物祖派与黄护相继辞世，一时群龙无首，施工断断续续，延宕十余年，安海人只能继续望“洋”兴叹。

天堑变通途。（陈英杰 摄）
The once insurmountable obstacle has been changed into a navigable pathway. (Photo by Chen Yingjie)

The "Crowdfunding" Mode of Anping Bridge

Anhai Town, positioned at the intersection of Jinjiang and Nan'an, is nestled against mountains and faces the water, with Shuitou Town in Nan'an on the other bank. During the Song Dynasty, as Quanzhou's foreign transportation and trade flourished, Anhai emerged not only as a strategic transportation hub geographically but also a bustling center for daily trade and the collecting and distributing of goods. However, prior to the construction of Anping Bridge, the transportation of both passengers and goods in Anhai heavily relied on boats and ferries, resulting in great inconvenience. This can be observed in historical descriptions that depict the challenges faced by the people here due to unpredictable hurricanes and tidal waves, which often trapped boats in the water, rendering them immobile and causing great difficulties since ancient times.

In the face of the formidable river, the inhabitants of Anhai made a solemn commitment to convert this insurmountable obstacle into a navigable pathway. In 1138 of the Southern Song Dynasty, a monk by the name of Zupai pledged to construct a stone bridge. This endeavor received significant financial support from Huang Hu, a prosperous merchant from Anhai, who generously contributed 10,000 strings of copper cash. Another monk named Zhiyuan managed to raise an additional 10,000 strings of copper cash. Consequently, the construction of the bridge commenced. Regrettably, the project encountered a setback when both Zupai and Huang Hu passed away, leaving the endeavor in a state of chaos. Lacking a leader to guide the project, the construction became sporadic and was plagued by numerous delays, extending the timeline by more than a decade. The people of Anhai could only continue to gaze upon the sea, their hearts heavy with longing and disappointment.

绍兴二十一年（1151）十一月，新上任的泉州知州赵令衿采纳民意，推举黄护之子黄逸和僧人惠胜负责安平桥的续建事务。历时一年，安平桥终于大功告成，赵令衿欣喜不已，撰书碑文《石井镇安平桥记》：“……其长八百十有一丈，其广一丈有六尺，疏为水道者三百六十有二。以栏楯为周防，绳直砥平，左右若一。隐然玉路，俨然金堤，雄丽坚密，工侔鬼神。”

值得一提的是，修建安平桥时，资金募集采用的是“众筹”模式，除了零散的捐款之外，捐资者还可以认捐桥墩或桥墩之间的一段工程，并在其上镌刻自己的姓名。如安平桥中亭西侧的石栏杆上，就镌刻着“浯洲屿颜达为考妣施此一间”的铭文。所以，赵令衿说：“斯桥之作，因众志之和，资乐输之费，一举工集，贻利千载。”这种众志成城的精神在后来安平桥重修的过程中也得以延续。安平桥中亭西侧存有两段明代题刻，分别是“安平颜哲舍桥梁壹间”“万历庚子颜哲五世孙嘉梧募缘重修中亭并修桥玖间立记”，都是民众捐资建桥和修桥的历史见证。此外，中亭西侧墙上镶嵌的清乾隆十三年（1748）《重修安平西桥碑记》中，也有“监生陈登高自修桥脚（桥墩）二座、板三孔，费银六十余两”“监生黄士善董首理银数，仝生员吴朝鹤修桥脚一座、板二孔”等相关记录。

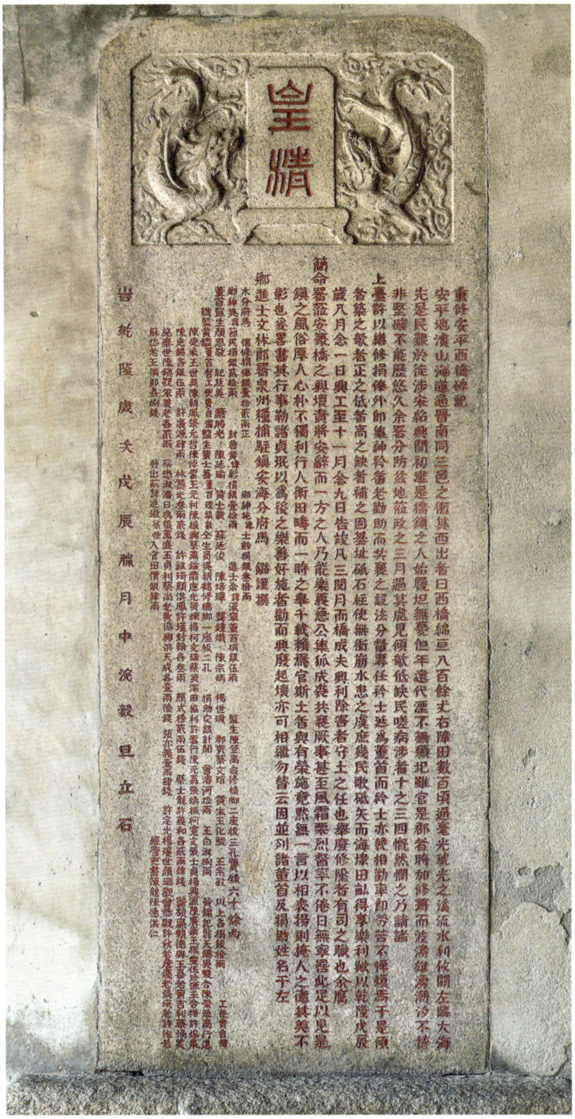

清乾隆十三年《重修安平西桥碑记》。（成冬冬 摄）
The 1748 *Inscription About the Renovation of the West Side of Anping Bridge*. (Photo by Cheng Dongdong)

In lunar November 1151, Zhao Lingjin, the newly appointed Quanzhou governor, responded to the prevailing public sentiment and appointed Huang Yi, the son of Huang Hu, and Monk Huisheng to oversee the rebuilding of Anping Bridge. Following a year of strenuous efforts, Anping Bridge was successfully completed. This achievement brought immense joy to Zhao Lingjin, who commemorated the event by inscribing a stone monument entitled *A Record of Anping Bridge in Shijing Town*. In this inscription, Zhao Lingjin provides a detailed description of the bridge, stating that it spans a length of 811 *zhang* (approximately 2.7 kilometers) and measures 1 *zhang* and 6 *chi* (approximately 5.3 meters) in width. The bridge consists of 362 water passages and is equipped with railings and shields for protection. The bridge is straight and smooth, and both the left and right sides of the bridge are identical in design. The bridge's appearance is likened to a indistinct jade road or a grand golden embankment. Its magnificence and solidity are deemed comparable to the work of supernatural beings.

It is noteworthy to mention that the construction of Anping Bridge was supported through a unique "crowdfunding" mode. Apart from those sporadic donations, contributors had the opportunity to donate towards a specific bridge pier or section, with the privilege of having their names engraved on the respective structure. A tangible example of this can be observed on the stone railing located to the west side of the middle pavilion on Anping Bridge, where an inscription reads, "This section was donated by Yan Da from Wuzhou Islet in memory of his deceased parents." Zhao Lingjin also emphasized the collaborative nature of the bridge's construction, stating that "The construction of this bridge was achieved through the collaborative efforts of the people, with funds contributed willingly, and the construction completed in one effort benefits future generations." This spirit of unity and collaboration persisted during the subsequent restoration of Anping Bridge. Inscriptions recording the identities of contributors and their beneficence made during the Ming and Qing dynasties can also be seen on the bridge, mostly to the west side the middle pavilion, which serve as historical witnesses to the donations made by the common people to build and repair the bridge.

建桥“六大功臣”

说到安平桥兴建的功臣，有六个人不能不提，即祖派、黄护、智渊、赵令衿、黄逸和惠胜。如果没有他们的贡献，可能如今我们也就见不到安平桥屹立的雄姿了。

祖派，泉州人，在开元罗汉寺落发为僧，后驻锡承天寺。祖派还是一位水利专家，绍兴六年（1136）曾受晋江县令洪元英委托，与晋江人李密、李国表和僧人体柔共同负责修建晋江湮浦埭，历时三年，殚精竭虑。事成之后，泉州知州刘子羽表奏朝廷，祖派获赐号“慈惠大师”。也正是因为祖派有修建水利工程的经验，黄护和智渊才愿意跟随他建造安平桥。兴建安平桥的消息传开，晋江、南安两地民众纷纷响应，有钱出钱，有力出力，形成一股强大的造桥力量。黄护不仅捐钱，还亲自参与监理建桥，操劳多年。可惜的是，在当时，建一座像安平桥这样的石桥，是个浩大的工程，纷繁芜杂的事宜耗尽了祖派、黄护的精力，他们竟没来得及等到桥梁竣工，便相继辞世了。

祖派和黄护的过早去世使得安平桥建设工程注定要成为一场接力赛。该桥在修建了近十四年后，仍未落成。不过这一状况在绍兴二十一年（1151）得到了彻底改变。是年，赵宋宗室赵令衿出任泉州知州，他应士民之请，与新任兴化县令黄逸、僧人惠胜再度筹集资金，续建安平桥。

泉州承天寺。（成冬冬 摄）
Chengtian Temple in Quanzhou City. (Photo by Cheng Dongdong)

The "Six Meritorious Figures" in the Construction of Anping Bridge

The six key men in the construction of Anping Bridge who cannot be overlooked are Zupai, Huang Hu, Zhiyuan, Zhao Lingjin, Huang Yi and Huisheng. Without their contributions, we might not be able to witness the majestic Anping Bridge today.

Zupai, a native of Quanzhou, was a monk at Kaiyuan Luohan (Arhat) Temple and later resided at Chengtian Temple. Zupai was also an expert in water conservancy. In 1136, he was entrusted by the county magistrate of Jinjiang, Hong Yuanying, to work with Jinjiang locals Li Mi, Li Guobiao and a monk named Tirou to build Yanpudai Dike of Jinjiang River, which took them three years of meticulous planning and efforts. After the completion of the project, Liu Ziyu, the governor of Quanzhou, reported to the imperial court, and Zupai was thus given the honorary title of "Great Master of Benevolence and Compassion". It was because of Zupai's experience in water conservancy projects that Huang Hu and Zhiyuan were willing to follow him in constructing Anping Bridge. As soon as the news of constructing Anping Bridge spread, people in Jinjiang and Nan'an responded enthusiastically, contributing money and physical labor, hence forming a powerful force. Huang Hu not only donated money but also supervised and participated in the construction of the bridge in person, working tirelessly for many years. Unfortunately, building a stone bridge like this was a massive project at that time, and the overwhelming tasks exhausted Zupai and Huang Hu. They passed away successively before the completion of the bridge.

The lamentable deaths of Zupai and Huang Hu transformed the construction of Anping Bridge into a relay race. After nearly fourteen years of construction, the bridge remained unfinished. However, this situation underwent a complete change in 1151. In that year, Zhao Lingjin, a member of the imperial family of the Southern Song Dynasty, was appointed as the governor of Quanzhou. In response to the requests of the local scholars and people, Zhao, along with Huang Yi, the newly appointed county magistrate of Xinghua County, and Monk Huisheng, once again raised funds to continue with the bridge's construction.

赵令衿一向是敢作敢当之人，靖康元年（1126）任军器少监时，就曾因直陈见解触怒皇帝而被革职。复官后，在坚持抗金主张的张浚被罢官时，他又挺身而出，疏求挽留张浚，再遭罢官。第二次复官后，赵令衿先至德安府任通判，后来才到泉州出任知州。有这么一位勇于担当的血性官员主政泉州并续建安平桥，可以说是泉州人的福气，也是安平桥的运气。

黄逸，字德后，黄护之子，南宋绍兴年间曾任兴化知县，为政“根于至诚，尤崇尚学校，建议道堂”，是位“有贤名”的好官。安平桥建造未半，祖派与黄护便相继离世，这对建桥民众的士气打击颇大。所幸经知州赵令衿援促，黄逸秉承父志，再度倡修安平桥，为安平桥的最终完工作出了不可磨灭的贡献。

有了赵令衿的主持、黄逸的倡建及监理，尚需一位“高级工程师”来负责安平桥的具体设计与建造，这项任务就落到了僧人惠胜的肩上。惠胜早在绍兴六年（1136）就已崭露头角。那一年，时任泉州知州的刘子羽策划重修州学。众所周知，古时州学乃州郡官办教育的主体，因此修建州学非同小可。刘子羽不敢大意，推选惠胜等人负责重修具体事宜。这次州学重修按左学右庙建制，增高旧基二尺余，在新址建成大成殿，殿前置东西两庑，殿东建明伦堂，殿后为议道堂。明伦堂前为东西十二斋，“御书有阁，祭器有库，祠房燕亭宾次庖廪之属，一新轮奂”。同时疏浚由东南方流经州学的南溪支流，使州学见山傍水，“江山增丽，亘古无前”。能把州学重修至“亘古无前”的地步，足见惠胜对于承建工程得心应手。正因如此，赵令衿在续建安平桥时，才会想到请惠胜出手相助。

果不其然，有了赵令衿、黄逸、惠胜等人的合力修建，安平桥于绍兴二十二年（1152）十一月告竣。安平桥建成后，“海港千帆百舸，乘风顺流，出入海门之间；渡头风樯林立，客商云集，转输货物山积，市镇之繁荣，不亚于一大邑”。险恶的海湾渡口变成坦途，与泉州内陆腹地紧密相连，四通八达，不仅为安海港运输提供便利，也吸引更多商户通过安平桥将货物运输到泉州、漳州及广州等地。

Zhao Lingjin had always been a bold and decisive person. In 1126, when he served as the deputy supervisor of Military Supplies, he was dismissed for expressing his opinions that offended the emperor. After being reinstated, when Zhang Jun, who advocated resistance against the Jin army, was dismissed from his official position, Zhao Lingjin once again stepped forward to plead for Zhang Jun's retention, only to be dismissed again. After his second reinstatement, Zhao Lingjin first served as the magistrate in De'an Prefecture before being appointed as the governor of Quanzhou. Having such a courageous and responsible official governing Quanzhou and overseeing the construction of Anping Bridge was seen as a blessing for Quanzhou people and a fortunate turn of events for the bridge's completion.

Huang Yi, the son of Huang Hu, who once held the position of magistrate of Xinghua County between 1131 and 1162, governed with sincerity and a strong focus on education. He actively advocated for the establishment of schools and lecture halls, earning a reputation as a virtuous and respected official. The construction of Anping Bridge faced a setback when both Zupai and Huang Hu passed away successively before its completion. This unfortunate turn of events demoralized the bridge-building team. Fortunately, Governor Zhao Lingjin provided crucial support and encouragement, and Huang Yi, following in his father's footsteps, took the initiative to resume the construction of Anping Bridge. His dedication and efforts played a pivotal role in ensuring the successful completion of the bridge.

With the supervision of Zhao Lingjin and the advocacy and direction of Huang Yi, the task of the specific design and construction of Anping Bridge fell on the shoulders of a "senior engineer", Monk Huisheng. Huisheng once made a name for himself in 1136 when Liu Ziyu, the governor of Quanzhou, planned to repair the state school. As is well known, the state school was the main body of official education established by states and counties in ancient China, and the construction of a state school was no small feat. Liu Ziyu did not dare to be careless, and selected Huisheng and others to be responsible for the specific matters of the repair. This repair of the state school followed the layout of a school on the left and a temple on the right, with the old foundation raised by more than two feet. Dacheng Hall was built on the current site, with wing houses on both sides in front of the hall, Minglun Hall to the east, and Yidao Hall to the rear. In front of Minglun Hall were twelve rooms on both the east and west sides, including "a library, a sacrificial utensil warehouse, a memorial temple, a guest house, a lounge pavilion, a kitchen and a granary, all renovated". At the same time, the South Creek branch flowing through the state school from the southeast was dredged, making the state school surrounded by mountains and water, "enhancing its beauty, unparalleled in history". The fact that Huisheng was able to bring the state school to such a level as "unparalleled in history" demonstrated his skills in construction projects. It was because of this that Zhao Lingjin thought of inviting Huisheng to help with the continued construction of Anping Bridge.

As expected, with the joint efforts of Zhao Lingjin, Huang Yi, Huisheng and others, Anping Bridge was completed in lunar November 1152. After the completion of Anping Bridge, it was said that "Thousands of sails and hundreds of boats in the harbor ride the wind and flow smoothly between the entrance and exit of the sea gate; masts stand tall at the ferry terminal, bringing numerous merchants and goods, and the prosperity of the town is no less than that of a large city." A once dangerous ferry at the bay was hence transformed to an easy path, which provided convenient transportation to and from the hinterland of Quanzhou in Anhai Port, stimulating increased trade and attracting merchants from Quanzhou, Zhangzhou, Guangzhou and other regions to transport goods through Anping Bridge.

横卧风波里。（陈英杰 摄）
Anping Bridge spanning the bay. (Photo by Chen Yingjie)

寻找东洋桥远去的身影

绍兴二十二年（1152）十二月，沉浸在喜悦之中的安海人决定趁热打铁，恳请赵令衿在东洋渡口再建造一座桥梁，连接安海港与晋江东南部的交通网络。恰巧安海人史清于前一年考中进士，被任命为漳州司户参军，尚未就任，愿意承担督造东洋桥的重任。因为有了之前建造安平桥的实践经验，众人又乐意捐资襄助，加上赵令衿极力促成，仅仅用了不到半年的时间，东洋桥就竣工了。东洋桥全长六百六十余丈，广一丈二尺，疏水道二百四十二间。赵令衿在《东桥碑记》中欣喜地写道：“一日肇兴，千古用壮。坦然砥平，四民帖泰。向之临深履危者，今则阔步徐行，无复留碍。”东洋桥建成之后，与安平桥交相辉映，“双桥跨海”成为“安平八景”之一，呈现出“海畔双桥芳草连，东西形胜锁长川”的壮丽景观。

元至正年间，因当地围海筑堤，东洋桥变成陆上桥。明嘉靖三十六年（1557），倭寇袭扰安海港，晋江县令卢仲佃命人拆卸东洋桥石材，用于建造安平城，东洋桥名存实亡。清康熙五十一年（1712），晋江富商施韬捐资重建东洋桥，至清乾隆年间，东洋桥又遭废弃。清道光元年（1821），晋江东石商人周仕泰倡议重建东洋桥，并以一人之力，率先修造176坎桥梁。在随后的十年间，安海港周边的商贾延续“众筹”建桥的传统，由蔡时绍、蔡笃志、黄信观、周兰观、萧元迪、黄庇观、陈尊观、林世忠、叶庆观等人捐资，共建造149坎桥梁。至道光十一年（1831），东洋桥基本恢复原貌。只可惜，随着安海港航运的衰退和东洋渡周边不断筑堤围垦，加之洪水侵袭，东洋桥的残损越来越严重。1966年，乡民拆掉东洋桥石料，用于修筑水利工程，昔日宏伟壮观的东洋桥仅存9座桥墩，残长54米。

今天的东洋桥仅剩残躯，每当落日的余晖映照在斑驳的桥板上，水草在晚风中摇曳，沙沙作响，似乎仍在述说着东洋桥历经沧桑的前世与今生。

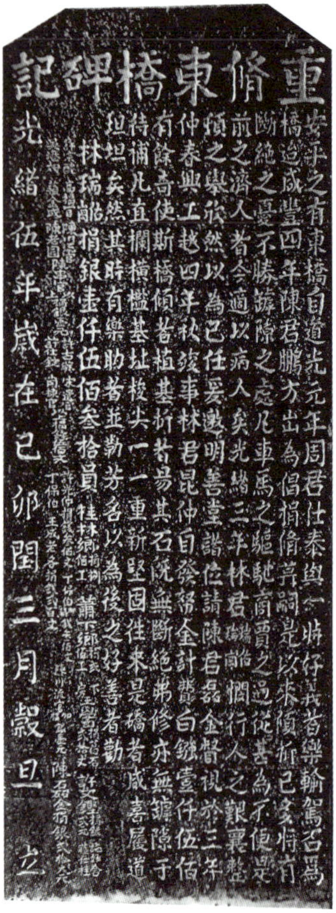

清光绪《重修东桥碑记》拓片。（李国宏 供图）

The rubbing of *Inscription About the Reconstruction of Dongqiao Bridge* of the Qing Dynasty. (Courtesy of Li Guohong)

Searching After the Fading Image of Dongyang Bridge

In lunar December 1152, the people of Anhai, immersed in joy, decided to strike while the iron was hot and earnestly requested Zhao Lingjin to build another bridge at Dongyang Ferry, connecting Anhai Port with the transportation network in the southeastern part of Jinjiang. Coincidentally, Shi Qing, a native of Anhai, had just passed the imperial examination in 1151 and was appointed as the secretary of census register in the Zhangzhou division. He had not yet taken office but was willing to take on the important task of overseeing the construction of Dongyang Bridge. Thanks to the previous experience in building Anping Bridge and the willingness of the people to donate funds, along with Zhao Lingjin's efforts, Dongyang Bridge was completed in less than half a year. The bridge was over 660 *zhang* (approximately 2.2 kilometers) in length, 1 *zhang* and 2 *chi* (approximately 4 meters) in width, with 242 waterways. In his *Inscription About Dongqiao Bridge*, Zhao Lingjin joyfully wrote, "It was started in one day and will be used for eternity. On such a smooth passaway, the four classes of people, namely, scholars, farmers, artisans and merchants, are at peace and harmony. Those who previously faced danger and difficulty now walk freely without obstacles." After the completion of Dongyang Bridge, it complemented Anping Bridge, and the "Two Bridges Across the Sea" became one of the "Eight Scenic Spots of Anping", presenting a magnificent landscape of "a connection between the two bridges by the sea, locking the long river in the east and west".

Between 1341 and 1368, due to the construction of dikes around the sea, Dongyang Bridge became a land bridge. In 1557, pirates attacked and disturbed the port of Anhai. Lu Zhongdian, the magistrate of Jinjiang County, ordered people to dismantle the stone materials of Dongyang Bridge and use them to construct Anping City. Dongyang Bridge existed in name only. In 1712, a wealthy merchant named Shi Tao from Jinjiang funded the reconstruction of Dongyang Bridge. However, between 1736 and 1795, Dongyang Bridge was abandoned once again. In 1821, Zhou Shitai, a businessman from Dongshi in Jinjiang, proposed the reconstruction of Dongyang Bridge. With his own efforts, he took the lead in building 176 sections. In the following decade, the merchants and traders around Anhai Port continued to uphold the tradition of "crowdfunding". Donations were made by individuals such as Cai Shishao, Cai Duzhi, Huang Xinguan, Zhou Languan, Xiao Yuandi, Huang Biguan, Chen Zunguan, Lin Shizhong, Ye Qingguan, etc., resulting in the construction of 149 sections. By 1831, Dongyang Bridge was largely restored to its original appearance. Unfortunately, with the decline of shipping in Anhai Port and the continuous construction of seawalls and reclamation in the surrounding area, coupled with flooding, Dongyang Bridge suffered further damage. In 1966, local residents dismantled the bridge's stones and used them to build water conservancy projects. Only 9 bridge piers of the once magnificent Dongyang Bridge remained, with a survival length of 54 meters.

Today, Dongyang Bridge stands only as a remnant. When the setting sun's afterglow shines on the mottled bridge deck, the water plants sway and rustle in the evening breeze, as if they still recount the past and present of Dongyang Bridge.

石井镇横空出世

安平桥和东洋桥见证了宋代安海作为港口市镇的繁荣。安海港位于泉州围头湾内，水域宽广，晋江东石澳和南安石井澳东西对峙，控扼海门，船舶进入后，可享天然的避风良港。泉州市舶司设立之后，在安海港设石井津，定期派遣榷税官到此征收税费。据《安平志》记载："安海于宋全盛时，东有新市，西有旧市……盖四方射利者所必趋，随处成交，惟直街为最盛。"新市、旧市隔着东洋渡，船舶驶入东洋渡后，停靠在新市附近的码头，"与居人互市"。为了便利新市与旧市之间的交通往来，东洋桥建成之前，乡民曾在东洋渡修建内市桥、佳板桥和甘棠桥三座小型跨港石桥。南宋建炎四年（1130），为了协调新市、旧市两处征税点的关系，朝廷下令在此设立石井镇（今安海镇），正式委派监镇官处理政务。安海成为宋代泉州湾沿海市集中唯一设立镇级建制的地方。

The Emergence of Shijing Town

Anping Bridge and Dongyang Bridge witnessed the prosperity of Anhai as a port town during the Song Dynasty. Anhai Port is located in Weitou Bay of Quanzhou, with a wide water area, whereas Dongshi Inlet of Jinjiang and Shijing Inlet of Nan'an face each other from east to west, controlling the entrance to the sea. Once entering the port, ships can enjoy a natural sheltered harbor. After the establishment of Quanzhou Maritime Trade Office, a tax collection station called Shijing Post was set up in Anhai Port, and tax officials were regularly dispatched there to collect taxes and fees. According to *Annals of Anping*, during the heyday of the Song Dynasty, Anhai had a new market in the east and an old one in the west... Merchants from all directions flocked there, and transactions were conducted everywhere, with the main street being the most prosperous. The new market and old market were separated by Dongyang Ferry. After ships sailed through Dongyang Ferry, they would dock near the new market's wharf and engage in trade with local residents. Prior to the construction of Dongyang Bridge, the local villagers had built three small stone bridges, namely Neishi Bridge, Jiaban Bridge and Gantang Bridge, in Dongyang Ferry to improve transportation between the new market and the old one. In 1130, the court ordered the establishment of Shijing Town (now Anhai Town) and officially appointed a supervisor to handle administrative affairs so as to coordinate the relation between the two tax offices of the new market and the old one. Anhai became the only place among Quanzhou Bay's coastal markets to possess an officially established town-level administration during the Song Dynasty.

今日安海。（陈英杰 摄）
Anhai today. (Photo by Chen Yingjie)

绍兴初年，朱松（朱熹之父）被举荐担任石井镇第一任监镇官，友人苏籀赋诗以赠，并期许他“衣被卉裳殊俗惯，解捐犊佩猾商驯”。“殊俗”与“猾商”反映出当时安海港海外贸易繁荣，商业活动频繁，社会风俗多元，各种利益纠葛错综复杂。所以，苏籀以“解捐犊佩”指代汉代名宦龚遂重本惜农的典故，鼓励朱松注重教化、有所作为。

朱松素怀高节大志，其诗文汪洋宏放、天然秀发。监镇石井对他来说可谓牛刀小试，举重若轻。闲暇之余，他还设立鳌头精舍，招录安海优秀学子，教以义理之学。种下希望就会有所收获。二十多年后，朱熹任泉州府同安县主簿，多次经临安海，寻访父亲朱松的遗迹旧事，“见其老幼义理详悉，遂与论说”。因此，泉州府文庙明伦堂曾悬挂一副楹联：“圣域津梁，理学渊源开石井；海滨邹鲁，诗书弦诵遍桐城。”以此纪念安海“二朱过化”这段学林佳话。南宋嘉定四年（1211），石井镇官游绛采纳安海民众建议，在泉州太守邹应龙的支持下，依照州郡学宫的建制，在石井镇公廨西侧建造石井书院，由时任泉州通判朱在（朱熹之子）负责具体事宜。从此，“石井书香”被列为“安平八景”之一。

明代安平镇舆图中绘有朱文公祠（石井书院）。（李国宏 供图）
The map of Anping County in the Ming Dynasty features Zhu Wengong Shrine (Shijing Academy) . (Courtesy of Li Guohong)

Between 1131 and 1134, Zhu Song (father of Zhu Xi) was recommended to serve as the first supervisor of Shijing Town. His friend, Su Zhou, composed a poem to congratulate him. Su Zhou also expressed his hope that Zhu Song would habituate himself to the distinct customs here, reject bribes and uphold justice like the virtuous official Gong Sui of the Han Dynasty (206 B.C.—220 A.D.), and subdue the cunning merchants. The phrases "distinct customs" and "cunning merchants" indicate that during that time, overseas trade in Anhai Port was prosperous, with frequent commercial activities and diverse social customs. There were various complex interests and conflicts. Therefore, Su Zhou used the reference to the story of Gong Sui, a virtuous official who valued agriculture, to encourage Zhu Song to focus on education and make a difference in his new role.

Zhu Song had great ambitions and a talent for literature. Serving as the supervisor of Shijing was merely a small test for him, as he was able to handle the complicated matters with ease. In his spare time, he established Aotou Academy to recruit outstanding students from Anhai and taught them Confucian classics argumentation. There will be harvest when seed is planted. Over twenty years later, Zhu Xi became the principal clerk of Tong'an County in Quanzhou Prefecture. He frequently visited Anhai to search for traces and stories of his father, Zhu Song. He found that the young and old in Anhai were well-versed in Confucian classics, so he engaged in discussions with them. As a result, Minglun Hall in Quanzhou Confucian Temple and School once hung a couplet, which commemorated the story of the "two Zhus' influence in edification" in Anhai. In 1211, You Jiang, the magistrate of Shijing Town, adopted the suggestions of the people of Anhai and with the support from Zou Yinglong, the prefect of Quanzhou, built Shijing Academy on the west side of the government office in Shijing, following the model of the county school. Zhu Xi's son Zhu Zai, who was serving as the deputy prefect of Quanzhou at the time, was responsible for the specific matters. Since then, the "literary atmosphere of Shijing" has been listed as one of the "Eight Attractions in Anping".

睡木沉基新技术的运用

建造安平桥的过程中，在洛阳桥筏形基础的启发下，南宋泉州工匠又创造出一项新型桥基建造技艺——睡木沉基。所谓睡木沉基，是在潮落水枯时，对墩基区域的泥沙进行平整，然后将杉木平列，分层交叉，固定在筑墩处，再在其上垒筑墩石；随着墩石的逐层增高，其分量亦不断加重，木基在重压下渐渐沉陷于泥沙之中，直到江底承重层，保证桥墩的稳固。

1980 年 11 月至 12 月，在对安平桥桥墩基础进行考古发掘时，发现了两项与睡木沉基相关的技术创新。一是睡木沉基与桩基础相结合的筑基方法。如呈船形的 185 号墩，墩底为烂海泥，墩也较小，发掘至墩底时发现 5 根杉木，间隔平行卧于海泥之上，每根杉木的两端分别架于打入海泥的桩木之上，作为桩基础。在靠南北两侧的睡木外侧，又加了两根木桩，可能是为了防止外侧睡木滚出墩外。墩的条石与睡木交叉叠砌，这种筑基法在安平桥船形墩和半船形墩中较为典型。

安平桥筏形基础示意图。（李国宏 供图）
The illustration of a raft-shaped foundation of Anping Bridge. (Courtesy of Li Guohong)

The Application of a New Technique: Sunk Foundations Made with Wooden Planks

Inspired by the raft foundation of Luoyang Bridge, craftsmen in Quanzhou of the Southern Song Dynasty created a new technique for bridge foundation construction called the "sunk foundation made with wooden planks". This technique involves smoothing the sediment in the pier foundation area during low tide, then fixing layers of crisscrossed wooden planks at the pier location. Stone piers were then built on top of the wooden planks. As the pier stones were gradually increased, their weight also increased, and the wooden planks gradually sunk into the sediment under heavy pressure until reaching the load-bearing layer at the riverbed, ensuring the stability of the bridge piers.

From November to December in 1980, during the archaeological excavation of the pier foundation of Anping Bridge, two technological innovations related to the use of sunk wooden foundations were discovered. One is the combination of sunk wooden foundations and pile foundations. For example, in the boat-shaped pier No. 185, the bottom of the pier was filled with soft mud, and the pier was relatively small. During the excavation, five Chinese fir planks were found lying parallel on top of the mud, with each end supported by wooden piles driven into the mud, serving as the pile foundation. Two additional wooden piles were added on the northern and southern sides of the wooden planks, possibly to prevent them from rolling out of the pier. The stones of the pier were interlaid with the wooden planks, which was a typical foundation construction method for the boat-shaped and semi-boat-shaped piers of Anping Bridge.

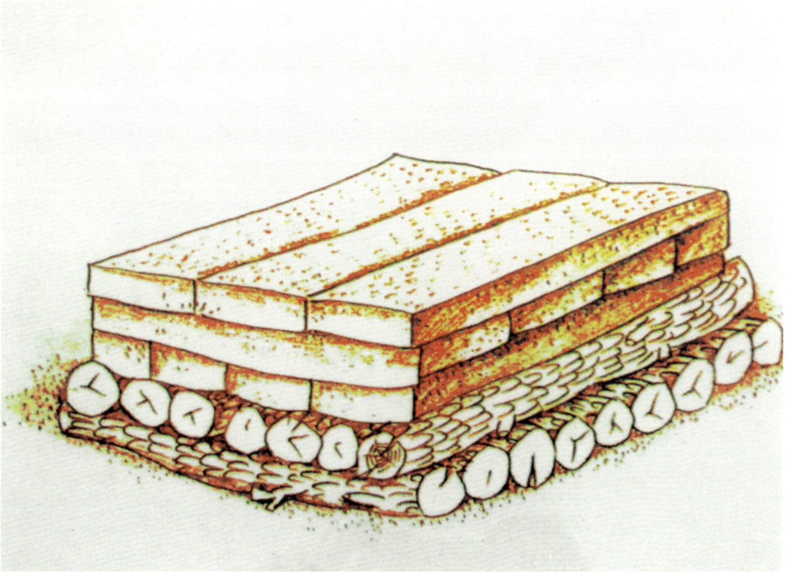

睡木沉基法示意图。（李国宏 供图）

The illustration of a sunk foundation made with wooden planks. (Courtesy of Li Guohong)

二是睡木沉基与沙基相结合的筑基方法。如呈船形的 312 号墩和呈半船形的 39 号墩，前者墩底层用直径 20 多厘米的杉木编成木排，作为墩基，墩石垒于基上；后者筑基方法与前者相似，但睡木长短不一，长出来的部分露在船形墩外，达 22 至 60 厘米。上述两处墩底海泥中均掺有粗沙、石片、石砾，显然是为了加大烂泥的摩擦系数，延缓下沉速度。

安平桥桥墩的施工技术也有新的突破，主要体现在桥墩砌法的科学性与桥墩形制的多样性。安平桥的墩台是用整块大石一层纵一层横垒置而成，不用人工胶凝材料嵌结，构造简单，施工便捷，整体性好，压重大，使浅基不易漂动和松散，还能有效应对江水冲蚀和浪潮拍击，更加坚固耐用。随着造桥经验的不断积累，南宋的桥工们已经能够根据不同桥梁的不同部位、不同需要建造不同形式的桥墩。如在安平桥的 362 座桥墩中，就采用了长方形、双边船形和单边船形 3 种不同的形制。在水流主干道上采用双边船形桥墩，可以有效分流，缓解来自江河与大海的水势，同时便于港道畅通；在滩涂或缓水区多采用单边船形与长方形桥墩，可以省工省料，加快建桥速度。这种因地制宜设计多种桥墩的理念，说明宋代泉州造桥工匠们对水文特征和桥梁功能的认识达到了相当高的水平。

安平桥墩台一横一纵的垒砌方式。（陈英杰 摄）
The pier of Anping Bridge built by stacking whole large stones in layers vertically and horizontally. (Photo by Chen Yingjie)

The second innovation is the combination of sunk wooden foundations and sand foundations. Take the boat-shaped pier No. 312 and the semi-boat-shaped pier No. 39 for example. For the former, a layer of wooden planks with a diameter of over 20 centimeters was used as the foundation, with the stones of the pier stacked on top. The construction method of the latter was similar to the former, but the lengths of the wooden planks varied, with the protruding parts exposed outside the boat-shaped pier ranging from 22 to 60 centimeters. In both cases, the mud at the bottom of the pier was mixed with coarse sand, stones and gravel, clearly to increase the friction coefficient of the soft mud and slow down the sinking speed.

There were also new breakthroughs in the construction technology of the piers of Anping Bridge, mainly reflected in the scientific method of construction and the diversity of their shapes. The piers of Anping Bridge were built by stacking whole large stones in layers vertically and horizontally, without the use of artificial cementitious materials for bonding. With this simple structure, convenient construction and good overall integrity, they could withstand heavy loads, preventing the shallow foundations from easily floating and loosening. They could also effectively resist water erosion and wave impact, making themselves more sturdy and durable. With the continuous accumulation of bridge construction experience, the bridge builders of the Southern Song Dynasty were able to construct different forms of bridge piers according to the different parts and needs of different bridges. For example, among the 362 bridge piers of Anping Bridge, three different pier shapes were used: rectangular, double-sided boat-shaped and single-sided boat-shaped. On the main waterway, double-sided boat-shaped piers were used to effectively divert the water flow from rivers and the sea, while facilitating the smooth navigation in the harbor. Single-sided boat-shaped and rectangular piers were often used in tidal flats or slow water areas to save labor, materials and accelerate the construction speed. This concept of designing multiple types of piers according to local conditions demonstrates that the bridge builders of the Song Dynasty in Quanzhou had a considerable understanding of hydrological characteristics and bridge function.

宋元中国建设的“基建狂魔”

据《八闽通志》记载，宋代泉州地区建造大中型桥梁共138座。其中，晋江区域内，集中在南宋绍兴年间建造的桥梁就有安平桥、东洋桥、石笋桥、普利大通桥、玉澜桥、苏埭桥、建隆桥、梅溪桥、古陵桥、长溪桥、适南桥等。玉澜桥由僧人仁惠修建，长达千余丈，横跨石狮玉澜浦，成为石湖港从陆路通往泉州城的交通枢纽。苏埭桥由僧人守徽建造于绍兴二十四年（1154），跨越晋江九十九溪，“长二千四百余丈，以通泥淖难行处”，解决了磁灶窑产品的运销问题。

玉澜桥和苏埭桥的长度都超过安平桥，如果没有足够的资金和先进的技术，是不可能完成如此宏大的桥梁建筑工程的。说起财力，因繁盛的海外贸易对泉州贡献颇大，朝廷也常对海外诸国入贡使臣给予奖励性的特赐。例如，绍兴六年（1136）八月二十三日，泉州市舶司提举奏请：“大食蕃国蒲罗辛造船一只，搬载乳香投泉州市舶，计抽解价钱三十万贯，委是勤劳，理当优异。”宋高宗于是下诏：“蒲罗辛特补承信郎，仍赐公服、履笏，仍开谕以朝廷存恤远人，优异推赏之意。候回本国，令说喻蕃商广行搬贩乳香前来。如数目增多，依次推恩。”同年十二月十三日，在泉州市舶司提举的又一次奏请下，泉州纲首蔡景芳因能招诱舶舟、抽解货物，自南宋建炎元年（1127）至绍兴四年（1134），收净利钱九十八万贯，按推恩例，“特予补承信郎”。朝廷对泉州“纳税大户”的表彰，提高了中外客商的社会地位，自然也调动了他们经营贸易的积极性，从而为泉州港带来源源不断的经济收入。

The Boom of Bridge Construction in Song-Yuan China

According to *A General Gazetteer of Fujian*, during the Song Dynasty, a total of 138 large and medium-sized bridges were built in the Quanzhou area. In its Jinjiang region alone, quite a number of bridges were built between 1131 and 1162 during the Southern Song Dynasty, including Anping Bridge, Dongyang Bridge, Shisun Bridge, Puli Datong Bridge, Yulan Bridge, Sudai Bridge, Jianlong Bridge, Meixi Bridge, Guling Bridge, Changxi Bridge and Shinan Bridge. Yulan Bridge, built by Monk Renhui, spanned over 1,000 *zhang* (approximately 3.3 kilometers) and crossed Yulan Bay in Shishi, becoming a transportation hub connecting Shihu Harbor and Quanzhou by land. Sudai Bridge, built by Monk Shouhui in 1154, spanned across Jinjiang Ninety-Nine Creek, "stretching over 2,400 *zhang* (approximately 8 kilometers) to pass through the muddy and unaccessible areas", providing a solution to the transportation and distribution problems of Cizao Kilns products.

Both Yulan Bridge and Sudai Bridge are larger than Anping Bridge. It would be impossible to complete such grand bridge construction projects without sufficient funds and advanced technology. Speaking of financial resources, since the prosperity of overseas trade had made significant contributions to Quanzhou, the court often rewarded envoys from foreign countries with awards. For example, on lunar August 23, 1136, the Maritime Trade Office submitted a request: "A ship built by Pu Luoxin from the Arab Empire has arrived in Quanzhou. It is loaded with frankincense and the estimated value is 300,000 *guan* (a currency unit in ancient China). His laborious efforts deserve recognition." Emperor Gaozong of the Southern Song Dynasty issued a decree, stating, "Pu Luoxin is appointed as a special 52nd-rank officer and is awarded official robes and accessories. This is to show the imperial court's care for foreigners and recognition of their outstanding contributions. When returning to their home countries, they should explain to the foreign merchants and encourage them to engage in the trade of transporting and selling frankincense. If the quantity increases, rewards will be given accordingly." On lunar December 13 of the same year, at another request was made by the Maritime Trade Office, Cai Jingfang, the chief of Quanzhou's maritime trade, was also awarded the title of 52nd-rank officer for his ability to attract foreign ships and collect goods, resulting in a net profit of 980,000 *guan* between 1127 and 1134. The recognition from the imperial court to Quanzhou's "major taxpayers" elevated the social status of both domestic and foreign merchants and naturally motivated their active participation in trade, thus bringing a continuous economic income to Quanzhou Port.

在泉州桥梁建筑史上，僧侣是一个不可或缺的特殊群体，清代乾隆版《泉州府志》就记载了 41 位僧侣桥梁建筑师的故事。除丰富的造桥经验和普度众生的功德之心外，僧侣建筑师们善于继承和勇于创新的科学精神也是推动宋元泉州造桥事业蓬勃发展的重要因素。例如，北宋皇祐年间，法超在晋江深沪湾建悲济桥，开创泉州僧侣筹资建造跨海桥梁的先河。北宋元符年间，为了改善石湖港、蚶江港与泉州城之间的陆路交通条件，怀应首创石路与石桥相结合的方法，“砌石为路，自北而南二十里”，中间建造前埭、林湾、高港三座桥梁，桥上架石为亭。

宋代泉州僧侣造桥大师除了义波、宗善、祖派、惠胜、道询等人之外，注重技术传承与创新的代表人物还有了性与守净。了性，俗姓黄，泉州安溪人，南宋淳熙年间重修开元寺镇国、仁寿两座木塔，积累了丰富的建筑经验。从南宋乾道八年（1172）至开禧三年（1207），了性修建了晋江县安济桥、龟山桥，安溪县双济桥、龙津桥和德化县化龙桥。

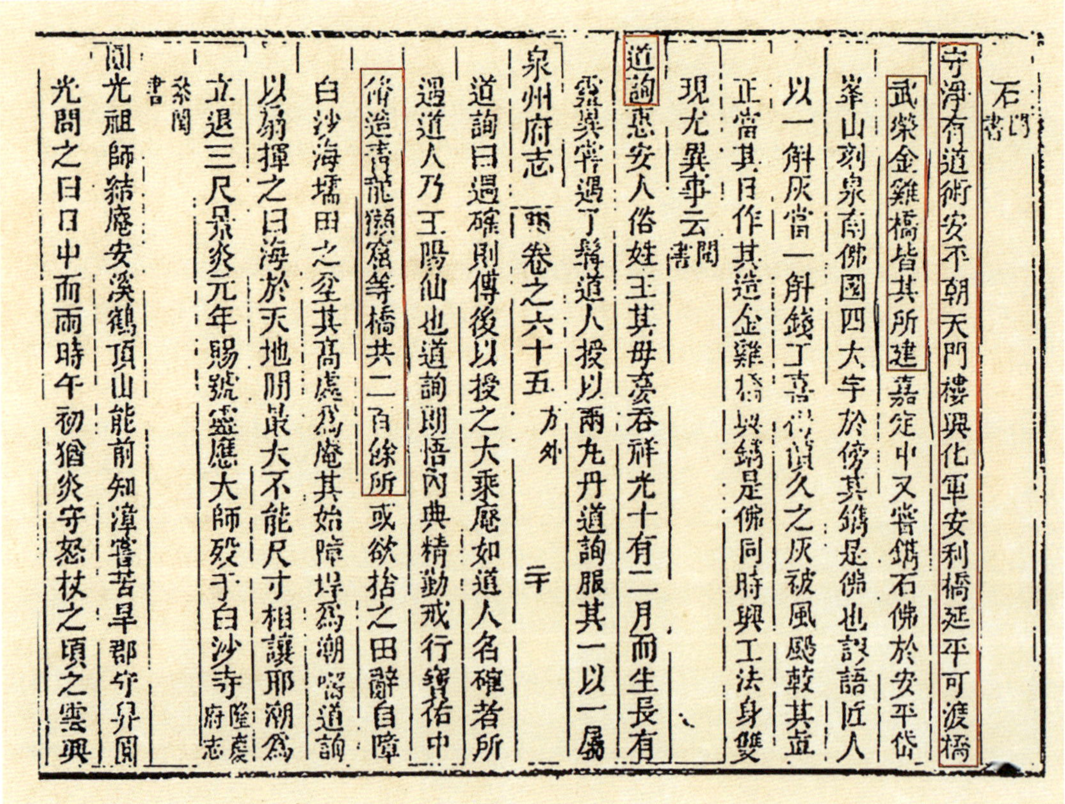
石 門書
守淨有道術安不朝天門樓興化軍安利橋延平可渡橋
武榮金雞橋皆其所建嘉定中又嘗鐫石佛於安平岱
峯山刻泉南佛國四大字於傍其鐫是佛也設語匠人
以一斛灰當一斛錢工喜得賞久之灰被風颺較其盈
正當其日作其造金雞橋與鐫是佛同時興工法身雙
現尤異事云 閩書
道詢惠安人俗姓王其母夢吞祥光十有二月而生長有
殊異嘗遇了翁道人授以兩丸丹道詢服其一以一屬
泉州府志 乾隆 卷之六十五 方外 三
道詢曰遇碌則傳後以授之大乘慶如道人名碌者所
遇道人乃王陽仙也道詢頓悟內典精勤戒行皇祐中
偕道者能獺窟等橋共二百餘所或欲捨之田辭自障
白沙海壖田之半其高處為庵其始障埕為潮嚙道詢
以扇揮之曰海於天地間最大不能尺寸相讓耶潮為
立退三尺景炎元年賜號盛應大師殁于白沙寺 隆慶府志
閩書
圓光祖師結庵安溪鶴頂山能前知漳嘗苦旱郡守昇圓
光問之曰日中而雨時午初猶炎守怒杖之頂之雲興

清代乾隆版《泉州府志》中关于宋代僧人守净、道询建造桥梁的记载。（李国宏 供图）
The record about monks Shoujing and Daoxun's building bridges in the Qianlong edition of *Local Chronicles of Quanzhou Prefecture*. (Courtesy of Li Guohong)

In the history of bridge construction in Quanzhou, monks are an indispensable group. The Qianlong edition of *Local Chronicles of Quanzhou Prefecture* records the stories of 41 monks engaging in bridge construction. In addition to their rich experience in bridge construction and their dedication to benefiting all beings, these monk architects' readiness in inheriting and courageous spirit of innovation are also important factors in promoting the flourishing development of bridge construction in Song and Yuan dynasties in Quanzhou. For example, between 1049 and 1054 during the Northern Song Dynasty, Fachao built Beiji Bridge in Shenhu Bay of Jinjiang, pioneering the fundraising and construction of sea-crossing bridges by monks in Quanzhou. Between 1098 and 1100, Huaiying first combined stone roads with stone bridges to improve the land transportation that connected Shihu Port and Hanjiang Port with Quanzhou City. Three bridges named Qiandai, Linwan and Gaogang were built with stone pavilions on top.

In addition to Yibo, Zongshan, Zupai, Huisheng and Daoxun, who were renowned bridge builders in Quanzhou during the Song Dynasty, there were also two other notable figures who emphasized on the inheriting and innovation of bridge-building techniques: Liaoxing and Shoujing. Liaoxing was from Anxi, Quanzhou. Between 1179 and 1189, he rebuilt Zhenguo and Renshou wooden pagodas in Kaiyuan Temple, accumulating rich experience in architecture. From 1172 to 1207, Liaoxing constructed Anji Bridge and Guishan Bridge in Jinjiang County, Shuangji Bridge and Longjin Bridge in Anxi County, and Hualong Bridge in Dehua County.

守净，俗姓翁，泉州晋江人，淳熙十三年（1186）追随了性修造开元寺镇国塔，逐渐成长为建筑大师，先后建造了资圣僧伽塔、安平朝天门楼、晋江南天寺石佛。他主持兴建了南安县金鸡桥、龙济桥，并将泉州先进的造桥技术传入莆田和南平地区，建造了仙游县安利桥、石马桥以及南平县可渡桥。了性师徒二人除广泛采用睡木沉基、船型桥墩、墩上叠涩等传统桥梁建筑施工技术外，还在桥梁的形制上有所创新，独具匠心地创造出梁上架屋的建桥形式。如了性在建造安溪县龙津桥时，“上覆以屋，凡四十三间”。这种形制的桥梁既可供行人歇脚、避雨，又增加了桥梁结构的稳定性，还使桥梁与周围的山水景观完美融合，集实用性、科学性和艺术性于一体。

今日安溪龙津大桥。（成冬冬 摄）
The present Longjin Bridge in Anxi County. (Photo by Cheng Dongdong)

Shoujing was from Jinjiang, Quanzhou. In 1186, he followed Liaoxing in the construction of Zhenguo Pagoda in Kaiyuan Temple and gradually became a master builder. He subsequently built Zisheng Sangha Pagoda, Anping Chaotianmen Gate Tower and the stone Buddha in Jinjiang Nantian Temple. He supervised the construction of Jinji Bridge and Longji Bridge in Nan'an County, and introduced the advanced bridge-building techniques from Quanzhou to Putian and Nanping counties, where he built Anli Bridge and Shima Bridge in Xianyou, as well as Kedu Bridge in Nanping. In addition to widely adopting traditional bridge construction techniques such as sunk foundations made with wooden planks, boat-shaped piers and corbelling, Liaoxing and Shoujing also innovated in the design of bridges. They created the unique bridge-building form of placing houses on beams. For example, when Liaoxing built Longjin Bridge in Anxi County, "The upper part was covered with houses, with a total of forty-three rooms." This design of bridge not only provided a resting place and shelter from rain for pedestrians but also increased the stability of the bridge structure. It also perfectly integrated the bridge with the surrounding landscape, combining practicality, scientific principles and artistry.

前身为安利桥的今仙游金凤桥。（中共莆田市委宣传部 供图）
Xianyou County's Jinfeng Bridge, its predecessor being Anli Bridge. (Courtesy of the Publicity Department of the CPC Putian Municipal Committee)

元代泉州桥梁建筑大师首推高僧法助。据《八闽通志》记载，元大德年间，法助主持建造的桥梁就有晋江县适南桥、陈翁桥，南安县梯云桥、卢溪桥、从龙桥、弥寿桥、潘坑桥等12座。元至正年间，法助又建造了晋江县下辇桥，桥孔共有620间，中亭两侧配置4座石塔，雄伟壮观，跻身于宋元泉州“十大名桥”之列。在此期间，法助还建造了晋江县御亭头桥，南安县竹溪桥、象头桥，惠安县大柘海径桥、马山桥等5座桥梁。

宋元时期，泉州桥梁建筑涉及区域之广、建造规模之大、施工技术之精、耗费资金之巨，在世界桥梁建筑史上堪称一绝。在这里，桥梁建筑师的聪明才智得到充分发挥，每一座桥梁都是一道亮丽的风景线，都是理性主义与浪漫主义的完美结合。从此岸到彼岸，无论走多远，泉州的桥总有一份长在骨子里的信仰和牵挂，虽渐行渐远，却又难分难舍。

晋江县下辇桥老照片。（泉州海外交通史博物馆 供图）
An old photo of Xianian Bridge in Jinjiang County. (Courtesy of Quanzhou Maritime Museum)

In the Yuan Dynasty, the master of bridge construction in Quanzhou was primarily the eminent monk Fazhu. According to *A General Gazetteer of Fujian*, between 1297 and 1307, Fazhu supervised the construction of 12 bridges, including Shinan Bridge and Chenweng Bridge in Jinjiang County, Tiyun Bridge, Luxi Bridge, Conglong Bridge, Mishou Bridge and Pankeng Bridge in Nan'an County. Between 1341 and 1368, Fazhu built Xianian Bridge in Jinjiang County, which had a total of 620 arches and was adorned with four stone pagodas on both sides of the central pavilion, making it magnificent and grand. It was listed among the "Ten Famous Bridges" in Song-Yuan Quanzhou. During this period, Fazhu also constructed Yutingtou Bridge in Jinjiang County, Zhuxi Bridge and Xiangtou Bridge in Nan'an County, and Dazhe Haijing Bridge and Mashan Bridge in Hui'an County.

During the Song and Yuan dynasties, bridge construction in Quanzhou was unparalleled in terms of the wide coverage, large scale, advanced construction techniques and enormous financial investment, making it matchless in the history of bridge construction worldwide. The ingenious talents of bridge architects were fully displayed, and each bridge became a beautiful landscape and a perfect combination of rationalism and romanticism. From one bank to the other, no matter how far in span, there is always a deep-rooted belief and concern embedded in the bridges of Quanzhou. Though time passes and distance grows, it is difficult to part with the bridges that hold such significance.

郑芝龙与安平桥

明成化八年（1472），泉州市舶司驻地迁往福州，泉州港从此失去官方贸易港的地位。泉州海商被迫转移到安海、月港等远离官府控制的走私港，冒着巨大风险继续他们的航行。面对海洋争霸时代带来的大变局，大明王朝温文尔雅地作茧自缚，西方海上列强咄咄逼人地张网以待。在接下来的海上角逐中，命运的天平已经悄然倾斜，谁能力挽狂澜？没想到居然是那个被贴上“海盗”标签的郑芝龙，他大声喊出“无海则无家”的响亮口号，建立以安海港为基地的“海上商业王国”，展示“依水作营，鼓声偕潮声而夜发”的实力，实现“临渊布阵，旌影合帆影以星驰”的愿景。

尽管姗姗来迟，郑芝龙终究站在了风口浪尖，捍卫泉州海商久违的尊严。明崇祯元年（1628），在泉州士绅的斡旋下，郑芝龙接受招安，进驻厦门。闯荡江湖多年的郑芝龙率领一支船坚炮利的舰队，衣锦还乡。他不仅取得了厦门港的控制权，也着手以安海港为基地，建立属于自己的王国。

Zheng Zhilong and Anping Bridge

In 1472, the Maritime Trade Office moved its headquarters to Fuzhou, and Quanzhou Port lost its status as an official trading port. Quanzhou maritime merchants were forced to move to smuggling ports such as Anhai and Yuegang, which were far from government control, and continued their voyages at great risk. Facing the great changes brought by the era of maritime hegemony, the Ming Dynasty bound itself in a cocoon with its gentle and civilized approach, while Western maritime powers aggressively laid their traps. In the ensuing maritime competition, the balance of fate had quietly tilted, and who might turn the tide? Unexpectedly, it turned out to be Zheng Zhilong, the man labeled as a "pirate", who loudly shouted out the resounding slogan, "No sea, no home." He established a "maritime commercial kingdom" based in Anhai Port, showcasing the strength of "building camps by the water, setting sail at night with the sound of drums and tides", and realized the vision of "deploying troops on the sea, merging the shadows of banners and sails and speeding like stars".

Despite arriving late, Zheng Zhilong ultimately stood at the forefront, defending the long-lost dignity of Quanzhou's maritime merchants. In 1628, under the mediation of Quanzhou gentry, Zheng Zhilong accepted the offer of amnesty and stationed himself in Xiamen. After years of wandering, Zheng Zhilong led a fleet of powerful and well-armed ships, returning in glory. He not only gained control of Xiamen Port but also started to establish his own kingdom based in Anhai Port.

郑芝龙画像。（李国宏 供图）
The portrait of Zhen Zhilong. (Courtesy of Li Guohong)

《雷希特伦航海日记（1628—1632）》收录了一幅荷兰人绘制的厦门湾海图，在这幅海图中，“安海大城”的图标特别引人注目，甚至还准确地绘有安海港的标志性建筑——安平桥。比利时传教士鲁日满也证实郑芝龙曾在安海港修筑城堡：“为了安全和秘密装卸运载珍奇和贵重商品的船只，他下令修造欧洲样式的高大建筑物，不妨称之为堡垒，一半筑在沙滩上，一半在海里，其大门内停靠华丽的船，好像一个神秘的港口。”

崇祯十年（1637），郑芝龙捐资重修开元寺大雄宝殿。见多识广的他突发奇想，竟然将来自一座废弃印度教寺院的须弥座雕塑和一对雕刻着印度教神话故事图案的大石柱迁移到开元寺，分别装配在大雄宝殿的月台和后廊，造就了建筑史上的一大奇观，也体现了泉州本土文化的多元包容及中华传统文化海纳百川的广博胸怀。

崇祯十一年（1638）正月，踌躇满志的郑芝龙顶着前军都督府右都督、潮漳副总兵头衔，踏上安平桥。那时，经他出面奖倡，安平商人吴寰宇、曾希止、郑心昂、陈跻宇等人捐资重修的安平桥水心亭正好修葺一新，石匠黄重镌刻的《重修水心亭记》石碑也刚刚竖立在安平桥中亭西侧的墙外。

开元寺刻有印度教神话故事图案的大石柱。（黄国炎 摄）
The stone pillars at Kaiyuan Temple with carvings of Hindu mythological stories. (Photo by Huang Guoyan)

Seyger van Rechteren's *Voyage to the East Indies (1628—1632)* includes a map of Xiamen Bay drawn by a Dutchman. In this map, the icon of "Anhai City" is particularly eye-catching, and even the iconic building of Anhai Port, Anping Bridge, is accurately depicted. Belgian missionary Francois de Rougemont also conformed that Zheng Zhilong had built a castle in Anhai Port, stating that, "In order to ensure the safety and secrecy of loading and unloading rare and valuable goods, Zheng Zhilong ordered the construction of a tall European-style building, which can be called a fortress. Half of it is built on the beach, and the other half is in the sea. Magnificent ships are docked inside the gate, creating the appearance of a mysterious harbor."

In 1637, Zheng Zhilong donated funds to renovate the main hall of Kaiyuan Temple. With his extensive knowledge and experience, he had a unique idea. He decided to relocate a sumeru pedestal sculpture and a pair of stone pillars carved with Hindu mythological stories from an abandoned Hindu temple to Kaiyuan Temple. These artifacts were then installed respectively on the platform and rear corridor of the main hall, creating a remarkable spectacle in architectural history. It reflected the diverse and inclusive nature of Quanzhou's local culture and the broad-mindedness of Chinese traditional culture in embracing different influences.

In the first lunar month of 1638, Zheng Zhilong, full of ambition, set foot on Anping Bridge, carrying the titles of right deputy commander of the Front Army Commandery and deputy general of Chaozhou and Zhangzhou. At that time, with his incentives, Shuixin Pavilion of Anping Bridge, which was funded for renovation by local merchants such as Wu Huanyu, Zeng Xizhi, Zheng Xin'ang and Chen Ji'yu, had just been restored to its original glory. The stone tablet with *A Record of the Renovation of Shuixin Pavilion* carved by stonemason Huang Chong was also newly erected outside the western wall of the central pavilion on Anping Bridge.

郑芝龙倡议重修水心亭碑刻。（李国宏 供图）

The inscription about the renovation of Shuixin Pavilion initiated by Zheng Zhilong. (Courtesy of Li Guohong)

时过境迁，碑记上镌刻的安平商人的事迹已经难以稽考，但是，安平商人的故事却如同波澜不惊的江水，静静地流淌着。

“每岁造舟通异域”的海洋视野，“涨海声中万国商”的开放盛景，造就了安平商人走向深蓝的文化自信。在强大海权的庇护下，安海港织就一张覆盖 17 世纪亚洲海域的贸易网络。事实证明，海洋活动所带来的风险和冲突虽然是不可避免的，却也是可以合理规避并有效管控的。当然，这需要足够的实力与坚强的意志，还有和平共处、合作共赢的海洋文明智慧。

历史云烟散尽之时，郑芝龙海商集团与安海港的故事依然令人神往，安平商人也始终带着对美好生活的向往，以坚定的意志力和顽强的适应力扬帆起航，走向深蓝。1926 年，历史学家、中西交通史专家张星烺在泉州访古时说：“泉州遂日行凋零，无人知其曾为古代世界第一大商埠也。试执泉州市人而问之，即彼亦不自知也。今日尚能维持，不致如邯郸、洛阳之凄凉者，南洋华侨不忘故乡之力也。”正是凭借一代又一代本地海商的勇毅前行和海外华侨的不懈努力，泉州才能竭尽全力地挽住刺桐港徐徐滑落的风帆，并在艰难的环境中默默积攒重振雄风的力量。在蔚蓝的历史舞台上，安平商人演绎的海洋传奇，无论悲喜，都是不可磨灭的海洋文明记忆。

安平桥水心亭。（成冬冬 摄）
Shuixin Pavilion at Anping Bridge. (Photo by Cheng Dongdong)

Time has passed, and the deeds of Anping merchants engraved on the tablet have become difficult to trace. However, the stories of Anping merchants still spread like the tranquil water.

The maritime perspective of "building ships every year to sail to foreign lands" and the open and prosperous scene of "merchants from all nations thronged to Quanzhou amidst the sound of rising tides" have fostered the cultural confidence of Anping merchants to venture into the deep blue sea. Under the protection of a powerful navy, Anhai Port wove a trade network covering the Asian waters in the 17th century. It has been proven that while risks and conflicts arising from maritime activities are inevitable, they can be reasonably avoided and effectively managed. Of course, this requires sufficient strength and strong determination, as well as the wisdom of peaceful coexistence and win-win cooperation shared in maritime civilization.

Even as the glory of history fades, the story of Zheng Zhilong's maritime merchant group and Anhai Port remains enchanting. The merchants of Anping have always carried a longing for a better life, setting sail with unwavering determination and resilience, and heading towards the deep blue sea. In 1926, Zhang Xinglang, a historian and expert in the history of Sino-Western transportation, remarked during his visit to Quanzhou that, "Quanzhou then fell into decline, and few people knew that it was once the largest trading port in the ancient world. Even the people of Quanzhou themselves were unaware of that. Thanks to the efforts of overseas Chinese in Southeast Asia who have not forgotten their hometown, Quanzhou can still sustain itself and does not end up like Handan or Luoyang in desolation." It is through the courage and perseverance of generations of local maritime merchants and the relentless efforts of overseas Chinese that Quanzhou has been able to desperately hold onto the slipping sails of Zayton Port and silently accumulate strength in the difficult times to revive its former glory. On the vast stage of history, the maritime legends performed by Anping merchants, whether joyous or sorrowful, are indelible memories of maritime civilization.

顺济桥：诸峰返照潮声远

顺济桥位于泉州古城南门德济门外，它是泉州古城与晋江南岸的陆运节点，是伴随着海洋贸易发展而建设的出入古城商业区的主要通道，完善了泉州水陆转运系统。顺济桥与德济门、天后宫共同体现了海洋贸易推动下古城南部商业性城区的发展，见证了商业拓展对交通系统的促进。

东有万安，南有顺济

顺济古桥如一架古琴横跨泉州城南的晋江江面，一座座桥墩就如一个个琴键，急湍而过的江水抚弄着这琴键，击发出一串串或急促或轻缓的音符。这涛声回响在晋江两岸，与晚风合奏出一曲悦耳动听的旋律，一直飘扬了千百年。

城南是泉州港的重要商贸区，也是宋元时期外国客商和侨民的主要聚居地。每当涛声远去，江水处于低位，船舶就难以靠岸停泊，码头也得以享受一段清闲。而当涛声渐响，江水回到高位，各种船只开始靠岸装卸货物，城南各个渡口也就繁忙起来了。如遇涨海之声响起，古渡口就会迎来一批批远航的客人，泉州古城也就洋溢着浓浓的异域风情。

顺济古桥。（成冬冬 摄）
The ancient Shunji Bridge. (Photo by Cheng Dongdong)

Shunji Bridge: A Bustling Transportation Hub

Shunji Bridge, located outside Deji Gate of the southern gate of Quanzhou City, served as a major land transportation hub linking the ancient Quanzhou City with the south bank of Jinjiang River. It served as the primary passage for entering and leaving the bustling commercial area of the ancient city, which flourished along with the growth of maritime trade, and enhanced the water-land transshipment system of Quanzhou. Together with Deji Gate and Tianhou Temple, it reflects the development of the commercial district in the southern part of the ancient Quanzhou driven by maritime trade, and bears witness to the advancement of the transportation system through commercial expansion.

In the East Lies Wan'an Bridge; in the South Lies Shunji Bridge

The ancient Shunji Bridge stretches across Jinjiang River in the southern part of Quanzhou City, resembling a horizontal ancient zither. Each bridge pier functions as a key on this zither, with the rushing river water gently caressing these keys, producing a delightful symphony of rapid or soothing notes. The sound of the waves resonates along the banks of Jinjiang River, blending harmoniously with the evening breeze to create a captivating and enchanting melody that has lingered in the air for hundreds of years.

The southern part held great significance as a commercial area of Quanzhou Port. During the Song and Yuan dynasties, it served as the main settlement for foreign merchants and overseas Chinese. When the tide receded and the river level dropped, ships encountered difficulties in docking, resulting in a period of tranquility for the docks. However, as the sound of the tide grew louder and the river level rose, various ships began to dock and unload goods, transforming the ferry terminals in the south of the city into bustling hubs. With the sound of the rising sea, the ancient ferry terminals warmly welcomed a constant flow of long-distance travelers, imparting upon the ancient Quanzhou a distinct and exotic atmosphere.

南宋绍兴年间，寓居泉州的诗人李邴曾在此写下传颂千年的名句：“苍官影里三洲路，涨海声中万国商。”城南聚宝街无疑是当年泉州最繁荣的街市之一。那些载着奇珍异宝的“蕃船”，趁涨潮时分沿晋江直入顺济古桥下的富美码头停泊，再用小船把货物载到车桥头进行交易。于是，各种香料、药材、金银珠宝、茶叶、瓷器、布匹绸缎聚集于此，聚宝街因此而得名。这种繁荣的景象也印证了南宋学者祝穆关于泉州“蕃人巷”的描述，他在《方舆胜览》中记载：“诸蕃有黑白二种，皆居泉州，号蕃人巷。每岁以大舶浮海往来，致象犀、玳瑁、珠玑、玻璃、玛瑙、异香、胡椒之属。”

随着城南商业区的发展，进出泉州城的交通压力越来越大，加之晋江流经城南，江水汹涌，通行不便。于是，建造跨越晋江的桥梁成为解决城南交通问题的当务之急。北宋皇祐元年（1049），泉州太守陆广在临漳门外建造浮桥，名为“履坦桥”。南宋绍兴三十年（1160），僧人文会募资将其改建为石桥，名为“石笋桥”。南宋庆元四年（1198），僧人了性募资重修甘棠桥、棠荫桥、龟山桥三座位于临漳门外的跨江石桥。

今日聚宝街。（成冬冬 摄）
Today's Jubao Street. (Photo by Cheng Dongdong)

Between 1131 and 1162, the renowned poet Li Bing, made his home in Quanzhou and once composed a verse that has endured for a thousand years. The verse, which goes "A road sheltered by pine trees connects three islets in the south of Quanzhou City; amidst the sound of rising tides, merchants from all nations thronged," beautifully captures the bustling trading scene that thrived in the city during that era. No doubt Jubao Street, located in the southern part of Quanzhou, boasted one of the most thriving market. At Fumei Wharf, nestled beneath the ancient Shunji Bridge, foreign vessels laden with exotic treasures would dock during high tide. These goods would then be transported via small boats to Cheqiaotou, in the end of Jubao Street, for trading. Jubao Street became a hub for a wide range of commodities, including spices, medicinal herbs, gold and silver jewelries, tea, porcelain and silk fabrics, hence the name "Jubao" (gathering treasure). This vibrant marketplace aligns with the description of Quanzhou's "Foreigners' Alley" provided by Zhu Mu, a scholar from the Southern Song Dynasty. In his work titled *The National Gazetteer of Southern Song Dynasty*, Zhu Mu documented the presence of both black- and white-skinned foreign merchants residing in Foreigners' Alley in Quanzhou. He further noted that large ships embarked on annual voyages across the sea for trade, bringing back coveted commodities such as ivories, rhinoceros horns, tortoise shells, jewelries, glass, agates, spices and pepper.

The expansion of the commercial district in the southern region of Quanzhou led to increased traffic congestion; the presence of Jinjiang River also posed transportation challenges. The construction of a bridge across Jinjiang River to solve transportation problems in the southern part of the ancient Quanzhou became urgent. In response, Lu Guang, the prefect of Quanzhou, built a floating bridge outside Linzhang Gate in 1049 during the Northern Song Dynasty and aptly named it "Lyutan Bridge" to symbolize a smooth journey. Subsequently, in 1160, Monk Wenhui initiated a fundraising campaign to rebuild the bridge using stone materials, resulting in its new name as "Shisun Bridge". Furthermore, in 1198, Monk Liaoxing successfully raised funds for the repair of three stone bridges situated across the river outside Linzhang Gate. These bridges, namely Gantang Bridge, Tangyin Bridge and Guishan Bridge, were restored to ensure efficient transportation flow in the area.

晋江上游的交通压力暂时得以缓解，但是，城南商业区正对的晋江江面更加宽阔，水流更加湍急，雨季甚至“阴风怒号，霖潦暴溢，巨涛翻天，惊雷撼地”。建桥之前，往来客商依靠渡船往返两岸，费时费力，又面临极大的风险。南宋嘉定四年（1211），泉州太守邹应龙在修缮泉州罗城之时，兴工建造跨江石桥一座，全长一百五十余丈，左右架设护栏，以临近顺济宫（今泉州天后宫）得名顺济桥，又以其建造时间晚于石笋桥，俗称新桥。

清乾隆二十二年（1757），顺济桥被山洪冲毁，泉州知府怀荫布主持重修，其间追忆顺济桥的历史贡献，说道：“泉州桥梁难更仆数，其跨江而当孔道者，东有万安，南有顺济……其地下通两粤，上达江浙，实海国之冲衢，江城之险要也。自斯桥（顺济桥）成，而肩摩踵接，直蹑风涛于足下，而恬然不知，厥功伟矣！”可见顺济桥继上游石笋桥之后建成，把晋江南岸的广大地区与泉州古城的陆路交通紧密联系在一起，由南部往来泉州不必再绕行至晋江上游的石笋桥，使泉州连接安海、同安、漳州等地的陆路交通更为便捷。此外，顺济桥的建成也方便了晋江南岸各港口与泉州古城之间的交通，进入石湖港的货物可沿建于南宋乾道年间、被称为海岸长桥的沿海大通道直抵顺济桥，再到古城南门；进入深沪湾、围头湾等其他港口的货物也可由陆路经顺济桥到达古城。顺济桥的建设体现了古城泉州作为国家口岸的水陆运输网络的逐步完善。

The construction of bridges across Jinjiang River alleviated the traffic congestion in the upstream area. The particular section of the river in face of the southern commercial district of Quanzhou, however, remained an obstacle. With its wide expanse and powerful currents, during the rainy season it turned into a tempestuous force, aptly described as "the wind howling ominously, the rain pouring relentlessly, the waves surging dramatically, and the thunder shaking the earth". Before a bridge was built, merchants and travelers had to rely on ferries to cross between the two banks, a tedious and risky endeavor. In 1211, during the restoration of city walls, Zou Yinglong, the Quanzhou prefect, took the initiative to construct a stone bridge that spanned the river. This impressive bridge, measuring over 150 *zhang* (500 meters) in length, had railings on both sides and was named Shunji Bridge after the nearby Shunji Palace (now known as Tianhou Temple or the Palace of Goddess Mazu in Quanzhou). It was also referred to as the New Bridge as it was built later than Shisun Bridge.

In 1757 during the Qing Dynasty, a devastating flash flood destroyed Shunji Bridge. In response, Huai Yinbu, the magistrate of Quanzhou, took it upon himself to oversee its reconstruction. During this process, Huai Yinbu recalled the historical significance of Shunji Bridge and acknowledged the crucial roles played by Wan'an Bridge to the east and Shunji Bridge to the south among the various bridges spanning the river. They served as vital connections between Fujian and Guangdong, Guangxi provinces, and extended to Jiangsu and Zhejiang provinces. They were pivotal hubs for maritime trade and strategically positioned the ancient Quanzhou City. Huai Yinbu specially lauded remarkable achievements of Shunji Bridge. It was constructed downstream of Shisun Bridge, effectively linking the expansive area on the south bank of Jinjiang River with the land route of the ancient Quanzhou. This new bridge eliminated the need for detours to the upstream Shisun Bridge, greatly improving land transportation between Quanzhou and neighboring regions such as Anhai, Tong'an and Zhangzhou. Moreover, the completion of Shunji Bridge facilitated transportation between various ports on the south bank of Jinjiang River and the ancient city of Quanzhou. Goods arriving at Shihu Port could conveniently follow the coastal highway, known as the Long Bridge Along the Coast, which was constructed between 1165 and 1173. This route would lead them to Shunji Bridge before reaching the southern gate of the ancient city. Similarly, goods arriving at other ports like Shenhu Bay and Weitou Bay could also access the ancient city via land transportation through Shunji Bridge. The construction of Shunji Bridge exemplifies the gradual improvement of the water-land transportation network in the ancient city of Quanzhou, solidifying its status as a prominent national port.

顶着状元光环的造桥太守

如果时间是条河流，古桥就是横跨在这条河流之上的历史的彩虹，是一个地方的文化光影。站在顺济古桥桥头，听逶迤东逝的晋江水低吟浅唱，这声音似乎伴着唐风宋韵从遥远的时空传来，讲述着南宋状元太守邹应龙的悠悠往事。

邹应龙，字景初，福建泰宁人，南宋庆元二年（1196）状元及第，声名鹊起。步入仕途后，邹应龙耿直敢言，勤勉于政务。南宋嘉定二年（1209），多地发生旱灾与蝗灾，粮食歉收，官府救灾不力，导致爆发多起民变。五月，帝诏群臣进言，邹应龙力陈必须重振朝纲、整肃吏治、薄赋宽民、抚集流亡。不料，他却因此得罪擅权专政的右丞相史弥远，被降职为宝文阁待制。十二月，邹应龙离开京城，出任泉州太守。

The Bridge-Building Prefect with the Title of Top Scholar

In the metaphorical sense, ancient bridges can be likened to historical rainbows that traverse the river of time, symbolizing the cultural legacy and heritage of a particular location. The ancient Shunji Bridge, when viewed from its starting point, evokes a sense of awe as one listens to the tranquil flow of the meandering Jinjiang River, which has been there since the Tang and Song dynasties, transcending the boundaries of both time and space. In this moment, the sound of the river serves as a conduit, narrating the story of Zou Yinglong, the scholar prefect of Quanzhou during the Southern Song Dynasty.

Zou Yinglong, a native of Taining, Fujian, emerged as a prominent figure in the late 12th century. In 1196, he achieved the highest score in the imperial examination, earning him the prestigious title of top scholar. His exceptional performance quickly garnered him widespread recognition. Upon entering the officialdom, Zou Yinglong became renowned for his unwavering integrity and diligent approach to government affairs. In 1209, a series of calamities, including droughts and locust infestations, resulted in poor harvests and inadequate relief efforts by the government, leading to widespread uprisings. In response, the emperor called upon his officials to provide advice in lunar May of that year. Zou Yinglong strongly advocated for the restoration of order, administrative rectification, tax reduction and relief measures for the displaced population. However, his outspoken stance offended the powerful and authoritarian right prime minister, Shi Miyuan, resulting in Zou Yinglong's demotion to the position of Baowen Ge retinue, a low-ranking official. Undeterred, Zou Yinglong left the capital in lunar December and assumed the role of prefect of Quanzhou.

邹应龙画像。（李国宏 供图）
The portrait of Zou Yinglong. (Courtesy of Li Guohong)

嘉定三年（1210），邹应龙抵达泉州，下车伊始便访察民情，并围绕海外贸易、城市建设、文化教育三大方面，雷厉风行地为泉州百姓办了不少的实事。当时，泉州是南外宗正司所在地，赵宋宗室聚居于此，在皇室特权的庇护下，有些人暗中与商人勾结，垄断贸易，牟取暴利。查明实情后，邹应龙敢于硬碰硬，将奸商首恶庄文宝绳之以法，以儆效尤。结果，与庄文宝有利益往来的宗室成员暗中整邹应龙的“黑材料”，对其大肆中伤诽谤。邹应龙无所畏惧，坦然应对，并借此优化泉州港的营商环境，促进外贸的持续发展。

嘉定四年（1211），邹应龙主持修缮泉州罗城与泉州府文庙，并建造顺济桥和安海石井书院。一年之内，四大工程顺利完成，充分显示其务实高效的施政能力。值得注意的是，这些工程的资金来源与泉州港海外贸易的兴盛有着莫大的关系。

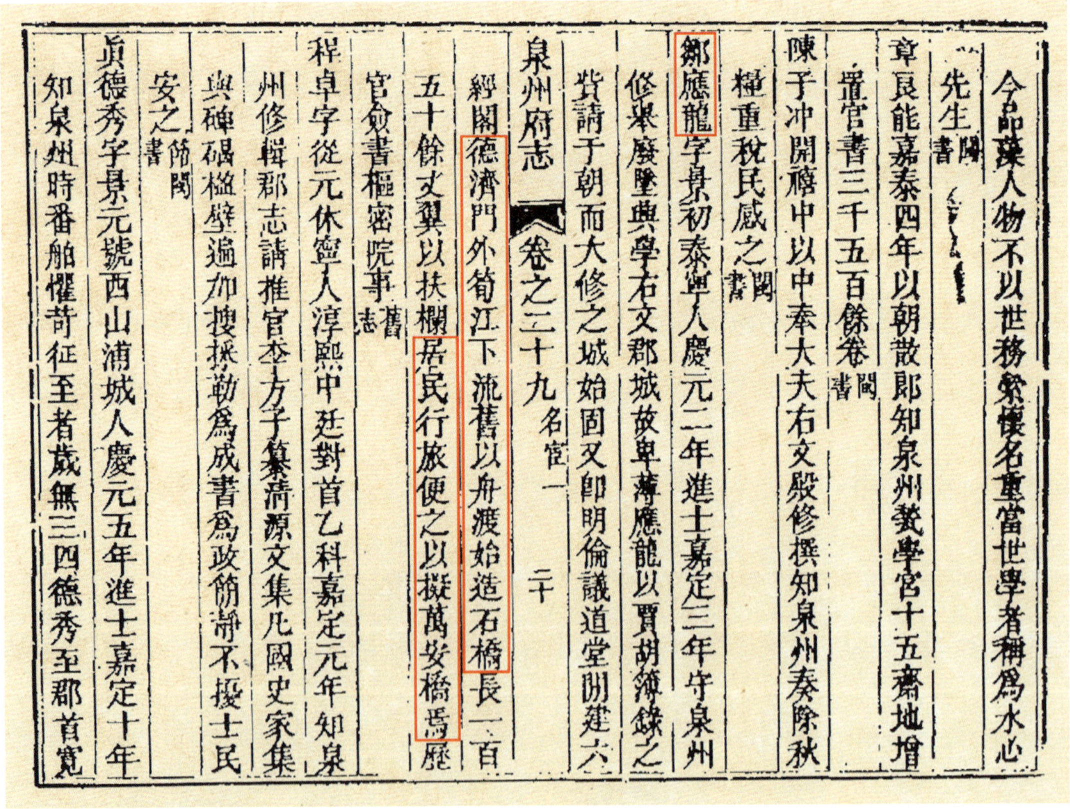
今邑藥人物不以世務縈懷名重當世學者稱爲水心
先生閩書
章良能嘉泰四年以朝散郎知泉州教學宮十五齋地增
置官書三千五百餘卷閩書
陳子冲開禧中以中奉大夫右文殿修撰知泉州奏除秋
糧重稅民感之閩書
鄒應龍字景初泰寧人慶元二年進士嘉定三年守泉州
修舉廢墜興學右文郡城故卑薄應龍以買胡簿錄之
貲請于朝而大修之城始固又即明倫議道堂剏建六
泉州府志 卷之三十九 名宦一 二十
齋閣德濟門外筍江下流舊以舟渡始造石橋長一百
五十餘丈翼以扶欄居民行旅便之以擬萬安橋焉歷
官僉書樞密院事舊志
程卓字從元休寧人淳熙中廷對首乙科嘉定元年知泉
州修輯郡志請推官李方子纂蒨源文集凡國史家集
與碑碣槪璧遍加搜採勒爲成書爲政簡肅不擾士民
安之閩書
真德秀字景元號西山浦城人慶元五年進士嘉定十年
知泉州時番舶憚苛征至者歲無三四德秀至郡首寬

清代乾隆版《泉州府志》中关于邹应龙建造顺济桥的记载。（李国宏 供图）
The record about Zou Yinglong's construction of Shunji Bridge in the Qianlong edition of *Local Chronicles of Quanzhou Prefecture*. (Courtesy of Li Guohong)

Upon his arrival in Quanzhou in 1210, Zou Yinglong wasted no time in conducting a thorough investigation of the local circumstances. He swiftly turned his attention to matters pertaining to overseas trade, urban development and cultural education, successfully accomplishing numerous practical tasks for the benefit of the people in Quanzhou. During this period, Quanzhou held significant importance as the site of the Southern Clan Office, and it served as a residence for the Zhao royal families. Some individuals colluded with merchants, exploiting their royal privileges to monopolize trade and reap excessive profits. Upon uncovering this truth, Zou Yinglong fearlessly confronted the wrongdoers and brought to justice the ringleader, Zhuang Wenbao, thus serving as a deterrent to others. Consequently, certain members of the royal family who had been associated with Zhuang Wenbao covertly gathered what they deemed as "evidence" to slander and defame Zou Yinglong. Nonetheless, undeterred by these attempts, Zou Yinglong remained composed and responded calmly, utilizing this opportunity to optimize the business environment of Quanzhou Port and further promote the continuous development of foreign trade.

In 1211, Zou Yinglong assumed the responsibility of overseeing the renovation of city walls, Quanzhou Confucian Temple and School, as well as the construction of Shunji Bridge and Anhai Shijing Academy. Remarkably, all four major projects were completed within a year, showcasing Zou Yinglong's practical and efficient governance capacity. It is noteworthy that the funding for these projects was closely linked to the flourishing overseas trade in Quanzhou Port.

据清代道光《晋江县志》记载，修建罗城的庞大资金来自“胡贾簿录之资”，也就是外国商人被依法查抄罚没的钱财，它从一个侧面反映了泉州港外贸的繁盛，也印证了当时的泉州港已经具备完善的涉外法律体系。而据《安海志》记载，石井镇官游绛请示建造石井书院，邹应龙拨款四十万钱作为启动资金，同时协调“漕、舶二使者”给予资助，连同安海商民的捐款，总共筹集资金四百万钱用于建造石井书院。《安海志》提到的“漕、舶二使者”中，“漕”指的就是管理催征税赋、出纳钱粮、办理上供以及漕运等事的福建路转运使，“舶”则是负责海外贸易事务的泉州市舶司提举。由此可见，泉州港海外贸易的繁荣既给泉州地方带来巨额的财政收入，也为城市公共设施的建设提供坚实的资金保障。

安海石井书院。（成冬冬 摄）
Shijing Academy in Anhai. (Photo by Cheng Dongdong)

According to the Daoguang edition of *Local Chronicles of Jinjiang County*, the huge sum of money for the construction of city walls was derived from the "confiscated assets of foreign merchants". This phrase refers to the money and assets confiscated from foreign merchants in accordance with the law, thereby indicating the prosperity of foreign trade in Quanzhou Port. Moreover, this evidence demonstrates the existence of a sound legal system governing foreign affairs in Quanzhou Port during that period. *Local Chronicles of Anhai* reveals that You Jiang, the magistrate of Shijing Town, sought permission to establish Shijing Academy. Zou Yinglong allocated an initial sum of 400,000 coins as start-up funds and coordinated with two officials: one was the Fujian Province transport commissioner, responsible for managing tax collection, treasury operations, tribute handling and water transportation, and the other was the superintendent of Quanzhou Maritime Trade Office, responsible for overseas trade affairs. Together with donations from local merchants in Anhai, a total of 4 million coins were raised for the construction of Shijing Academy. This illustrates that the prosperity of overseas trade in Quanzhou Port not only generated significant fiscal revenue for the local area but also provided substantial financial support for the construction of urban public facilities.

安溪清水岩宋代石刻上可见邹应龙落款。（成冬冬 摄）

The signature of Zou Yinglong can be seen in a Song Dynasty's stone inscription at Qingshuiyan in Anxi. (Photo by Cheng Dongdong)

天外帆樯估客来

伴随晋江北岸的自然淤积，泉州城市市域逐步向南部延伸。从1009年清净寺建成、1087年市舶司设置至1196年顺济宫（天后宫）建成，古城南部的商业性城区逐步发展起来。而1211年顺济桥的建造正是城市南部商业聚居、贸易发展、交通需求旺盛的体现。此后，1230年沿江翼城的建设及城南德济门的拓展，标志着泉州古城南部商业性城区形态的确立，顺济桥与德济门、天后宫共同成为泉州古城南段的重要地标。

古城今貌，图中可见天后宫、德济门、聚宝街、顺济桥等。（黄国炎 摄）
The present appearance of the ancient Quanzhou City, where you can see Tianhou Temple, Deji Gate, Jubao Street and Shunji Bridge, etc. (Photo by Huang Guoyan)

Sails and Masts from Afar Herald the Arrival of Merchants

As the urban area of Quanzhou gradually expanded southward due to the natural siltation on the north bank of Jinjiang River, the commercial district in the southern part of the city began to take shape. This development can be traced back to the construction of Qingjing Mosque in 1009, the establishment of the Maritime Trade Office in 1087 and the completion of Shunji Palace (Tianhou Temple) in 1196. The construction of Shunji Bridge in 1211 was a clear indication of the thriving commercial settlement, the growth of trade and the increasing transportation needs in the southern part of the city. Subsequently, the construction of ramparts along the river in 1230 and the expansion of Deji Gate in the southern part of the city solidified the presence of the commercial district. These sites, namely Shunji Bridge, Deji Gate and Tianhou Temple, emerged as significant and recognizable landmarks in the southern part of ancient Quanzhou.

元至正年间，顺济桥重修。当时，顺济宫已是天妃信仰的重要发祥地，“自是水旱灾盗贼，有祷辄应，历代遣官斋香诣庙致祭”。顺济桥附近的沿江码头成为“蕃舶客航聚集之地”。城南一带街市繁华，“午街喧杂闹交厢”，随处可见“毶丝缠髻西洋客”。随之而来的还有琳琅满目的舶来品，“象犀珠翠海南香，万里归来水路长”。元至正十年（1350），翰林学士张翥作为朝廷的代祀官莅临顺济宫，祭祀天妃。由此，与寓居泉州的航海家汪大渊、文学家吴鉴相识，并应邀为汪大渊的《岛夷志略》作序。泉州港的旖旎风光与海外贸易的繁华景象给张翥留下了深刻的印象，其《怀清源洞旧游》诗云：“漫漫涨海际天涯，万里乘来使者槎。紫泽重寻仙客洞，碧山长醉故侯家。人多熟酒烧藤叶，市有生蛮卖象牙。安得梦中时化蝶，翩翩飞向刺桐花。”

Between 1341 and 1368, a renovation took place on Shunji Bridge. Concurrently, Shunji Palace had already established itself as a prominent site for the veneration of Tianfei, also known as Goddess Mazu. During times of natural disasters or banditry, prayers were offered at the temple, and government officials were also dispatched to make sacrificial offerings. The docks near Shunji Bridge became bustling hubs for foreign ships and travelers, while the streets in the southern part of the city were teeming with vibrant markets. The presence of Western visitors with coiled hair became a common sight, and with them came a diverse array of exotic goods, including ivories, rhinoceros horns, jewelries and incense, sourced from distant lands. In 1350, Zhang Zhu, a Hanlin academician representing the imperial court, visited Shunji Palace to perform sacrificial rites for Tianfei. During the visit, he encountered two notable individuals residing in Quanzhou, namely the seafarer Wang Dayuan and the writer Wu Jian. Zhang Zhu was subsequently invited to provide a preface for Wang Dayuan's work titled *A Brief Account of Island Inhabitants*. The picturesque scenery of Quanzhou Port and the bustling scene of overseas trade left a profound impression on Zhang Zhu, inspiring him to pen the following lines in his poem Recalling a Visit to Qingyuan Cave:

"The endless sea stretches to the horizon,
Thousands of miles traveled by emissaries on boats.
I search for caves where immortals inhabit around Zize Academy,
And get drunk in Bishan where the old marquis lives.
People enjoy drinking old wine brewed with vine leaves,
And there are foreigners who sell ivories in the market.
If only I could transform into a butterfly in my dreams,
Fluttering towards the erythrina flowers."

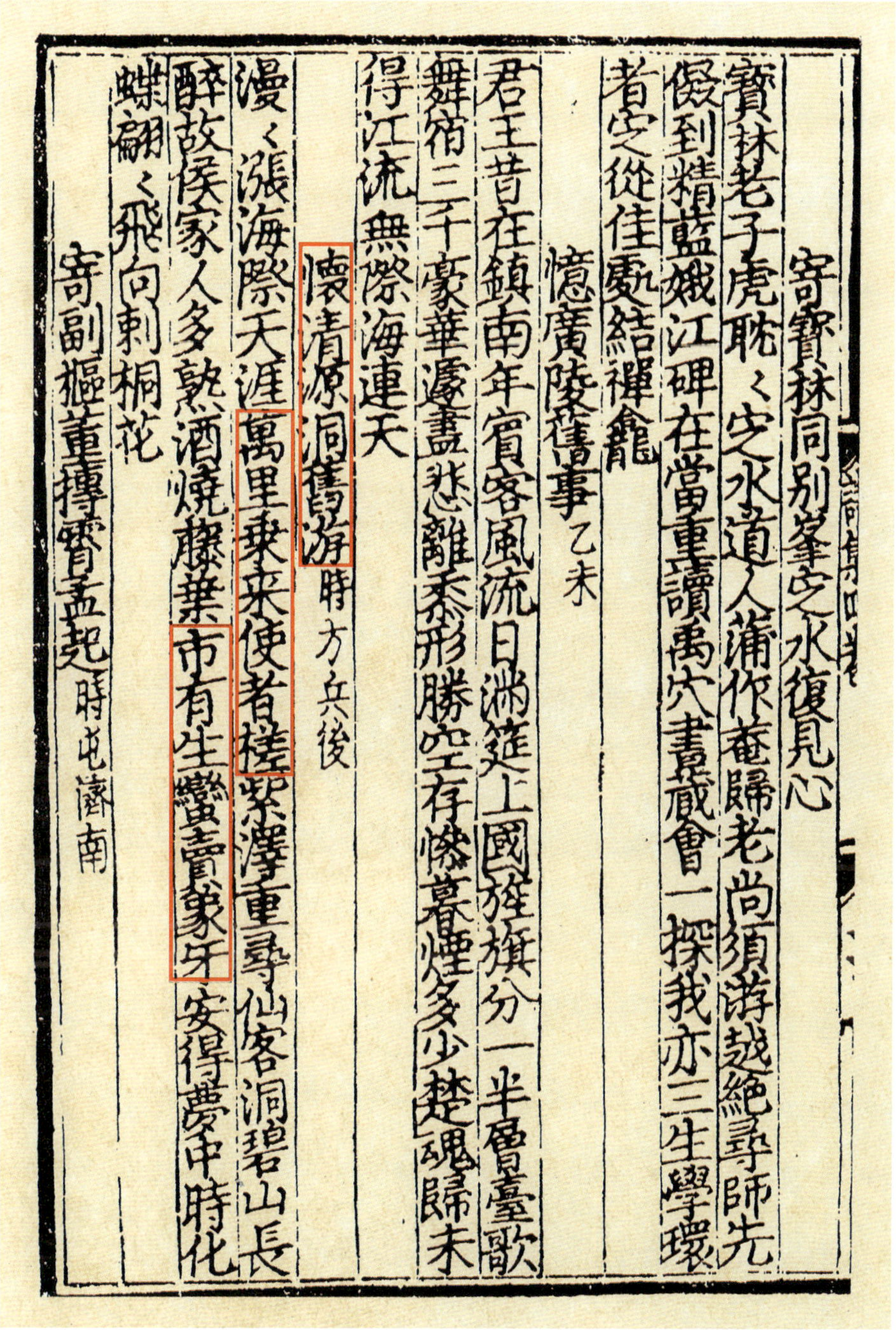

寄寶林同別峯定水復見心
寶林老子虎眈眈定水道人蒲作菴歸老尚須游越絕尋師先
假到精藍娥江碑在當重讀禹穴書藏會一探我亦三生學環
者定從佳處結禪龕

憶廣陵舊事 乙未
君王昔在鎮南年賓客風流日滿筵上國旌旗分一半層臺歌
舞宿三千豪華遽盡悲離黍形勝空存慘暮煙多少楚魂歸未
得江流無際海連天

懷清源洞舊游 時方兵後
漫漫漲海際天涯萬里乘來使者槎紫澤重尋仙客洞碧山長
醉故侯家人多熟酒燒藤菜市有生蠻賣象牙安得夢中時化
蝶翩翩飛向刺桐花

寄副樞董摶霄孟起 時屯嶺南

张翥《蜕庵诗集》中收录的《怀清源洞旧游》。（李国宏 供图）

Recalling a Visit to Qingyuan Cave included in Zhang Zhu's *Mr. Tui'an Poetry*. (Courtesy of Li Guohong)

明洪武三年（1370）二月，泉州置福建市舶提举司，“掌海外诸蕃朝贡、市易之事”。明永乐元年（1403）八月，福建市舶提举司改由福建布政司直接管理。永乐三年（1405），泉州城南聚宝街车桥头建来远驿，专门用来接待抵达泉州港的外国贡使。永乐十三年（1415），少监张谦出使渤泥之时，遵照礼仪前来顺济宫行香祈祷。仪式结束后，他从顺济桥东的沿江码头登上宝船，沿着晋江驶出泉州港，一路顺风顺水，抵达渤泥。完成使命时，张谦奏请朝廷重修顺济宫。明成化八年（1472），福建市舶提举司从泉州迁往福州，泉州港失去了国际贸易港的官方地位，却也由此开启私商海上贸易的时代。成化十五年（1479），泉州知府徐源重修顺济桥，“复疏桥东小浦，引潮入城濠，以通舟楫”。“惟桥之东，海船所凑”，顺济桥再次成为进出泉州城南商贸区的重要交通枢纽。顺济桥下的“天外帆樯”也成为明代泉州诗人作品中挥之不去的文化符号，如黄克缵的“江间箫鼓游人少，天外帆樯估客来”，郑之铉的“天外帆樯遮旅雁，石间风雨下寒潮”。

In lunar February 1370, the Supervisorate of Fujian Maritime Trade Office was established in Quanzhou, which played a crucial role in managing foreign tribute and trade. In lunar August 1403, the Supervisorate came under the direct management of Fujian Provincial Administration, further solidifying its importance. In order to accommodate foreign tributary envoys, Laiyuan Post was set up at Cheqiaotou, Jubao Street in the southern part of Quanzhou in 1405. This period also witnessed the use of Shunji Palace as a ceremonial site, with the vice supervisor Zhang Qian following the established ritual, departing from Shunji Bridge's eastern dock on a treasure ship to Brunei and returning safely in 1415. Upon the completion of his mission, Zhang Qian petitioned for the renovation of Shunji Palace. However, the relocation of the Supervisorate of Fujian Maritime Trade Office to Fuzhou in 1472 marked a shift in Quanzhou's official status as an international trade port. Nonetheless, private maritime trade began to flourish from then on. Efforts to maintain and improve Quanzhou's infrastructure were still made, such as the repair of Shunji Bridge and the dredging of the small harbor east of the bridge by Quanzhou prefect Xu Yuan in 1479. This revitalized the importance of Shunji Bridge as a transportation hub in the southern commercial district of Quanzhou. The imagery of "sails and masts from afar" under Shunji Bridge became a recurring theme in the works of the Ming Dynasty poets from Quanzhou, reflecting the bustling maritime trade and the anticipation it brought.

天后宫门前为德济门遗址。（陈英杰 摄）
Tianhou Temple, with the remains of Deji Gate in front. (Photo by Chen Yingjie)

闽台郊商接力修桥

顺济桥跨越晋江，直通泉州城南商业区，起着重要的交通枢纽作用。同时，考虑到城市防卫的需求，顺济桥建造时采取与众不同的设计方案，在桥北增设吊桥，遇到紧急情况即可升起吊桥，阻断来人，还建有桥头堡，设置戟门，加强防守。清乾隆四十九年（1784），朝廷指定泉州府蚶江港与台湾府彰化县鹿港对渡通商，许多泉州商人前往鹿港进行贸易，鹿港商户也纷纷在泉州设立商行，促进了闽台两岸商贸往来的逐步繁盛。当时，顺济桥附近的泉州南门浯渡铺建有一座浯渡宏济院，因寺院前有座窣堵波式佛塔，俗称塔堂宫。此处左通富美码头，右接顺济桥，地理位置非常好，便于商贸，因此吸引了大量闽台郊商在此设立贸易商行。

清乾隆四十二年（1777），顺济桥吊桥损毁，在鹿港开设日茂行的永宁（今石狮市永宁镇）富商林振嵩捐资修复。清嘉庆八年（1803），吊桥被洪水冲毁，林振嵩之子林文时捐资重修。林文时，名元考，号敦崖，家道殷实，乐善好施。嘉庆九年至十年（1804—1805），他还参与重修赐恩岩观音寺大雄殿山门、石笋桥、清源山蜕岩、泉州府督学试院等公益设施。

林振嵩画像。（李国宏 供图）
The portrait of Lin Zhensong. (Courtesy of Li Guohong)

Merchants Engaged in Trade Between Fujian and Taiwan Jointly Repaired the Bridge

Spanning Jinjiang River, Shunji Bridge, a crucial transportation hub in Quanzhou City, facilitated trade and played a significant role in urban defense. Constructed with a unique design, the bridge featured a drawbridge to the north, which could be raised in emergencies to prevent incoming enemies. Furthermore, a bridgehead with a portcullis was built to enhance defense capabilities. In 1784, the imperial court designated Hanjiang Port in Quanzhou and Lukang Port in Penghua, Taiwan for trade. This decision fostered trade between Fujian and Taiwan, as Quanzhou merchants journeyed to Lukang for trade while Lukang merchants established businesses in Quanzhou. Located near Shunji Bridge, Wudu Ferry housed Hongji Temple, locally known as Tatang Palace due to a stupa-style pagoda at the gate. This strategic location connected Fumei Wharf to the left and Shunji Bridge to the right, attracting numerous merchants from Fujian and Taiwan to establish trading enterprises in the area.

In 1777, the drawbridge of Shunji Bridge was in need of repair, and Lin Zhensong, a prominent merchant from Yongning (now Yongning Township, Shishi City), generously donated funds for its restoration. However, in 1803, the drawbridge was once again destroyed by floods. Lin Wenshi, the son of Lin Zhensong, stepped forward and provided financial support for the reconstruction of it. Lin Wenshi, born in a wealthy family, was renowned for his philanthropy and benevolence. In addition to his contribution to the restoration of Shunji Bridge, he also played a role in the reconstruction of other public facilities in Quanzhou between 1804 and 1805, including the gate of the main hall of Ci'enyan Guanyin Temple, Shisun Bridge, Tuiyan Cave of Qingyuan Mountain and Quanzhou Prefectural Examination Hall.

民国时期的顺济桥老照片。（李国宏 供图）

The old photograph of Shunji Bridge during the Republic period of China. (Courtesy of Li Guohong)

嘉庆二十二年（1817），顺济桥一段石板断裂，铺锦（今石狮市宝盖镇铺锦村）郊商黄清和（曾任福建延平府学训导）捐资修复。嘉庆二十四年（1819），狂风巨浪折损顺济桥护栏，林振嵩之子林文献重修。在巡视桥梁之时，林文献发现第十、十一两座桥墩出现倾斜开裂的险情，且吊桥也有损毁。于是，他联络塔堂宫附近的郊商黄清和、王日曜、陈鸿谟、石焕章等人，倡议众商行捐银二千二百两，对顺济桥整体进行修缮。此外，南安富商黄伦恩独资修造三座石塔并修补吊桥。

综上可见，顺济桥不仅是泉州港海外贸易兴盛的历史见证，也承载着闽台郊商情系桑梓、热心公益的情怀。时间的淘洗已使顺济古桥成为断桥，但它仍然如一道风景伫立，让人们去追忆那些与涛声有关的往事。如今，举目望去，在顺济古桥的东西两侧，顺济新桥与泉州大桥如长虹般飞架在晋江两岸，彰显着新时代的风采。“沉舟侧畔千帆过，病树前头万木春”，这就是时代进步的象征吧。

今天的晋江飞虹胜景，左为顺济新桥和古桥，中为泉州大桥，右为田安大桥。（陈英杰 摄）
Today's magnificent view of the rainbow-like bridges across Jinjiang River, with the new and old Shunji bridges on the left, Quanzhou Bridge in the center, and Tian'an Bridge on the right. (Photo by Chen Yingjie)

In 1817, the flagstone of one section of Shunji Bridge suffered damage. Huang Qinghe from Pujin (now Pujin Village, Baogai Town, Shishi City), the former instructor at Yanping Prefectural School in Fujian, generously funded the repair. However, in 1819, strong winds and waves caused further damage to the bridge's railings. Lin Wenxian, the son of Lin Zhensong, took it upon himself to repair the railings. During his inspection, Lin discovered additional structural dangers, including tilting and cracked piers, as well as the need for repairs to the drawbridge. Lin proposed a collective effort among merchants residing near Tatang Palace, including Huang Qinghe, Wang Riyao, Chen Hongmo and Shi Huanzhang, to contribute 2,200 taels of silver for the complete restoration of Shunji Bridge. Furthermore, Huang Lun'en, a wealthy merchant from Nan'an, generously funded the construction of three stone pagodas and the repair of the drawbridge.

This historical account underscores the significance of Shunji Bridge, not only as a symbol of Quanzhou Port's thriving overseas trade but also as a reflection of the deep-rooted connection between local merchants and those from Taiwan, as well as their altruistic spirit. These individuals maintained a strong bond with their hometown and demonstrated their unwavering dedication to public welfare. Despite the passage of time, Shunji Bridge, even though broken, stand as a picturesque landmark, evoking nostalgia for a bygone era accompanied by the soothing sound of the waves. Adjacent to the ancient Shunji Bridge, the new Shunji Bridge and Quanzhou Bridge now gracefully span Jinjiang River, resembling vibrant rainbows that symbolize the allure and progress of the modern era.

参考文献

[1] 黄仲昭 . 八闽通志 [M]. 福州：福建人民出版社，2006.

[2] 何乔远 . 闽书 [M]. 福州：福建人民出版社，1994.

[3] 曹春平 . 福建石狮姑嫂塔 [J]. 建筑史，2012.2.

[4] 王寒枫 . 泉州东西塔 [M]. 福州：福建人民出版社，1992.

[5] 蔡永蒹 . 西山杂志 [M]. 晋江市图书馆藏本 .

[6] 中国海外交通史研究会，泉州海外交通史博物馆 . 泉州海外交通史料汇编 [M].1983.

[7] 黄凤翔 . 万历泉州府志 [M]. 台北：台湾学生书局，1987.

[8] 方鼎 . 乾隆晋江县志 . 中国方志丛书 [M]. 台北：成文出版社，1967.

[9] 周学曾 . 道光晋江县志 [M]. 福州：福建人民出版社，1990.

[10] 郭赓武 . 乾隆泉州府志 . 中国地方志集成 [M]. 上海：上海书店出版社，2000.

[11] 孙原 . 析泉州石狮六胜塔的建筑艺术特征与传承 [J]. 建筑与文化，2013.10.

[12] 真德秀 . 真西山文集 [M]. 上海：商务印书馆，1937.

[13] 庄为玑 . 海上集 [M]. 厦门：厦门大学出版社，2020.

[14] 杨德卿，许宗音 . 泉州古港史 [M]. 北京：人民交通出版社，1994.

[15] 林水强，林为兴，傅金星 . 蚶江志略 [M]. 香港：华星出版社，1993.

[16] 沈有容 . 闽海赠言 [M]. 北京：商务印书馆，2017 年 .

[17] 傅恩凤 . 泉州府后山遗址与文莱甜桔子河遗址出土瓷器之分析 [J]. 福建文博，2019.2.

[18] 福建博物院，石狮市博物馆 . 石狮市石湖码头考古发掘报告 [J]. 福建文博，2020.1.

[19] 泉州市文管办，泉州市博物馆 . 泉州法石古渡口遗址清理 [J]. 福建文博，2003.1.

[20] 福建省文物管理委员会考古队，泉州市丰泽区文化发展中心 . 泉州文兴、美山古码头发掘报告 [J]. 福建文博，2003,2.

[21] 中国科学院自然科学史研究所，泉州海外交通史博物馆 . 泉州法石古船试掘简报和初步探讨 [J]. 自然科学史研究，1983.2.

[22] 陈鹏 , 杨钦章 . 泉州法石发现宋元碇石 [J]. 自然科学史研究，1983.2.

[23] 泉州市文物保护管理所 . 洛阳桥石刻 [M]. 福州：海峡书局，2016.

[24] 蔡襄 . 端明集 [M]. 台北：台湾商务印书馆，1986.

[25] 贺威 . 宋元福建科技史研究 [M]. 厦门：厦门大学出版社，2019.

[26] 邵庆国 . 宋代科技成就 [M]. 郑州：河南科学技术出版社，2014.

[27] 安海乡土史料编辑委员会 . 安平志校注 [M]. 北京：中国文联出版社，2000.

[28] 许著华 . 安平碑拓录 [M]. 香港：香港风雅图书出版有限公司，2010.

[29] 陈鹏 . 宋代泉州桥梁及其建筑技术 [J]. 南方文物，1994.4.

[30] 中共泉州市委宣传部 , 泉州市社会科学界联合会 . 泉州与世界海洋文明 [M]. 北京：海洋出版社，2022.

[31] 安海港史研究编辑组 . 安海港史研究 [M]. 福州：福建教育出版社，1989.

[32] 陈彬强，陈冬珑 . 泉州海上丝绸之路历史文献汇编：初编 [M]. 厦门：厦门大学出版社，2020.

[33] 吴拏云 . 兴建安平桥的六功臣 [J]. 泉州晚报，2021.8.13.

[34] 吴拏云 . 顺济桥：状元邹应龙主持修建的南宋名桥 [J]. 泉州晚报，2021.4.9.

[35] 郑剑文 . 顺济桥头的涛声 [J]. 闽南网，2020.8.31.

图书在版编目（CIP）数据

向海而歌：宋元泉州的交通网络：汉英对照 / 中共泉州市委宣传部编．--福州：福建人民出版社，2024.6（2025.3重印）

（世遗之城：泉州）

ISBN 978-7-211-09040-2

Ⅰ.①向… Ⅱ.①中… Ⅲ.①交通运输史—泉州—宋元时期—汉、英 Ⅳ.①F512.9

中国国家版本馆 CIP 数据核字（2023）第 078999 号

向海而歌——宋元泉州的交通网络

XIANGHAI ER GE——SONGYUAN QUANZHOU DE JIAOTONG WANGLUO

特约撰稿： 李国宏
翻　　译： 倪秀华
责任编辑： 孙　颖
美术编辑： 陈培亮
责任校对： 林乔楠
装帧设计： 雅昌（上海）设计中心
出版发行： 福建人民出版社　　**电　　话：** 0591-87533169（发行部）
网　　址： http://www.fjpph.com　　**电子邮箱：** fjpph7211@126.com
地　　址： 福州市东水路 76 号　　**邮政编码：** 350001
经　　销： 福建新华发行（集团）有限责任公司
印　　刷： 雅昌文化（集团）有限公司
地　　址： 深圳市南山区深云路 19 号
电　　话： 0755-86083235
开　　本： 787 毫米×1092 毫米　1/16
印　　张： 15.25
字　　数： 390 千字
版　　次： 2024 年 6 月第 1 版
印　　次： 2025 年 3 月第 2 次印刷
书　　号： ISBN 978-7-211-09040-2
定　　价： 68.00 元
